HOW
SAILBOATS
WIN or LOSE
RACES

REVISED
EDITION

HOW SAILBOATS WIN OR LOSE RACES

REVISED EDITION

WILLIAM ALLEN SMITH

VNR VAN NOSTRAND REINHOLD COMPANY

NEW YORK   CINCINNATI   TORONTO   LONDON   MELBOURNE

Van Nostrand Reinhold Company Regional Offices:
New York   Cincinnati   Chicago   Millbrae   Dallas

Von Nostrand Reinhold Company International Offices:
London   Toronto   Melbourne

Library of Congress Catalog Card Number   64 – 17956

Published by VAN NOSTRAND REINHOLD COMPANY
450 West 33rd Street, New York, N.Y. 10001

Published simultaneously in Canada by
VAN NOSTRAND REINHOLD LIMITED

3   5   7   9   11   13   15   16   14   12   10   8   6   4   2

Contents

Illustrations

SECTION I

PURPOSE AND PROBLEM

1 THE PURPOSE OF THIS BOOK

This book's purpose is to show by simple towing and wind-tunnel tests on a class of one design sailboats, how much speed is gained or lost by hull, sail, and rig variations. Also to show that sailors compete under unseen handicaps of their ability to perform standard racing maneuvers.

Because each departure from perfection within a class has its cost in feet-lost per mile, the text shows sailors how to total their boat-and-skill failures for a personal "Race-Rating"—a distance they will on the average finish astern of class leaders in race after race.

The high rating of an expert helmsman can help him cure minor inefficiencies; the very low one of a beginner will show where to work for most improvement; even the losing sailor, obstinately wedded to methods long proved wrong, must in his mediocre rating, concede the cost.

2 BASIS OF THE VARYING RACE RESULT

Although the attractions of sailboat racing stand out in the sunshine—the healthy marine surroundings, a sporting tradition, the ability of sailors to win glory far into their sixties—we need only ask why one helmsman regularly leads his fleet, or one boat outruns her sisters, to see fogs of confusion drop from all compass bearings. A further paradox is that the racing approach beloved by cruisers and novice sailors guarantees they shall win few races.

Ego Is Out

The cruising sailor as he dips away to sea is pressing to his bosom a mistress of whom he can never tire. He may expand his romance in any way HE desires. The sea lies open before him. He may view it as a field of adventure across which he will surge like a new Sir Francis Drake; or with oceanographers he may study marine life, the tides and changing weather. The vastness of the sea consoles him, for its timeless ways foreshorten human problems. But always the complete choice of means and of methods is HIS alone.

Novice racers take even hotter pride in steering a personal course. Because sailing seems an inexact science they believe that techniques of their own invention will prove more gratifying and as effective as any others. Consequently, the businessman will buy a new hull, the best sails, and read a book or two, and the youngster with less equipment, but even taller hopes, will follow him to the starting line; and for several years

4

both will finish near the bottom of their class, while deluding themselves that it was all due to bad breaks, to wind shifts, or to someone else's trickery.

This book hopes to show that serious racers can not afford the warmly expanded ego. Even the most gifted crews in one design classes soon find that there are *best* ways of performing each racing task and that these skills can be most quickly acquired by careful imitation of the race-habits of those who finish above them. Margins of superiority are small, yet they govern so firmly that an experienced racer moving into a new class expects to go back to school. The good S-boat skipper racing for the first time in frostbite dinghies, knows that his surest path into the top third is through copying the habits of his new class leaders until *their* ways are also *his* ways.

The racing creed of the cruiser/novice differs most from that of the winning class boat sailor in that the novice thinks all sailing an Art, whereas the winner sees much Science forced upon him. Amateurs think taking a racing boat to windward is the highest kind of Art and something hardly teachable. But experience forces a majority of sail and hull trimming decisions. And crews who perform these slowly, sloppily, or not at all, find themselves left astern by regular distances in race after race. There is a reason for each gain or loss, and even the mysterious "taking a boat to windward" can be broken down into component acts of Science. Of course, some men will always outsail others, but it is correct technique that supports their superior skill and flair. Most also-rans approach sailing purely as a relaxation and do not relish close study of details. Experts, however, study continually and enjoy it.

A further confusion for sailors lies in the absence of firm doctrine on delicate adjustments such as tiller-touch, or whether a certain boat should be headed high or footed fast. While a few experts are indeed qualified to speak on these matters, for the best sailing methods are well-known to them, why is their expertise not more readily available?

Simply because, since the coming of the steamboat in the mid-nineteenth century, fast propulsion by sails has been a backwater with no big money in establishing its details. The last sailing vessels upon whose day-to-day speed large amounts changed hands were probably the Gloucester mackerel seiners. These crews doubled their take when they led the fleet home to T Wharf with a new catch. Consider how minutely such concerns are examined in the aviation industry, where upwards of three million dollars rides on each experimental airplane, and where, before that new model is wheeled out for first flight, its pilot already knows through simulators and wind tunnel data eighty per cent of the details on how to trim, maneuver, and land it. The best sailing practices would also be available if one Navy or Air Force life a year depended upon our knowing how to obtain the very maximum drive from cloth sails. Problems of sailboat handling are simple compared to those of aviation. Sails operate at the bottom of the wind speed ladder, and, regardless of size, their characteristics are similar; hulls and rigs need not withstand the crushing forces of high speed maneuvers; there is no varying altitude to consider, no Reynolds' Number.

This is not to imply that design of a new racing sailboat is simple. For Design *is* an art involving delicate compromises, plus the uncertainties of creation. But the problems of handling a new sailboat, once she is delivered to those who will race her, are of a lower order. For a tenth of the cost of testing one military airplane, a full sized wind tunnel, such as that available to NACA technicians at Wright-Patterson Air Force Base, could clarify all major questions of power derivation from cloth sails; and not for one class only. For $5000 any racing class, for example the Atlantics, might have their standard hull tested at a towing basin to determine its fastest trim on major points of sailing, or have this done full size.

Is it likely that such tests will soon be made? No, it is very unlikely. Even after *America's* Cup years the knowledge gained through building several defenders, plus challengers, remains largely proprietary and seeps down only slowly into general use. It is because of this lack of urgency, because no one seems to have tackled the broader aspects of racing in concerted fashion, that we make the simple tests outlined in this book.

Even Major Components of Racing Success Are Doubtful

As a final example of the fogs surrounding speed causes in sailboats, there has never been an accepted system of handicapping racers in one design classes. Winning is attributed either to luck or to some unnatural tinkering with the winning boat. Books on sailing attempt such rough evaluations of speed factors as: Helmsman and Crew—40%, Hull Condition—30%, Sails and Rig—30%.

The proportions vary with the writer, but are never advanced as concrete. They apply to only one theoretical racing situation—when a particular crew sails a hull of particular speed, using sails of specified value. The percentages can govern only one race, and during that race no values may change. Over a period of even two days, Helmsman and Crew should probably rate 75% or higher. For the second time out a good crew will start improving a bad hull and rig, and after a week even transform them completely, having by then polished the bottom to a mirror, or bought the very best sails. Conversely, a poor crew never improves poor equipment and in a short time brings good sails and a fine hull down to its own level.

There are a number of excellent books on sailboat racing, all doubtless mines of general information for the beginner. Based on their own distinguished records, the authors recommend routines that they hope will apply in all classes. They do not try to assign time or distance values to specific acts of rig tuning, nor to say in yards how much skill or ineptness in rounding a downwind buoy or tacking upon an enemy's wind will gain or lose; for it is assumed that such values must vary widely in different boats. The results are catalogues of recommended practice, with the various racing situations as headings. For example, under *Starting* the reader may be advised to: Get out to the line early; Establish the better end; Have stopwatches checked and ready; Read Circulars; etc. All worthwhile considerations. But they are hard to rate for importance against a background of no-specific-sailboat-class.

Once we resolve to look hard into why one sailboat defeats another, we note two obvious fields for the search:
1) In the boats themselves.

In their hull shapes, gear and adjustments. Here included are minor hull variations, such as bottom smoothness, shape of deadwood, and all fixed and semi-fixed tunings of rig. In a normal one design class these cumulative superiorities are larger than suspected.

2) In the sailing skill of helmsmen and crews.

Equally large superiorities are here concealed. And until human nature changes they will stay concealed; it being rare to hear a loser concede: "Lewis really outsailed us today"; although after every race we hear: "Lewis ran right into that new breeze off the shore; it hit him long before it did us."

Part of the service this book performs is the establishment of useful sailing handicaps, or "Race-ratings." Before they could be contrived it was necessary to view both boats and sailors in a sharper focus by:

1) Checking the gain/loss potential of various acts of tuning and tactical sailing against the background of a *known* class.

2) Providing a scale upon which to handicap, or Race-rate, boats and crews.

Simply as a convenience to the author we use the class of 19½ foot keel knockabouts now racing at Small Point, Maine. These thirty boats are of conventional design by Starling Burgess; all have been freely available for tests; and they are so normal that the reader will have no trouble in comparing their test results to his own fleet, be it of wooden boats, fiberglass, or, as at Small Point, a mixture of both.

The Race-Rating Scale

For the "Race-Rating Scale" a time interval over some standard distance might have served; but since time varies greatly in winds of different strength, a space interval was chosen. It is a minus figure: "Average loss in feet per racing-mile against *perfect* competition." A racing-mile is seen as including some proportion of windward work, reaches, and off-wind sailing, as well as part of a start and some buoy rounding. Widest possible loss over such a mile is estimated as *one foot in three sailed,* or minus 1760 feet. So great a loss would be very rare, and could only occur when a very bad beginner sailed a real clunker hull with atrocious sails, against Saint Peter (that great sailor) with Messers Knapp and Mosbacher trimming the Saint's sails. The average skipper loses far less: Class B, or second flight skippers, an average of 100 feet a mile to the Class A men. Note that this hundred foot gap between classes reflects differences in sailing skill alone, and assumes hulls and sails of equal value. With a poorer hull it would be more; with a better hull, less.

The material in this book will be presented as follows:

SECTION II gives brief details on the Small Point One Design Class, which serves as our background for hull/rig tests and for racing ability. Its sailing area in Casco Bay, Maine, is sketched, and the reader is told how the class began, the boat's characteristics, and those of the sailors who compete in her. How small hull variations started is considered, as well as the owners' opinions thereon. Human nature being the same in all racing areas, the reader should have no trouble in seeing behind this group his own fleet.

SECTION III tells how simple towing tests and a homemade wind tunnel were used to come up with speed ratings for Hulls, Sails and Rigs. A number of fixed and adjustable items were checked, each against our scale of possible "feet lost per racing-mile," after which Race-Ratings were assigned to each Small Point One Design. For example, when several were found to reach half a knot faster in moderate airs with the vang on than with it off, boats minus vangs were handicapped that amount. The reader should apply similar Race-Ratings to craft he knows well.

In SECTION IV we move out upon the course to study sailors' skills. How the Small Pointers sail each part of a race is told, from the start, on through the windward leg, and so to the finish. Again, racers will see their own fleet. Here once more, after widest possible loss is established, Race-Ratings are assessed.

SECTION V shows readers how to rate themselves in their own boats. Since many may not like what they find, several methods of confirmation are offered.

Now as we turn to our Background Class in search of what wins, let us remember that to hundreds of average racers the vital pleasures of sailing lie in the freedom they find there for competing casually under their own methods, while *imagining* they retain an equal chance.

SECTION II

A TYPICAL SMALL RACING CLASS CHOSEN FOR
BACKGROUND. ITS MINOR VARIATIONS.
ITS SAILORS' SKILLS

3

THE SMALL POINT ONE DESIGNS:
OUR GUINEA PIG CLASS

Casco Bay extends eastward some twenty miles from the city of Portland to the long, dangling finger of Cape Small. As one sails down-east across the bay, the Atlantic Ocean is open all the way to Spain on one's right, while many large islands and spiny points, such as Harpswell and Bailey's Island, claw out from the Maine coast on the left. The area is only half sheltered to the southwest, and it is from this sweep of ocean that prevailing summer winds blow at twelve to fifteen miles an hour. Light southeast winds that bring fog are also common, and fresh northwesterlies in the fall with air so clear that Mt. Washington stands out a hundred miles away. For racing purposes Casco Bay winds are less puffy than those of Buzzards Bay, and are generally of least velocity in the mornings. Both seas and swells are strong enough to affect racing sailboats; and because of a back eddy along the Small Point shore, concentrations of boats working to windward occur there with occasional groundings, collisions, and profaning of the rules.

The Small Point summer people have come to their colony since 1890, and are of five family groups. One branch stems from Philadelphia, one from New York, and the rest from New England. Over the years they have prospered and proved fertile. Where at the turn of the century there were less than thirty summer visitors in all, there are now more than a hundred children under twelve alone.

Before 1937 there was no class racing at Small Point, although the summer colony maintained half a dozen motor-

13

boats and one or two forty foot cruising sailboats. It is typical of the individualistic viewpoint of even the summer people in Maine that when they decided to promote sailing there was never the slightest consideration given to acquiring boats of an established class such as the Alden O's, or Winabouts, which were popular in those days. Nor was the Pine Tree, a round bilged cousin to the Lightning that was used on the New Meadows River nearby, thought seaworthy enough for the occasional heavy going in the open ocean off Cape Small.

At that time Mr. Starling Burgess had a summer place on Harpswell Neck in Casco Bay. Three senior Small Pointers contacted him. Their idea was to use a local boatbuilder, one Charles Gomes, of whom they all were fond, and who had turned out many of the local strip-built lobster boats and some sailboats.

Mr. Burgess chanced to own a fine little twenty foot knockabout of his own design that he called *Bunny*. She was a lively racing boat of rather short overhangs, planked yacht-type construction, and about four foot draft.

Mr. Burgess paid a call to Charles Gomes' boatyard at Sebasco, Maine, near Small Point. Several years before, Charley, as he is everywhere known, had built a twenty foot knockabout with a gaff rig, called *Arenjay*. Like his lobster boats, she was of strip construction and of the soft white pine known as "Maine mahogany." Charley had built several slightly smaller sailboats, and like all those who live where their grandfathers have lived and who use boats every day, he felt that he knew exactly what was required for those waters.

Mr. Burgess said little in Charley's yard, as was his custom, but studied the *Arenjay*. Some time later he sent to Small Point his "Design #80," which is roughly a compromise between his own *Bunny* and the *Arenjay* of Charley Gomes.

The Small Point 19½' One Design Class is a clever adaption. It is a hull suitable for Maine strip-building, a seaworthy boat of small draft, somewhat heavy with its 400 pound cast iron keel, and a moderate rig of 160 square feet in jib and mainsail, but with provisions for a 60 square foot genoa jib

Starling Burgess' Small Point One Design

Charley Gomes' original *Arenjay*, showing bilge and dead rise

if desired. This is about the sail plan of the Lightning Class on a heavier, round bilged hull.

Gomes built five of these boats in the winter of 1937–38, and their hull cost, less sails, was $385. Two more were ordered in the second year, and ten in all had been built before the war in 1941, by which time their hull price had risen to $800.

The boats were most successful. Not only did they prove to be sturdy day sailers, with fine accommodations for picnickers in their large cockpits, but they furnished close and spirited racing. After the war more boats were turned out by Gomes and several other builders, until twenty-nine have now been made to the original plans, with the going price, less sails, at $2800. Twenty-five of these boats sail at Small Point, four in Harpswell Sound.

Small Point racing, while sharply contested as to personalities, was at first rather low pressure. The boats were sailed with few genoas and only after 1955 with parachute spinnakers. There is no clubhouse at the Small Point Sailing Club, and the committee boat has often been a voluntary affair. Because it is inter-family sailing, there are basic differences on how racing should be run. All boats come out for a series of forty races during July and August. Different boats commonly win, the year's title being gained by whichever of the better sailors happens to be in Maine for the longest vacation that year.

The particular value of the Small Point fleet for such a study as the present one, is precisely its difference from so many "absolutely" uniform racing classes today, stamped it would seem out of so many miles of fiberglass sheet: the Small Point boats have sufficient variation to make the differences accessible, interesting and valid for a wide spectrum of other classes, from frost-biting dinks to Solings.

4
VARIATIONS IN THE SMALL POINT CLASS

Hearsay and Hull Differences

Of recent years there have been protests that the Small Point sailboats are only in theory a one design class. These complaints ring loudest from Harpswell, where the six boats comprising their fleet do have considerable differences.

It is well to indicate how, over a period of twenty years, hull changes took root. If these have altered the speed of the boats over what would obtain in a closely regulated class, such as the Lightning or International 210, we should be able to say where and how much. Or, our forthcoming towing tests may find no speed differences between any of these hulls, indicating that minor changes are of no importance.

In 1937 Starling Burgess was at the peak of his fame as a yacht designer. He was internationally known for his *Enterprise* and *Rainbow,* which had both successfully defended the *America's* Cup, and as co-designer with Olin Stephens of *Ranger,* the fastest J Class sloop ever built. But when he stepped from his car into Charley Gomes' boatyard, Mr. Burgess might as well have passed through a magician's doorway into another world. And in that world, restricted though it was, Charles Gomes was king.

Gomes had been building strip fishing boats for thirty years, as his father had before him. There are other builders of strip fishing boats in the area, but Charley has made the most—perhaps a hundred in his lifetime—and these up to forty feet in length. He had also built many small outboard boats for

Starling Burgess, designer of Small Point One Designs

inshore lobster trap hauling, and a dozen sailboats. He assembles his boats in the story and a half structure shown on the right, launching them on completion through the rear door when the tide is high.

His boats are all designed in his mind, with nothing on paper; for they are the result of a lifetime of experience, both his and that of his lobstermen and tuna fishing clients. His

Gomes' boat building shed

hulls have high bows, much flare and sheer, and are sea boats primarily, as befits craft that must live in the heavy Maine swells of winter.

The strip-built boat has no frames. A series of shapes are set up prior to construction, and around them the one inch strips of soft white pine are tapered to give the desired hull form. When the sheer line is reached the shapes are removed to allow decking over. The trimming of each strip is by eye. The strips may run to lengths of twelve feet, and are sawed out as needed from large boards. Fastenings normally are galvanized nails several inches long, driven down through the strips at intervals of a foot, and staggered over nails in the lower strips so that each passes through and secures several strips. Such nails last fifteen to twenty years, after which a strip lobster boat is considered worn out and likely to crack. When this happens at sea it is hazardous, for an entire seam may open. Small repairs, however, are easily made. Of late, copper hold-fast nails have been used.

It is illuminating to watch an old-fashioned hand craftsman. Charley Gomes will run an old boxplane the entire length of

Forms around which strips are built

Building up the strips. Forms will be removed later.

a twenty-five foot spruce mast and bring up an absolutely even shaving ⅛″ thick, while apparently paying little attention. Alvin Brewer, who builds boats next door using modern ma-

Charles Gomes, original builder of the class

chine tools, says that Charley can shape an oak stem by hand adz far quicker than he can do a like job by power.

Talk to Charley about the sailboats he has built and it is

easy to see that he is proud of them, and particularly of the
way they handle to windward. So, when Mr. Burgess came
down to look at his *Arenjay* before drawing the Small Point
One Design plans, Charley may have felt disappointed that the
boat was not left entirely to him. After all, he knew the waters
and he knew the owners.

One romantic account holds that when Burgess sent in his
drawings, Charley merely glanced at them, noted the length as
19½ feet, the beam and draft, then tossed them with some
lumber into a locker. Another is that when he made up two
sets of mold frames so as to erect two boats at once, he made
each of them slightly different from the other. Both stories are
doubtful; but he talks freely of the Small Point hull shape,
comparing it to the one he favors, and has never made it a
secret that he thinks his own *Arenjay,* and a newer version of
it, the *Royal Tern,* to be much abler boats that tack faster and
are better to windward. He compares the two sheers, remark-
ing that he did vary Burgess' design just a "little mite to make
her sharper forward, so she would hold onto the wind better."
He certainly made the rudders of all first five boats smaller
than the plans call for, and deepened the stem from the waterline down to the deadwood to give a little more lateral resistance.

Showing Gomes' design of stem.

Charley saw no reason why he should not improve upon Mr. Burgess' design. He was building a sailboat for local use that would carry his reputation. And in this he was quite right; for the Small Point Class have always been known as "Goomz boats," not as "Burgess boats."

The first five boats proved fine little sailers. No one ever came down from Mr. Burgess' office to check on their construction. And no Small Point owner ever checked Charley's hulls against the plan. The same applied to all ten hulls that Charley built before the war. They were essentially Burgess Design #80—as modified by C. Gomes—and everyone was satisfied.

In their early races the boats proved evenly matched. Some had seats and partitions inside, some did not. The first change from Charley's construction was in rudder shape, when one owner extended his slightly to conform to a suggestion he had received from M.I.T. for quicker response. This was not considered worthy of comment by others at the time. Maintenance of all boats was simple. One owner used Marblehead Green on his bottom and had the smoothest surface due to fine sanding; the others used a reddish Pettit paint much favored by lobstermen.

After the war Charley Gomes had a period of ill health. By that time the Small Point One Designs were considered entirely his. He did build three hulls, on the last two of which he exercised his creator's privilege by making their keels "a *strong* 400 pounds, and on the deep side," just for a change. Two of these went to Harpswell to start their fleet, but one of the heavy boats remained at Small Point, where she is noticeably at her best in blustery weather and stiffer than the others to windward.

For several years Charley Gomes was unavailable. But the Small Point summer colony was expanding and there was demand for new boats. Edward Sonia, a Bath construction man, had set up a boatyard with the aid of Governor Sumner Sewall, one of the founders of the Small Point Class. Sonia secured the help of a well known local boatbuilder named Blaisdell, and

together they built five boats to the Burgess plans. Sonia, being
a true son of Maine and 100% free under the U.S. Constitu-
tion, also felt that Mr. Burgess' lines could be improved upon.
As a result his boats were more rounded forward than either
the plans or the Gomes versions.

Sonia did not cut his stems in the deep Y that Charley favored, but ran them flush with the bottom ahead of the deadwood. In several boats he substituted watertight bulkheads fore
and aft for flotation tanks prescribed in the plans. His cockpit
rails were four inches higher, and his seats and floorings heavier. An unfortunate mistake was that in casting the Sonia keels
all came out with only 300 pounds of iron, as against the 400
pounds called for. Again no one considered checking them
against the Burgess plan.

An amusing example of boatbuilder's Freedom of Conscience
occurred when Edward Sonia decided that the Small Point One
Designs would be improved if built planked, rather than strip.
He started such a boat for himself to sell on speculation. The
Commodore of the Small Point Sailing Club took this strongly
amiss and told Sonia that the Burgess plan belonged to Small
Point and that if he persisted he could be sued. Such dogma-
tism confirmed Sonia in his enterprise. With great care he completed his new hull exactly to the Small Point lines, but with
a bare inch of tumblehome in the stern, which meant that its
sternboard at the deck was that much narrower than the others;
obviously a change of zero importance. This boat never sailed
at Small Point, so it is not known whether her planked construction made her faster or slower.

At Small Point the rounded Sonia boats proved faster than
the Gomes versions in reaching, but far slower to windward.
Some of their failures were due to poor rigging and sails. But
because their keels were 100 pounds light they were very
tender and rolled out badly in a breeze until they had proper
keels installed. Up to that point they had been thought logy
and slower than the Gomes boats.

Governor Sewall, who had purchased a Sonia boat, did not

win with her his first year, and sold her to the Harpswell area. Now that there were both Gomes and Sonia hulls racing together at Small Point, there began to be talk of "differences from the plans." Governor Sewall decided to have a boat built that he knew would conform. He commissioned the builder, Charles Blaisdell, to make him such a boat, and during construction had it carefully checked by Mr. Geerd Hendel, a young naval architect who had drawn the original plans for Design #80 while employed in Mr. Starling Burgess' office. This was to assure that all details of the new boat should be precisely as specified.

The new boat came out almost halfway between the Gomes V and the Sonia U forward sections. The Governor had been unable to obtain the original drawings, and so asked Mr. Hendel to trace out a new set from an old blueprint. For some unspecified reason it was decided to build this new boat planked, not strip, and to substitute ¾" cedar for ⅞" white pine. Mr. Hendel certified that the boat was exactly in accord with his new plan.

Governor Sewall was satisfied. But everyone else assumed that his boat was two or three hundred pounds lighter than the others—even Charley Gomes guessing that "she'd be a little lighter." So when the Governor won, as he did frequently, they said he had a better boat. This was clearly upon presumption, not knowledge, for the comparative weight of planked versus strip construction remains to be examined in these pages. While perhaps no faster than the Gomes boats, she is close winded and beautifully balanced. From which one may deduce that Mr. Burgess knew his business.

Of recent hulls, three have been by Gomes, all of which have done well in races, their only difference from his earlier ones being that they were copper nailed. Five more have been turned out by Captain Alvin Brewer, the ex-herring fisherman, who now operates a boatyard beside Charley Gomes' building shed. Alvin Brewer's hulls stick closely to the Burgess lines, and are edge-glued as is customary on strip boats built in Holland to add strength. One is of cedar strip, three of pine, and one of cypress taken from a dismantled brewery beer vat. All have raced successfully.

Twenty-nine hulls have been built to date to the Small Point One Design plans, with the differences noted, whose effects upon speed we shall presently evaluate. During the past few years several owners, whose primary concern is racing, have undertaken modernization of their boats. Simultaneously it has been observed that a few have done poorly in competition as a result of allowing theirs to degenerate into picnic craft or romance barges for moonlight sailing—both of which categories help to improve community growth in their own ways. Several boats have been left in the water over long periods, and as a result seem to have grown heavy in comparison with those class winners that are kept in the boatyard until just before the racing starts. One Sonia hull, which had previously never won, has been greatly improved by its owner carefully removing all excess fittings, planks, high cockpit combing, and any weight-adding material, including changing the floorboards into seats, for a total reduction of sixty-seven pounds. Since this boat won the class championship several years running, much comment ensued, it being felt that excess lightening was the reason. We shall check into the value of such reductions. One of the original Gomes boats, now thirty-five years old, has been given a thin fiberglas skin. Comment was mixed regarding the legality and advantages so derived.

If the reader's class is closely regulated, it is probable that variations in the Small Point hulls exceed those in his. It is interesting to state local opinion as to the value of such hull differences. Your author has sailed all the Small Point boats, and, excepting the handicap of a light keel to windward in a blow, found little speed difference when sails and fittings were equal. The fatter Sonia hulls do seem faster on reaches and slower to windward. Heavier boats seem at their best to windward in breezes over twenty-five knots. But whether this is due to the extra deadwood that Gomes says he put on one particularly heavy boat, or to its keel being on the fat side, remains to be determined here in our tests.

Local racers feel that while the original plans call for a weight of 2275 pounds, some of the boats are much lighter, and that this is an advantage. There are at least six different rudder shapes, and the most recent have trailing edges finely thinned. This is also felt to be an advantage; but how much is uncertain.

There is little regard for bottom smoothness. Half a dozen owners religiously burn off all paint every two years; others never do. Some smooth their keels each year; others don't. Some leave their boats in the water five or six months a season; some only for the actual races, and think this helps.

In fine, conjecture on hulls among Small Pointers might run this way:

1) The hull itself is the most important speed factor.

2) Whoever wins has the fastest boat; and probably illegally.

3) Just what makes the difference is uncertain; but it is probably lightness.

Mast Differences

Should a reader be shocked at the down-east free handling of Starling Burgess' hull plans for the Small Point Class—not only by boat builders, but by the owners—he will bow his head in despair at their disregard for Mr. Burgess' rigging instructions.

Starling Burgess was an undisputed genius at mast support and stress analysis. His work on the first aluminum spars for the J Class sloop *Enterprise,* as detailed by Harold Vanderbilt, entitled him to the veneration of even schoolboy sailors. But the riggers of the original five Small Point One Designs did not even examine his blueprint. It was unfortunate that the mast sticks procured for these first boats were green native spruce and somewhat whippy. But the riggers made them limber out of all proportion by placing the single side stays by eye, and deciding that a spot two feet below the one marked by Mr. Burgess would be about right.

The first sailing trial came on a windy day, and the masts

bent alarmingly. The riggers decided that Mr. Burgess was a bad guesser, and to better support the masts they added wide cross-trees and masthead shrouds. No check was made with the Burgess office. Galvanized wire was used with hand splicing; and the masts, now doubly supported, of course held.

Mast sizes were uniform, except on one boat that obtained a very light stick of small diameter. The only pre-war complaint resulted when the boatyard mixed up the masts one spring, so that some who had formerly had fine straight ones, ended with badly twisted spars that they were never able to unload upon the original owners. After the first half dozen whippy sticks, cut on a nearby hill, masts were of good quality spruce. All the Sonia boats had very good masts, held by $\frac{3}{16}$" stainless stays and cross-trees copied from the first ones, strong enough for a 10 Metre. Sonia masts were at first so large that two seagulls could sit upon their tops at once, a ludicrous sight. When Governor Sewall had his second boat built, it was rigged exactly according to the Burgess plan, except that double jumper stays, which by then had become fashionable, were added instead of the plan's single jumper. Owners who wished to improve their boats have since gone to a copy of Gov. Sewall's rig with its reduced windage and better set to the mainsail before the wind; for on any run the wide spreaders cut far into the mainsail.

The new Gomes and Brewer boats have exaggerated double jumpers with struts too wide and too far apart. It is interesting that six of the most recent boats with the single side stays called for by Mr. Burgess' plan, still have not followed it in attaching these stays to the mast; instead, they have again put them two feet too low as was done by error on the first boats, with the result that even in light winds all these masts curve badly. One owner has even gone back to the clumsy spreader rig in consequence. Thus we see mistakes first made through ignorance, perpetuated through custom.

All boats built by Gomes have their masts several inches forward of the spot recommended on the Burgess plan. With increased lateral resistance to the water forward, due to Charley's deeply cut Y stems, they may need such a small forward shift of the sail plan to counteract what would otherwise give increased weather helm. This detail Charley seemed to sense without being told.

The mast rake of Gomes boats varies considerably. All Sonia boats had their masts originally a full foot aft of the plan, and as a result had extreme weather helm. The mast placement of Gov. Sewall's boat, as checked by his naval architect, was precisely according to the plan, as have been those of the boats recently built by Alvin Brewer. One of the Brewer boats first had excessive aft rake to its mast and consequent weather helm, until corrected. We may therefore assume that, except where a slight forward placement is needed to balance out an increased lateral resistance in the stem of the Gomes boats, the Burgess mast placement is about correct.

General sailing opinion at Small Point pays little attention to masts until they break. Only a few have in thirty-five years, and those were due to tang failures. Several owners of early boats say their masts have warped so that the sailtrack no longer runs up straight near the top. They suspect that this hampers them on one tack; but they do not take the obvious step of simply unscrewing and straightening the track. The mast of one Sonia-built boat, when found to be thirteen inches aft of proper location, was moved forward, which necessitated cutting the deck. A few protests were made, not because the mast was moved, but because cutting the deck was somehow thought to have speed-giving implications.

Sail Differences

The original Small Point One Designs all had sails by the late Prescott Wilson. They were well made, on the flat side, with their greatest arch about in the middle. Some were small; and the word "small" is putting it mildly, for two measured 15% undersized. As a result, these boats only placed well in heavy breezes. Although the sail plan calls for four battens in the mainsail, the class got started with only three, and for some

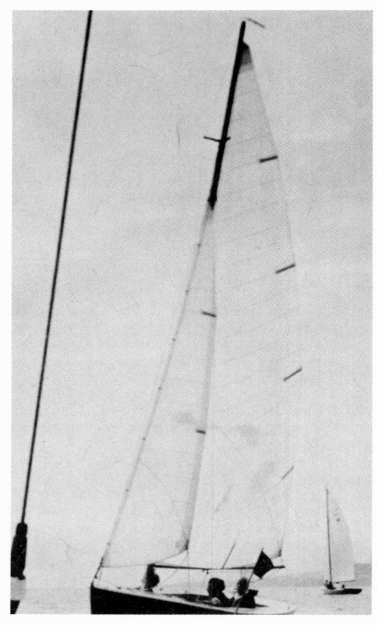

Sail plan of Small Point One Designs

reason, only three have been supplied by any sailmaker until recently.

The first set of pre-war Ratsey Egyptian cotton sails seemed very full. But since they were plainly faster in winds up to twenty miles an hour, more boats ordered them. There were two colored sails by Ratsey, one red and one blue, that were of extremely light material and which excelled in drifting conditions but soon stretched badly. No one questioned their use, even when they were six inches long on the boom. As happens in every class, several owners tried to save $30 by purchasing sails from unknown local makers. These proved hopeless in competition. One of the Sonia boats in particular was so penalized by them that she was considered a "real dud" and eventually sold away from Small Point. Her jib was fat and contoured like a ham. She could reach with it; but after rounding any leeward mark the boat felt as if she had run into a snowbank. She would simply fall away to leeward as everyone drove by.

Around 1957 the Small Point fleet became about two-thirds equipped with Ratsey dacrons. When first introduced, these sails proved outstanding to windward and others soon bought them. Several of the early sets arrived ten inches short in the hoist. It is curious that owners did not seem greatly interested in this, nor did they feel that in ordering sails they should specify exact dimensions. That is the sailmaker's business, they said.

A few general statements about sails may interest owners in other fleets. The Small Pointers first tended to stabilize on Ratsey dacrons. These were fine sails. In the intervening years sets by Hard have done even better, and one from the Hood loft quite well. Since 1970 Lowell North's products have become common. The Small Point sail plan of 160 square feet in working sails is almost that of the Lightning Class, where one sailmaker wins one year and another the next. Owners at Small Point are likely to use a single set of sails and not to order extra sets cut very full for light weather, or very flat for heavy. The larger genoa jib has recently caught on, and does speed up the boats.

Present canvas seems adequate in heavy weather, considering the
crews available, which are predominantly mothers and children.
Parachute spinnakers were bought on a fleet order from Hard,
and are cut on the small side to be suitable for reaching and
running.

As to opinions on sails, the Small Pointers give them little
thought. They do not measure their sails carefully, nor check
their construction. For some reason the larcenous possibilities
in sails do not strike the Small Point imagination with the
same impact as do those affecting the hull, such as removing
weight or greasing the bottom by moonlight. An owner who
went about boasting that his sails were extra large might draw
a few growls.

Differences in Fittings

The jib of Burgess Design #80 was originally club footed
and operated on a traveller with a single sheet. Few boats retained this arrangement for more than a year; although one
was moderately successful with a half club. All use loose footed
jibs today with either single or two part sheets.

A majority make some effort when going to windward to
trim their jibs along approximately the 12° line, following the
advice of Mr. Prescott Wilson and various books. But there is
no uniformity in this regard. Jib sheet leads were once checked
on all boats as a result of complaints that several would not "go
to windward on anything but the port tack." The reason
proved to be that on the bad tack the jib sheets were trimmed
out on about the 16° line, which made it impossible to head
up. Only six boats have adjustable jib sheet leads; a few trim
the jib further out for reaches than for windward work.

The mainsheet on some boats leads from the end of the boom
to a block exactly amidships, and is without a traveller. But
others with adjustable mainsheet travellers seem to get better
results.

There are only two snubbing winches in use, and since
the 1950's all use cam cleats extensively. Two boats have bars

across the forward end of the cockpit so that crews can sheet in their jibs more effectively. A number have filled in the forward corners of the cockpit for this purpose.

One way of arranging jib sheet controls

Clew outhauls are generally fixed, or cleated where they are impossible to adjust. Two-thirds of the boats have sliding goosenecks, but only a few tighten or loosen the main downhaul as winds vary.

Because the ladies who crew often have gentle hands and cannot hold a single part jib sheet in a twenty-five knot breeze, the following equipment, at one time rare, has now come to be quite standard: pivoting camcleats, jib reaching leads, geared trimming winches for outhauls, downhauls and the jib luff, wire halyards and halyard latches, carefully marked sheets, boom vang on trimming winch for use to windward, adjustable mainsheet traveller, tacking lines, large compass to aid tacking on headers, aluminum mast track.

In 1950 the vang, as a result of being used successfully by one boat, was adopted by seven others. In those days, whisker and spinnaker poles were often too light and too short for best adjustment. Some tillers were stubby and loose. Extra iron cleats dotted the decks where they could only serve to qualify owners to sing in the Vatican Choir. It is fair to say then, that the early Small Point sailors, in common with many of their brothers across the country, considered trimming and adjusting devices to be of little value and largely gadgetry. Camcleats were at first thought dangerous by some as a result of two boats filling up when distrusted skippers forgot to free the main-sheet as they rounded downwind marks. Children were warned against them, and many fathers piously held the tugging main-sheet as they steered. Hiking straps or hiking sticks were thought foolish; wind indicators such as masthead flies were too fancy; telltales were indeed to be found on some half of the fleet, but the helmsmen tended to sail more by sight and feel than by watching them.

In the meanwhile the reader may conclude that the old Small Point One Design class was certainly crudely rigged, incon-venient for green crews to learn in, or for ladies with their small hands, and lacking in sail adjustments to improve speed.

5
SKILL LEVELS AND BELIEFS OF SMALL POINT SAILORS

Since those who race sailboats are more important than the boats they sail, in that a skipper soon transforms a boat into his own image, we now briefly outline the characteristics of those who sail the Small Point fleet. The reader will, of course, contrast them with his own competitors.

At Small Point twenty-five boats sail forty races a summer. As few of the male owners average more than three weeks in residence, there is a large turnover in the handlers of each family's boat, with a total of about sixty skippers participating.

Class	Sailing ability	Equivalent golf score	No. at Small Point
A	Place high in any average fleet	75	4
B	Competent, steady sailors	85	10
C	Of moderate skill, but erratic	95	14
D	Of some experience, but skills undeveloped	105	20
E	Beginners	115 and up	12

Visiting skippers in Class B often stop by; only two Class A visitors have competed in recent years, one a lady champion from Cold Spring Harbor, and one *Weatherly* crew member.

Crews total another sixty. These include mothers, friends, visitors, children and a few dogs. They may be classed as both Experienced and Inexperienced; but largely Inexperienced, since those fairly advanced like to skipper and can generally pick up an unused boat.

Boats seldom race with less than three persons, for participation is general. And, of course, in heavy weather "everyone loves a fat man."

Small Point helmsmen operate under limitations that apply at many summer colonies: the men are only there during their vacations, the season is short, and the skipper of a borrowed or family boat does not feel free to alter or adjust. Numbers and proportions of sailors in the five skill classes above seem about standard. As to the numbers of each class who take part in the average race and their normal order of finish:

1) It is seldom that more than two of the Class A sailors are on hand at once.

2) The four Class A sailors win two-thirds of all races, and rarely finish worse than third.

3) There will normally be about three Class B helmsmen; and they win virtually all other races and finish in the top third.

4) Class C has some good, but decidedly erratic performers, who win an occasional race in weather exactly suiting their skills, or when for some combination of circumstances they have a good boat and let it sail itself; otherwise they finish in the middle or lower.

5) Class D helmsmen almost never win. Occasionally they stay up with the leaders for a leg or two.

6) Class E sailors are in constant trouble with their sail trimming, and are satisfied to get around the course.

Typical sailing experience of the five classes is:

Class A—all have had at least twenty years of competition. All are men, and steady sailors to whom racing is the ultimate pleasure. They are very keen to win, and will take endless trouble with their boats. They think of racing during the winters; and when competing are jumpy and extra alert.

Class B—The USNR type. They have what seems to the Class A helmsmen the quaint idea that other things are equally as important as racing. They may be as experienced, but spend less time on their boats and have fixed ideas about technique. They are often even better seamen and cruising sailors than the Class A operators, and they sail more calmly.

Class C—these helmsmen may be good in specific races. But they have some unsteady quality that leads them to mistakes under pressure, so their performance varies greatly. They have more chance to rise to Class A than the Class B men, whose skills seem fixed. Some women are in this class, who are good in light weather but lack aggressiveness.

Class D—in their formative years.

Class E—in their first or second season.

Characteristic Beliefs

It is interesting to contrast the opinions of our classes of sailor, regarding the very existence of skill-levels and Race-Ratings. Those of medium accomplishment doubt that they exist, and anyone can win a given race if he is lucky. The few Class A helmsmen all know that they have a lot to learn and that they can easily find someone to trounce them in a tighter class elsewhere. They are more open minded than the Class B's, all of whom are sure they could win half the races too, if only they wanted to take the time. Male skippers in Class C are even more sure of this, and recall how they "used to win as a boy down on the Cape," and how they beat the Class A sailors at tennis and make more money too, "So there *can't* be any sailing skill difference, and it must be in the boat." The most vocal of all are the wives of moderately skilled sailors who insist that *their* families sail for fun, and who want to keep their boat fully equipped for picnics and midnight sails, but still to win races in her. Class D's don't worry much about winning; and Class E's not at all, being well satisfied to finish a race without incident.

Over thirty years of racing in Maine, no Small Pointer has ever been heard to concede that a winner came in first because "he beat me upwind," or "he sailed a fine race." He (or she) always won because his boat was faster. From which we deduce that racers tend to over-rate their own skills, and not to believe that Race-Ratings apply to them.

Now before turning to our Tests, we summarize opinions on boats and sailing skill as held in our Background Class. The reader will see his own area and class as he reads.

As to *Hulls,* Small Point opinion says:

Gomes boats are the fastest. The important thing is a light hull—the degree of lightness is unknown. The weight of any boat can only be guessed at; but winners are certainly illegally light. Since Sonia-built boats have been proved slower in the past, for anyone to win with one is proof of skull-duggery. Gov. Sewall's planked boat is lighter than the rest. So when he wins it is due to that; of course any losing is up to him.

As to *Bottoms* and *Surface Smoothness:*

This is a matter of indifference. The weight of water absorbed into a hull by long immersion is simply guesswork. Foulness of bottom is unimportant until grass is plainly visible.

Masts, Stays, and *Trimming Leads:*

These are seldom considered. A stiff mast with cross-trees and extra stays is preferable to any whippiness with small windage. Sailors below Class B ignore the angle of sheet leads and simply sail a boat as they find it.

Sails:

Sails are thought much less important than hulls. Oversize is not checked, and undersize up to 10% of area seldom mentioned.

Tuning of *Boats:*

Tinkering or excess working upon a boat is considered a bit naive, and likely to be unsuccessful. If successful, it is thought somewhat unfair.

Respect for *Winning Efforts:*

Certain sailors are acknowledged to win a large percentage of the races, but are not necessarily admired on this account. To finish in the top five or six is creditable.

Additional "Sailors' Hallmarks":

Competitors recognize little difference between their own abilities and those of persistent winners. Women are less aggressive than their husbands on starts and crossing situations, and are more rule abiding.

Little or no study is made of local phenomena, such as tides or currents. Areas of favorable countercurrent and wind slants are known; but a sailor 100 yards behind will still tack away from these areas in a gamble to beat any leaders who are sailing in them.

No effort is made by the less successful to learn from the more successful; although the winners are quite willing to pass along their personal recipes. Since all prefer to sail by their own methods, and persist in these, even when proven wrong, a winner can reveal his every practice with the certainty that it will not be copied.

The less a sailor knows, once he is grown up and established in his life style and livelihood, the less he desires to test the validity of his racing knowledge and the more closed his nautical mind becomes.

An open mind characterizes the top sailor.

SECTION III

TESTS TO SHOW SPEED DIFFERENCES BETWEEN SAILBOATS

6 HOW BOATS ARE RATED

We have sketched our Background Class. The reader may object that there are more exaggerated differences in the Small Point One Designs than in his own fleet. This is no doubt true. *Fortunately, we can put these variations to use.*

The best way to study speed controlling factors in sailboats is to use a class in which only single items vary. The Bembridge Redwings of the Isle of Wight have identical hulls; sail plans are limited to exactly two hundred square feet of area; but they may be lateen, dipping lug, Bermudan, or hermaphrodite brig if the owner fancies. In the Moth Class it is the hulls that are free. The Small Point One Designs have small changes throughout, but because pairs of boats often differ in single items only, through contrasting these we may obtain a body of knowledge.

To confirm information taken from the larger Small Point One Designs, an active class of eight-foot sailing prams is also available there.

In this Section we try to resolve major speed uncertainties in boats alone. And because Hulls, Sails, and Trimming Devices each ask special treatment, we consider them in turn. Having demonstrated the *widest possible* performance gap for each item, handicaps in feet may be assigned particular boats. Such footage, when combined with what we later assess against their handlers' skills around the course, will allow complete Race-Ratings.

The reader will view all tests as if made upon his own boat. A pleasure of sailing is the entertainment of firm opinions; so

before each test let him state flatly what he believes its out-
come will be. As Ted Wells, the Snipe champion, says: "It is
not that sailors are ignorant: it is just that they *know* so many
things that aren't so."

7
ASSEMBLING AND CALIBRATING A TOW TEST RIG

This is an account of Hull Tests run in the summer of 1961. Owners of the Small Point sailboats were only mildly interested to see theirs being pulled about at strange angles of heel. Several did ask why anyone was foolish enough to scant the really important things of life, such as cocktail parties, or the production and rearing of children. And two suggested that the whole thing might be done more easily with models.

Unfortunately, accurate models are hard to come by. Estimating sailboat speed by towing them in a tank is a magical art practiced by naval architects at Stevens Institute. Experts spend their lives refining model simulations and devising corrections for scale. With so many sailboats available at Small Point in the shape their builders made them, it seemed best to test these full size at once, and even though results might be rough, no imaginative corrections would be required.

Only those matters about which sailors are strongly divided were tested. And those on quite obvious differences in weight, hull shape, bottom smoothness, trim, leeway and rudders. Besides securing access to hulls, some test equipment had to be assembled. Hulls had to be weighed to find whether displacement differences actually *did* exist. Fortunately, contour variations in underbodies or deadwood stood out to the eye and were measurable. But the most important part of each hull test was proof of whether an acknowledged alteration changed speed. This required the ability to *tow* hulls and to compare the forces needed to move them.

The Towboat

A week passed before satisfactory towing operations were
established. First resort was to a fifteen foot outboard boat with
a 7½ hp. Evinrude motor. It could tow sailboats thirty feet
long up to their normal hull speeds of six or seven knots. But
a chunky twenty-five foot cruising motorboat proved able to
hold a much steadier course when so burdened.

Numerous ways of towing by lines and outriggers were tried.
The best was to lash a T-bar across the foredeck of the motorboat, which drew the sailboat along well out to the side in
smooth water, clear of the towboat's bow wave and propeller
currents.

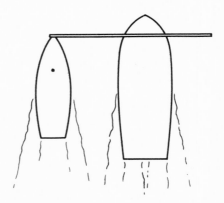

Placing the sailboat squarely alongside gave good observation and control. A towing bar so used must be well fastened
to the motorboat. Several times the Small Point T-bar broke
lose on passing through the wakes of lobsterboats, and came
aft like a scythe ready to lop off heads and the top of the outboard motor.

The towline led in through a low friction pulley on the end
of its bar, and so to a Chatillon meatmarket scale, whose "60
lbs." top reading was quite enough for a Small Point One De-

sign up to six knots. Except in moderate seas, this scale performed steadily without damping.

The Speedometer

An accurate speedometer proved the heart of these tests, for without one no repeat results were possible. Throttle and rpm settings varied too much under load to serve, and while a few expensive marine speedometers are on the market, they were judged insensitive over the low one-to-two knot speeds that are important to sailboats.

A towed device, using a dampened spring scale seemed indicated; so floats and vanes of several shapes and sizes were tried. Some would hop from the water, some would dive, while the Devil ruined all by draping them periodically with seaweed to cause ridiculous readings. Clearly, whatever was used had to be drawn along *over* the surface, while still maintaining a moderate pull. The solution was to tow a standard rowing pram with a stern skeg long enough to assure straight track-

Calibrating the dinghy

ing. The first pram tested gave steady readings that increased progressively with speed. It was secured to the opposite end of the motorboat's towing bar, where it slid along in smooth water of its own, half counter-balancing the pull of the sailboat under test and allowing the motorboat to hold a straighter course. The towline ran to another scale with readings up to 20 lbs., that covered speeds of seven knots.

Because the Speedometer Pram had to give accurate speed readings day after day, its exact calibration was vital. This consumed a full morning, and was achieved by pulling it to and fro past measuring stakes on the shore, with time-to-pass taken on a stopwatch. One man ran the towboat and pram up and down, he noting pounds-pulled by the pram at each change of speed, while two wives ashore took time-to-pass between the stakes. An interval of 88 feet was used, because 88 feet a second equals 60 mph, and it is easy to make up a chart for sailboats that at a glance converts seconds-to-cross this gap into miles an hour.

Calibration of the Speedometer Pram over its one-to-seven knot range had to be repeated until an accurate curve was obtained. Runs were made in each direction and their average taken to cancel out current or wind. As many as half a dozen confirmation checks were made at each low speed. When at last a smooth speed-curve for that pram was in hand, it was

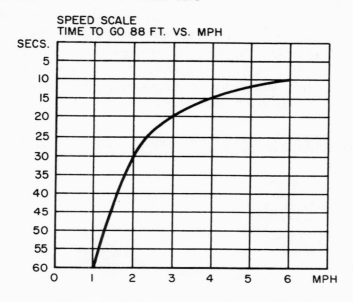

SPEED SCALE
TIME TO GO 88 FT. VS. MPH

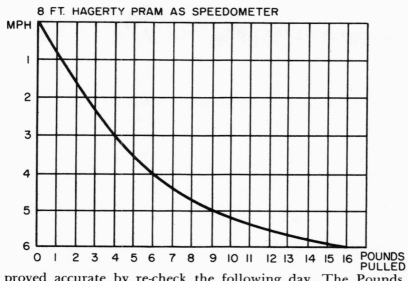

8 FT. HAGERTY PRAM AS SPEEDOMETER

proved accurate by re-check the following day. The Pounds figures were then covered by an overlay showing Miles per hour directly.

To begin a tow test it was now only necessary to hook up the calibrated pram, adjust the towboat's throttle to a speed somewhere within the 1 to 7 knot range, and read speed directly off the pram scale. Damping of this scale was satisfactory, if not perfect, and steady readings could always be obtained when they were given time to settle down.

Towing one design with dinghy to measure thrust, etc.

The same personnel performed each test:
1) A towboat helmsman to steer a steady course and change speed.
2) A light boy to ride the towed sailboat, heading it straight as required.
3) A wife with good handwriting to keep notebooks, take readings, and draw fair curves of Pounds pulled vs. Speed.

Incidental Towing Gear

Extra lines were needed so that the sailboat hull might be pulled askew at the stern for simulated leeway, or heeled from up its mast. In displacement tests the means of progressively adding weight was to center an empty 55 gallon oil drum in the sailboat, then pour in fifty pounds of water at a time by bucket.

Early Use of Towing Equipment

Anyone wishing to duplicate these tests might start with the Pounds pulled curve of a light rowboat. Ninety-five percent of all towing is in smooth water, which is most likely in the early morning. Once there is experience in hooking up all gear—the tow bar, Speedometer Pram, and towed hull—and after a simple rowboat test has been re-run with identical results, the larger sailboats may be attacked. For example, when sailors of a fleet are convinced that two hulls differ widely in speed (in the pounds they pull when towed at equal speeds), such assumed difference may be checked out.

Constructing the two speed curves here will be easy enough, so long as towboat speed is carefully noted against Pounds pulled by each sailboat, and enough readings are taken at low, middle, and high points to fill in the curve shape over six knots, approximately the speed range of these hulls. When occasional rogue readings distort a curve, re-checks must be run. The speed scale may have stuck, or the towed sailboat have ploughed into a mass of floating seaweed.

Routine procedure in such tests at Small Point was:
1) State a cause that in local opinion *surely* affects sailboat speed; e.g., Excess Weight, or Foul Bottom.
2) Determine by weighing or visual inspection whether this condition truly exists.
3) If it does exist, find where and, to the extent possible, why.
4) Now run tow tests to learn whether the proven difference does in fact alter speed.

Where harmful effects were believed to lie in Overweight alone, only one hull was towed under progressively greater loads of water. But when a slow-down was attributed to Poor Bottom, either one boat had to be towed in her rough bottom state, then shined and re-towed; or two otherwise identical sisters were chosen, one with mossy, one with glistening flanks.

Care was always taken to proceed at a leisurely pace, using rigorously standard procedures, remembering that the goal was not micrometer accuracy so much as reliable and consistent results from a full-sized hull that would be impossible to argue with.

8

TESTING SAILBOAT HULLS

FOR HULL WEIGHT

Few sailboat owners know within two hundred pounds what their boats weigh. Checks of gross weight are commonly made on small craft, such as Snipes, at the end of construction as part of the measurement certificate. These hulls may be set upon scales. Expensive 12 Metre boats receive displacement checks on launching, and their flotation lines are further verified before important races and after changes in trim. Builders of intermediate sized hulls check displacement carefully on the first few, then assume that others made of like materials will weigh the same. Weight checks during the competitive life of class racing boats are seldom made. Even the tightly regulated International One Designs do not establish poundage gained or lost during a season.

Because sailors are hazy on the weight differences between their hulls does not mean they hold vague opinions on the rewards of lightness or heaviness. Racers firmly believe that a light hull is faster than a heavy one under average conditions, but that in rough going the heavy hull will gain because it maintains better momentum through breaking seas. These opinions are rationalizations of what has been seen upon the course, and may confuse primary speed causes with collateral effects. For the owner of a heavy boat may well be a good heavy weather skipper who would place high then in any hull, and the weight of his boat only a reflection of his disregard for low weight as the fetish of light wind sailors.

The opinion of Ted Wells is characteristic of the expert.

Ted feels that although a heavy hull loses less momentum in passing through high seas than a light one, it will also recapture lost way more slowly, and so in the end average to be slower in rough going. Jack Sutphen, a champion in the numerous and extremely even Larchmont Interclub Dinghies, says that heavy hulls in his class suffer no light weather handicap so long as winds remain steady and seas flat—so long as momentum of the heavy hull, once established, is not repeatedly checked and forced to rebuild. It does appear that no matter how small the friction (and a sled towed on slick ice would be about the minimum), it must require more work to pull a sled or boat loaded with 800 pounds than one with under a hundred. But in sailboats the complications are not resolved by the common sense answer that a heavy hull sitting low is slow because it must push more water aside than a light one. Certain J. Class boats have upped their light weather speed by *adding* ballast. And this speed was not improved by better stability, but under flat drifting conditions. Sinking the hull to some faster underwater profile may have contributed.

Weight Test A. Do weight differences exist in class sailboats?

We now examine the effects of extra weight in two Small Point classes: the 8′ sailing prams, about whose poundage no one argues, and the Small Point One Designs, about which even naval architects who drew the plans disagree.

Twenty 8′ sailing prams are raced in the Small Point Back Bay by children. A half are copies of the old Hagerty rowing pram, shown in the photograph on page 66, while those built more recently have taken the hull shape of the International El Toro Class, which features more beam and a lifted bow. Fifteen are of plywood, four of colored fiberglas sheet, and one of plywood heavily covered with fiberglas. These prams are raced by any and all children, some of them skillful, some complete beginners. Class A and B adults rarely sail them except as a joke, for they are too small to support heavy tonnage. The prams are beached when not in use. There is no proof that one wins more races than another. And since they are not regarded as proprietary possessions, any skipper thinking a particular boat faster due to lightness, heaviness, or anything else, simply sails that boat.

All prams were weighed upon a bathroom scale. Including rig, oars, rudder and daggerboard, their all-up displacement came to:

No. of boats	Weight	Materials
1	95 lbs	Plywood
11⁻	100–105 lbs	Plywood
4	105–110 lbs	Fiberglas sheet
3	110–115 lbs	Plywood
1	130 lbs	Plywood with thick fiberglas skin

Prams with sides and bottoms of colored ⅛" fiberglas sheet averaged 5 lbs. heavier than their sisters of ¼" fir plywood. The one really heavy boat was the grandmother of the fleet, and to give this ancient Hagerty model strength it had been cased in a full fiberglas skin. No boat has proved noticeably faster than another; even the very heavy one wins as much as any. Average weight difference between these prams was less than 10%. The very heaviest, a special case, is 30% heavier than the very lightest, which is also alone in its class.

Weighing the larger Small Point One Designs presented complications. The boats are 19½ foot keel knockabouts that sit in cradles when ashore and require several men to move them. They are by different builders, each of whom interpreted the plans differently as to scantlings. Both strip and planked construction exist. Woods are white pine, cedar and cypress. Boats vary in age from ten to thirty-five years, so that water-logging due to immersion differs. Some boats sit overboard five months a season, some only two. Partitions, floorboards and seats vary. Paint thickness is dissimilar.

The 1937 Burgess plan for the Small Point One Designs called for a weight of 2275 pounds at Waterline 2. Mr. Geerd Hendel on retracing the plans in 1949, reduced this figure to 1705 pounds 1¾" below waterline 2, which is with the counter touching the surface. A majority of Small Point owners think the plans are accurate on hull weight, but that winning boats have been reduced several hundred pounds through recourse to a dark art known to New England school children as "jippery." Capt. Brewer, who moves all the Small Point hulls about his boatyard, declares that none weighs over 1600 pounds. No one frets about different specific gravities in the woods, although this is .32 for cedar, about .35 for cypress, and .37 for white pine. All believe that Governor Sewall's boat is light by 200 pounds because it is planked, not strip-built; even Charley Gomes guesses "she's a little lighter," on this account. Again Capt. Brewer disagrees, for he balances off the 35 pounds of nails used in a strip boat against the substantial frames of one planked. Owners are so sure of big weight differences that they classify boats as "light weather" and "heavy weather" on this assumed factor. But no one *knows* what a single boat weighs by actual test.

A large platform scale was borrowed from a junk yard and set into a trench at the head of Capt. Brewer's launching ways. The Small Point One Designs were jacked up free of their cradles and weighed with masts and booms aboard, first as they went overboard in the spring, then again on haulout in the fall, to establish any gains due to moisture absorption over the summer.

Hull types	Pounds
7 Gomes hulls 12–25 years old	1425–1670 lbs
2 Sonia hulls 12 years old	
1 Gomes hull 10 years old with heavier keel	
3 Gomes hulls 7 years old	1355–1400 lbs
4 Brewer hulls 1–6 years old	
1 Gomes hull 18 years old, very well kept	
1 Brewer hull, strip built of cedar, 5 years old	1100 lbs
1 Blaisdell hull, planked of cedar, 10 years old	1025 lbs

This is far greater difference than even the wildest guess of the uninformed, and shows no similarity to the hull weight called for in any plan. A maximum gap of 645 pounds exists between the oldest boat in the fleet, loaded down with paint, and the planked cedar hull—about 60% variation!

No boat displaces anything near the 2275 pounds called for in the 1937 plan. Even the 1708 pounds called for by Mr. Hendel for a cedar boat at a lower waterline is not reached. The heaviest and oldest white pine hull displaces 605 pounds under its plan, the planked cedar boat 683 pounds below its suggested figure. The hull that Gomes built with a slightly heavier keel weighed 1550 pounds, placing her about in the middle of the heavy group. She had all paint burned off before her test, so otherwise might have been near the top. She is classed as a "heavy weather boat." The Sonia hull that many felt had been excessively lightened, weighed 1525 pounds, also well in the heavy group, in spite of her always being outstanding in light weather. One twenty-five year old Gomes hull, that had been given a complete fiberglas skin, after much discussion as to its legality, weighed 1475 pounds. All paint had been removed and fiberglas materials put on totalling 75 pounds. One Gomes boat seventeen years old that had never been allowed to accumulate paint weighed no more than her duplicates seven years old.

Less weight difference than expected was found between strip and planked hulls of the same material; but more than expected between cedar versus white pine hulls. The Specific Gravity of cedar, at .32 versus .37 for white pine, means that 870 pounds of cedar can replace 1000 pounds of white pine in a boat, a saving of 130 pounds. The strip cedar hull did weigh 75 pounds more than her planked sister. But Mr. Hendel's 1949 plan called for planks $3/4''$ thick, whereas the strip cedar boat was built to the original thickness of $7/8''$. This is a ratio of 6 to 7; so 75 pounds could lie here. Planked hulls of the *same wood* as strip ones should therefore weigh virtually the same, and the lightness of the two cedar hulls should reflect their materials.

Weight Test B. What Causes Weight Differences?

Since weight differences averaged less than 10% of total displacement in the 8′ Sailing Prams, but almost 60% in the Small Point One Designs, we shall tabulate the sources of higher weight in each class.

8′ Sailing Prams

A maximum difference of 5 pounds was found in the water content of similar 1/4″ plywood hulls. Boats built of 1/8″ colored fiberglas flat-sheet averaged 5–7 pounds heavier than plywood hulls. The one extra heavy boat had been covered with fiberglas cloth and thick resin, adding 8 ounces per square foot, or 30 pounds in all.

Small Point One Designs

At the start of the racing season the following sources of varying displacement existed:

Difference	Max. Weight Gain
A few inches in overall length, or girth, which may cancel out, leaving possible bulk variations up to 2%.	100 lbs
Keels vary 25 lbs. in casting, and one is slightly fat.	75 lbs
Masts vary in materials and diameters.	25 lbs
There are strip and planked hulls, with strip assumed a shade heavier.	50 lbs
Cedar, cypress and white pine have different Specific Gravities.	150 lbs

Planking thickness varies from $\frac{7}{8}''$ down to $\frac{3}{4}''$.	50 lbs
Amount of paint differs; 15 coats of oil based paint is maximum, two of thin epoxy, minimum.	100 lbs
Waterlogging due to moisture held in planking over the years, with no effort to dry it out, can vary.	100 lbs
Widest displacement difference between the heaviest Small Point clunker and the lightest boat.	650 lbs

This table shows possible weight differences between hulls as they are launched in *the spring*. It is uncertain how much more a wooden racing boat can take on when she is sailed "wet" over several months; that is, when she lies all summer at her mooring without extended haulouts. Small Point sailors ignore this possibility. But experts in hot classes, such as Stars, sail their boats "dry," keep them out of water to the extent possible, and feel this is necessary in their grade of competition.

Relative to keeping weight low, it is worth observing that a racing boat can absorb as much moisture from within as without, if she is unpainted under her floorboards, as are a majority of the Small Point One Designs. Rain and water shipped during a race are quickly sucked in, for none of these boats use cockpit covers.

Weight Test C. How Much Moisture Does Untreated White Pine Absorb?

Identical blocks of white pine, one unpainted, but the rest given three thick coats of the best marine deck and bottom paints, were submerged thirty days in a kettle. Weight of each block was regularly checked, with these results after a month:

Paint used	Gain as % of first weight
None	85%
Oil based, highest figure	25%
Oil based, average figure	16%
Oil based, lowest figure	12%
Epoxy paints	9%

Unpainted cedar and cypress blocks were also checked, and one white pine block completely sheathed in fiberglas. As compared to the weight gain above of 85% by white pine,

Cedar gained	Considerably less
Cypress gained	Much less
Fiberglas covered gained	Almost nothing

Weight Test D. Seasonal Absorption

8' Sailing Prams

When not sailed, these little boats are pulled up on the bank where they dry out easily, but do take in rain. Gains over a summer from all causes were:

Plywood hulls	1 to 3 pounds
Fiberglas flat-sheet hulls	0 to 1 pounds

Small Point One Designs

Greatest gain by any hull	255 pounds
Average weight gain	150 pounds
Minimum weight gain	65 pounds
Gain by hull with full fiberglas skin	50 pounds

The Small Point One Design with the greatest summer gain was a Gomes hull fifteen years old that had sat drying in the open sun for two months prior to spring launching. She had no paint under her floor boards and only two thin coats on her bottom. Boats with paint under their floor boards averaged to absorb 50 pounds less than those that were unpainted. Boats with widely spaced floorboards, allowing sunlight and air to circulate and dry them out, also showed lower gains. The boat with a minimum gain of 65 pounds had vinyl based bottom paint, no floorboards at all, and a skin of fiberglas inside her garboards that had been put on to check small leaks. Epoxy paints were used on her topsides.

It appears that more moisture than expected is absorbed over a season by racing boats sailed wet. Owners wishing minimum weight gain at a mooring must give thought to painting inside beneath all floorboards, preferably with epoxy paints. A cockpit cover will exclude rain. An outside fiberglas skin keeps out approximately its own weight in water that would otherwise enter the hull. If it stops leaks, it promotes further lightness around the course.

Cumulative Absorption over the Years

It is not only possible for boats to absorb water when they are overboard, but old ones may *retain* it under thick layers of paint and never dry out. The possibility that an old boat may be guarding its moisture was investigated by removing a strip of white pine from the garboard of one built twenty years ago, sanding off all paint, then weighing and comparing this strip with new ones of identical size.

The old strip was brown after sanding, and weighed 60% more than new white ones. After a month in the sun the old strip had still not returned to equal lightness; although this was eventually achieved by baking it slowly in an oven.

How much weight can be saved if all paint is carefully removed each year? And, since it is clear that boats that are caked with paint do not win races, at what point does a boat become "paint sick"?

The weight of removable paint was easy to establish. Some Small Point hulls have been gathering it for years, where others have it burned off each spring. As a rule, only sides and bottoms are taken down to the bare wood; paint inside a cockpit is difficult to remove and so seldom is. A gallon of deck paint weighs 12–15 pounds. So these hulls add approximately fifteen pounds of paint a year. In ten years, if none has been burned or sanded off, 150 pounds of paint must ride free around the course. Of course few are so handicapped; but a Lightning Class racer with half this load would not be a winner in good competition. Slough off her heavy skin and there is 75 pounds less for the sails to move, plus a smoother racing finish of un-caked paint.

Weight Test E. Gains by Removing Paint from an Extra Heavy Boat

The heaviest Small Point One Design weighed 1670 pounds at spring launching. After two months at her mooring, and a number of poor finishes in races, she had gained another 200 pounds. The exasperated owner ordered all paint burned off in the fall. This cost what the boatyard called a "pot full," but the boat lost 140 pounds. She was left unpainted to dry out, but covered against rain. A month later she had lost another 100 pounds of entrapped moisture, and two months later, in spite of cold weather, 50 pounds more. She was then given a priming coat and covered for the winter.

When refinished in the spring she had lost a little more, and went into the water 200 pounds under her spring weight of the year before. This left her still in the heavy section, but near the bottom of that.

Are Heavy Hulls Necessarily Slow?

We now come to the weight question asked by both duffers and class champions: "Does it pay to lighten a racing boat?"

The following tests were run with towing equipment previously described.

Weight Test F. Increased Pull of Rowboat as Weight Is Added

This is the simplest possible test for change in pull of a row-boat, towed along at set speed, in this case three miles an hour, with weight added in 100 pound increments.

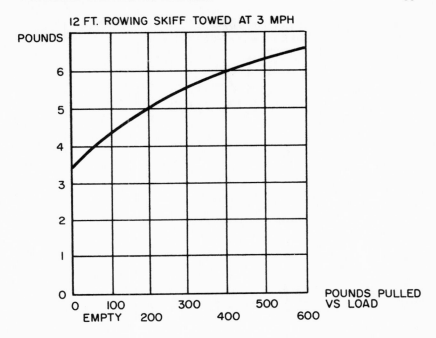

When unloaded, the rowboat asked 3½ pounds of pull from the towboat.

When fully loaded to 600 pounds, 6½ pounds were needed— an increased pull with added weight of almost 90%.

Conclusion: The heavier the rowboat grew, the more power was needed to tow it.

Weight Test G. Pull Change of an 8′ Sailing Pram as Weight Is Added

In this first check of a sailboat hull, a standard 8′ sailing pram was towed in smooth water without leeway or heeling. After enough pull figures were obtained to yield her curve at zero load, 50 pounds were added at a time.

Pounds-to-pull in three load states show clearly that as load was increased the pram became harder to pull at any set speed.

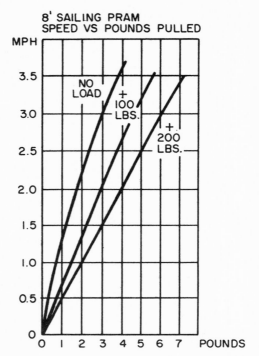

Weight Test H. Pull of a Small Point One Design Under Increased Load

Using standard tow procedures, and neutral trim, a Small Point One Design had her load progressively increased. Speeds covered were 1–6 knots. The chart shows Pounds-to-pull in "unloaded" and "heaviest" condition, the latter being plus 700 pounds.

Again the heaviest condition demanded most propulsion. Near the top of each curve, or at high speeds, the heavily laden boat was almost a knot slower. At low speeds the gap was smaller, but roughly the same, percentagewise.

Weight Test I. Heavy vs. Light Hulls in Moderate Seas

An effort was made to compare the pull of heavy against light prams, and of like pairs of Small Point One Designs in a

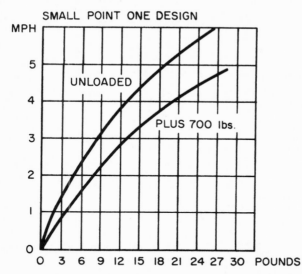

SMALL POINT ONE DESIGN

moderate seaway. Accurate readings were not obtained, since scales proved insufficiently damped, nor could towboat speed be guaranteed as constant. It was noted, however, that heavy hulls of both types did not show the extreme pull fluctuations of the light; yet power requirements for the heavy hulls between peaks were steadily higher. So it would appear that Ted Wells is correct in his belief that, although heavy hulls retain better momentum through breaking waves, they still lose to light ones over the course by not recapturing way as quickly after each check. Observation of one extra heavy sailing pram at Small Point shows that in a breeze this boat helps green sailors with her more-than-normal stability, but that when a new gust whips in she does not get up and scoot like her lighter sisters.

Clearly, whenever weight is added as load, that hull *becomes slower*.

HANDICAP FOR EXCESS WEIGHT

It being our announced purpose to handicap hulls for excess weight, let us not base this penalty upon some freak overload,

such as 250 pounds in a sailing pram or 700 in a Small Point
One Design. Rather let us choose an amount that can be carried around the course through carelessness. Fifty extra pounds
in a pram and 200 in a Small Point One Design can ride free
every day in half each fleet due to bad maintenance. And our
tests show that so much useless weight can cost—150 FEET A
MILE.

Tests of Hull Shape

A second source of variation in hulls lies in their shape.

Small Point Sailing Prams are of two basic shapes. The
photograph shows both.

The leader is a descendant of the Hagerty rowing pram with

Hagerty and El Toro dinghys

maximum beam aft and chines submerged full length. The following boat is an El Toro with greatest girth amidships, more
rocker in her keel, and chines out of water fore and aft.

Small Point One Designs are by four builders with three
minor but noticeable variations in forward sections. Gomes
hulls are slightly more "V'd" forward than the Burgess drawing. Blaisdell and Brewer hulls reproduce the Burgess lines
closely. Sonia hulls are "U" shaped forward.

The owner of a racing boat is limited to his class hull. But if
he seems to have a slow boat he will wish to know whether this
may be due to some small change from approved shape. To establish the value of such changes, hulls were towed that differed
only in these, and were identical in displacement, bottom
smoothness, and waterline length.

Textbooks and racing experience teach two things regarding
Hull Shape:

1) Of two boats in light going, the faster will offer less skin
friction through a more slippery bottom, and also less wetted
surface.

(This means that in drifting conditions we shine our bottoms
to reduce drag, and, if choice is allowed, use a hull that will
float us and itself with least bottom area exposed to the clutch-
ing fingers of passing water. Disregarding stability, a hull
shaped like A. will float its load on less area than one shaped
like B.)

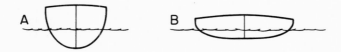

2) At higher speeds in strong winds, the wave-making properties of displacement hulls govern maximum speed. A rough
formula for top speed in displacement boats, which pass
through, rather than over the water, is in the nature of:
"1.4 × square root of the waterline." So a heavy sailboat 25
feet long will have as its top speed: $1.4 \times 5 = 7$ knots. This
formula does not apply exactly, since some hull forms are
lustier wave makers than others. But in no case can a displace-

ment boat sail faster than the wave system she generates, which is determined by her waterline length. The Planing boats that skim the surface may reach top speeds of three times the square root of their waterline, and cigar-like catamarans, that slit the surface with almost no wavemaking, about the same. Ballasted sailboats, however, are natural wave makers, and can go really fast only when they are very long; for waves with long periods move faster than short ones, as ocean swells demonstrate. One design racers, in consequence, can increase the top speed of their class hull only by such devices as sinking them in the water, or by heeling, if either will materially increase length. But short ended hulls, like the Small Point One Designs, only slow down under added ballast, since their waterline does not lengthen as the boat squats lower.

At Small Point local opinion says that small changes in hull shape alter speed: in the sailing prams, not at all; in the Small Point One Designs, very little, and certainly less than does weight.

Shape Test A. Does Speed Change Materially with Shape?

Hagerty and El Toro prams of identical weight were towed to give a direct contrast at slow, medium and fast speeds for those hulls. Comparisons were also attempted in two foot waves.

Speed	Better hull	Gain per mile
1 knot	No difference	0′
2 knots	El Toro, barely	appx. 50′
3 knots	El Toro, clearly	appx. 100′

The rough seas test was repeated several times, with the El Toro riding more easily and showing less tendency to bury her nose. The El Toro was more responsive in higher waves, where her advantage could have been 150′ a mile.

The Small Point One Designs were also towed in contrasting pairs. Hulls of equal weight and bottom smoothness were chosen. Speed range was one to six knots, and again figures in rough water were attempted.

Speed	Better hull shape	Advantage per mile
Up to 3 knots	The "U" shaped Sonia hulls to a small degree	75'
3 to 4½ knots	No type showed a gain	0'
Above 4½ knots	Burgess lines and Gomes "V" slightly faster	75'

It was hard to damp the scale enough to get exact readings when the hulls were pulled through breaking waves. But Gomes hulls plunged less than the fatter Sonia versions, nor did they snake, worm, and cast out spray to the same degree. The Burgess lines also gave a more level ride in moderate seas.

Shape Test B. Best "U" vs Best "V" Hull

The most successful Sonia "U" hull was towed up to 6 knots and her Pull-curve obtained. The most successful "V" hull had a similar bottom and equal weight. Her Pull-curve is shown in contrast.

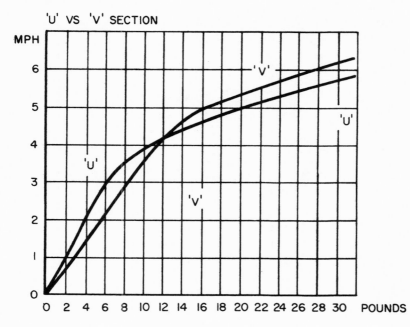

As if to confirm their racing records, up to 4 knots the "U" bow sections towed faster; above that, the "V".

HANDICAP FOR DIFFERENCES IN HULL SHAPE

When boats are well built to the same plans, speed or slowness due to small divergences therefrom can hardly exceed:
50 FEET A MILE

TESTS ON BOTTOM SMOOTHNESS

The bottom surfaces of racing sailboats vary tremendously. Losses come from marine growths, or from eddies set up by roughness.

Marine growth on keel and hull

On Small Point sailboats marine growths and deposits include:
Mud. Blackish, fairly thin and observable after two weeks. Not a living substance.

Grass. Fine textured and brilliant green. Forming along water-lines that dip in and out of the air. Visible on white boot-topping after a month, and luxuriant after two months.

Algae tufts. First sprouting in scattered tufts of golf ball size. But if unchecked, covering whole areas in masses large as a tennis ball. Well below the surface.

Barnacles. Small at first and well below the surface on areas starved of paint, but eventually dime sized.

All these are found on moving sailboats. (Stationary mooring lines after three months can triple in diameter under myriads of tiny mussel shells.)

A few Small Point enthusiasts broom off marine growths regularly, or swim beneath their boats with scrubbing brushes. The majority disregard them, even when during a race heeling shows their rudders to wave under thick green nightgowns. By Labor Day any boat that has not been hauled out at least once has slowed down. And when these are stored at the boatyard they sport extensive growths, particularly along the bottom of their iron keels.

Haul outs have always been limited by yacht clubs. Visits to marine railways are expensive and inconvenient for boats of moderate size. For small ones the problem is less bothersome today, since they may be pulled out on trailers or sailed dry. An owner can always borrow a snorkel, or even an aqualung, to clean his boat's bottom. But those who like to give orders and simply leave their boats at the yard in the fall, never see them hauled out and have no idea of the beards they carry.

Anti-Fouling Paints Used on Racing Sailboats

Anti-fouling paints are roughly of two types: the defoliating, and the hard surfaced. Fresh water sailors often dispense with protection against marine growths, but a sailboat moored in salt water soon requires it. The standard copper bottom paints are of the defoliating, or chalky type. These flake off bits of their thickness from week to week, so that growths hardy enough to take root upon their toxic surfaces, are soon sloughed off with the chalking paint. Copper oxide is the standard anti-fouling agent against barnacles and algae; mercury against weeds. All of the better defoliating paints discourage underwater growths, but because of their softness do not take a piano shine.

The "hard racing" finishes, particularly those based upon fine copper powder, can be burnished to a beautiful sheen if one has super-patience. They give the slicker bottom asked by the racing buff, but do not average the protection against salt water growths of the pungent, old-fashioned copper.

The best paint for a particular boat is always a compromise. No coating seems able to defeat inorganic slime of fresh water, or the mud that floats like an emulsion off Maine and deposits its skin on everything. Limiting the number of haul-outs is an obvious class economy measure. The International One Designs even restrict themselves to one brand of bottom paint. But the paint brand is only one factor in a fine racing bottom; the number and thinness of coats and the degree of sanding being far more important.

Few tests have been made on how much sailboats slow down under marine growths. Twenty years ago an article described tests made in the fresh waters of Lake George, which concluded that for two weeks a slime formed there upon moored sailboats that speeded them up, much as the Lord speeds up His fish through endowing them with a like natural ooze. After two weeks the increasing slime became harmful and the boats slowed down.

At Small Point one boat used a hard white bottom paint with no anti-fouling properties at all. For ten days she was very fast, but thereafter a brown scum was seen along her entire bottom and she grew plainly slower. It did no good to rub at this scum with steel wool: it stayed put, while the ends of the steel wool buried into the paint and after a few days oozed rust in innumerable brown flecks. Only when she was hauled out and scoured with Dutch Cleanser did the brown blanket fade. Another owner made his bottom paint by stirring fine copper powder into clear epoxy. This gave a slick and fairly cheap bottom that for a month proved fast. But as a result of amateur mixing the anti-fouling properties of the brew varied. After six weeks the boat slowed down, and on haul-out her flanks were found capriciously tufted with algae. Two-thirds still sparkled; but the rest resembled the rump of a maiden bear.

Marine Growth Test A. Foul Skiff vs Clean Skiff

The 8′ sailing prams are hauled out on the bank at Small Point, so they do not accumulate marine growths. A ten foot rowing skiff that had put on an Arctic overcoat during three months at the club float was substituted in this size class.

Growth on unprotected skiff bottom

This skiff is an extreme lesson in fouling, for she had no anti-fouling paint whatever. She carries at least two hundred algae tufts up to three inches long. She was first towed with this entire load. Then the tufts were scraped off, and without further cleaning she was re-towed so that any reduction in power needed to move her could be shown in two Resistance vs Speed Curves.

This is an exaggerated case of the fouling load possible on a

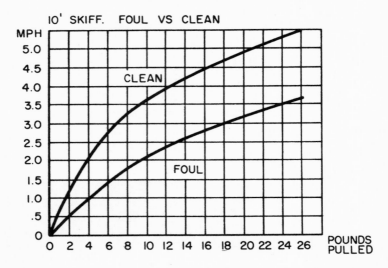

small boat. Yet careless racers tow similar loads without suspecting them. By pointing a ruler up from the "Pounds pulled" figure of "12" on the bottom line, we see that a sailboat having that amount of sail power in a fresh reaching breeze, would go only 2.4 miles an hour with her bottom dirty, but 4.0 if it were clean. This is a loss of 1.6 mph, or forty per cent of clean speed.

If only 4 pounds of sail power were available—for example to windward in a light breeze—the foul speed is only 1 mph as against 2.3 clean. Less than *half* the speed of a clean boat.

Marine Growth Test B. Pull of Single Algae Tufts

Resistance test were made with a letter scale on single, double, and triple tufts of algae taken from the bottoms of Small Point sailboats. When the tufts were separated along a towing string their resistances were cumulative, so the power to pull only one is given.

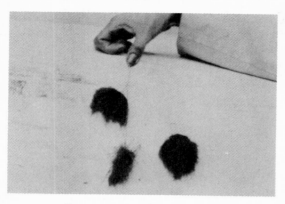

Separate tufts of marine growths

Drag of a single large algae tuft	Mph
1 ounce	1.2 mph
3 ounces	2.
4½ ounces	3.
11 ounces	4.

Tufts were three inches long by one and half inches at their hard bases. A considerable number massed together would offer less resistance than the same number spaced apart.

The photograph shows the rudder of a Small Point One

Marine growths on rudder

Design that had slowed down badly late in the season. Similar growths covered her entire bottom. Note some five major tufts and fifteen minor ones. Total drag of such growths on one side of her rudder alone must have absorbed *one pound* of available sail power at three miles an hour. So losses to all growths wasted a high fraction of it.

Marine Growth Test C. Losses on a Well Painted Bottom

A Small Point One Design with smoothly sanded bottom painted with hard racing bronze was towed at varying speeds when first launched, after two weeks, and after a month. Power to move her at like speeds was:
  After two weeks—Not appreciably more than at launching
  After one month—Slightly higher, but speed loss did not exceed 50′ a mile
The boat was not scrubbed or sponged off during this interval, and growth was limited to a muddy darkening of her bronze bottom.

Marine Growth Test D. Losses on an Ill Painted Bottom

A Small Point One Design that did poorly on the rare occasions she raced, and which after two months at her mooring had accumulated a green hula fringe along her waterline, was towed with this marine load, then again after it had been cleaned away. The underlying paint was not smoothed or sanded; only material that could be removed by scrubbing was taken. This included: a grass belt two inches wide at the water line, fifty large algae tufts and a hundred small ones, four large barnacles, a mud film, visible, but not feelable.

The "dirty-bottom resistance" of this hull to towing at speeds between one and six knots was high enough to give her a speed inferiority to the well painted hull tested in #C above *four hundred feet a mile*.

Cleaned of her grass and algae, she gained back *three hundred feet* a mile of her handicap.

Bottom Roughness and How It Cuts Speed

Bottom losses on racing boats are not restricted to marine growths. Paint roughness, gouges, or keel dents also slow a boat. Half the Small Point One Designs have fairly slick bottoms; the rest have rough ones in varying degrees.

Even among experts there is disagreement as to the value of extreme bottom slickness. Is it enough to have only what is known as "hydraulic smoothness?" Or is mirror gloss an advantage in light going? If gloss *is* necessary for speed, then how much is best? For example, are bronze paints worth burnishing in an automobile body shop? If hard racing finishes are faster than chalky paints, by how much? Small Point sailors shrug off such questions and race their boats as they come from the boatyard. "It's the yard's business to do my painting," they say.

Some dinghy experts disagree and will laboriously apply lanolin and stove polish to their hulls, or varnish mixed with graphite. We all remember tales of potleading (graphiting) before 1900, when those unsightly messes were conceded to be useless after three days. So accomplished a race winner as Harvey Flint advises sanding a bottom with wet-and-dry paper, following with pumice and oil, and lastly, rottenstone, a process that he repeats until shells on the shore are mirrored in the bottom and, "If a fly lights on it, he breaks his leg!" Are these old timers all deluding themselves for nothing? It hardly seems likely.

There is no standard smoothness test for the bottoms of racing boats. If a pingpong ball is set between the earpieces of a doctor's stethescope and the ball scraped over a bit of paint, the rasping scratch gives some measure of comparative roughness. Bottom nicks and gouges make whorls in the passing water, and we know that anything that sets up eddies will cause drag and slow a boat. Keels often show rust bulges or deep slots where bolt heads bed in their under sides. How harmful are these splinters and flow diverters?

Roughness Test A. The Drag of Holes and Knobs

Holes. A streamlined wooden shape, four feet long with a very smooth surface was towed at 3 and 6 miles an hour, and its drag established.

Holes were then dug into it, until a size was found for single indentations that increased drag by 2 ounces at 3 mph. This proved to be, one inch deep, by two inches wide, by two inches long.

At 6 mph the same hole dragged 8 ounces.

Knobs. Small bits of cork were tacked to the shape to simulate the roughness of a badly painted sailboat bottom.

One square foot of these eddy-makers raised drag by 3 ounces at 3 mph, and to just under 12 ounces at 6 mph.

Roughness Test B. Smooth Hull vs Rough Hull

A Small Point One Design with a distinctly rough bottom, paint ridges on her rudder, grooves in her iron keel, and caked paint along her topsides, was towed to establish Pull-curves between one and six miles an hour. She had no marine growths. If slow, it was because of the poorly prepared bottom.

She was then beached, carefully sanded, all cracks and keel gouges filled, and her entire bottom given two coats of clear epoxy paint. After drying, the surface was further smoothed and polished. She was then launched, and a new set of towing figures taken over the same speed range.

The boat was now faster by an average of *200 feet a mile.*

Deductions on Bottom Losses

If no anti-fouling paint is used, slow-down due to marine growth after six weeks can reach grave proportions—up to *one foot in two sailed.* Even if good anti-fouling paint is applied, there is none that may be trusted to give a top racing bottom for more than a month when much mud or slime is in the water. Bronzes and other hard racing finishes give a bit less protection than the defoliating types; but even chalky paints should be hand rubbed with a Turkish towel every two weeks to remove mud, and the boat hauled out at least monthly. Each algae tuft that roots itself to a bare spot will drag more than 3 ounces at 3 mph, so the under sides of keels where paint holidays are common must be checked.

Marine growths slow a sailboat most seriously at low speeds and to windward. On reaches and in big winds more sail power is available, so it is in soft going that the competitor with a shiny bottom moves away the fastest. When growths become more than an inch long they are clearly evident. So the widest loss that a sailor of any pretensions should suffer to them is 400 feet a mile.

Rough bottom paint is a handicap, but not to the same degree as unchecked marine growth. If the ultimate shine is desired, hard racing finishes are needed, not chalky paints. Many thinned down coats and much sanding mean that the owner must expect to produce this gloss himself; boatyards simply can not take the time to fill tiny holes or smooth away each rust bump. Liquid Lux is felt by Arthur Knapp to speed a hull up to one per cent; which is two boat lengths a mile. When tried at Small Point, first day results seemed good, but after a week the soaped bottom felt gummy. Loss of a rough against a mirror bottom seems about 200 feet a mile.

HANDICAP FOR BOTTOM GROWTH AND ROUGHNESS

The racing boat that starts her season with a poor bottom to which no further care is given, can after two months owe her sleek and shiny sister—

300 FEET A MILE

STABILITY AND TRIM TESTS

The attitude at which a sailboat moves through the water can importantly affect her speed in—

Resistance to Heeling
Fore and aft Trim
Centering of Weight
Weight shifts to ease Helm Pressures

Resistance to Heeling

To novices the heeled boat looks fast: to experts it is the one foaming along upright. Doctrine for best heeling angle varies between classes. Lightnings, with their hard chines, are felt to go fastest with the windward chine just clear of the surface; scows with long overhangs need enough heel to drop their lee sides into the water, at which point the 30% longer waterline gives them potentially higher speed. Of two similar hulls, if one heels appreciably more, it is deemed the slower. At anything over 25° a boat lifts her deadwood or centerboard out to windward, where its drag tends to spin her into the wind. To compound such luffing tendency, the center of effort of her rig now drops well to leeward, so both keel-drag and rig-push combine into a strong windward-turning couple.

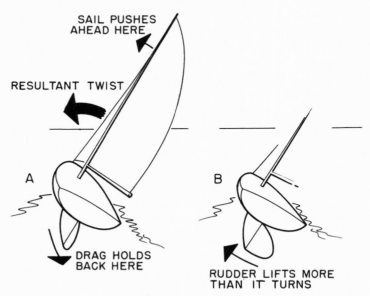

SAIL PUSHES
AHEAD HERE

RESULTANT TWIST

A

DRAG HOLDS
BACK HERE

B

RUDDER LIFTS MORE
THAN IT TURNS

To stop a luff, as in A, now asks more rudder across the boat. But the rudder blade is canted too, so instead of pivoting its hull in a circle level with the horizon, it lifts the stern and buries the bow, as in B. The consequence of high heeling, therefore, is a slow profile through the water, and up to 20° of braking cross-rudder.

Heeling Test A. Does Heeling Differ Within a Class?

The 8′ sailing prams were tested for sidewise stability by placing a hundred pound boy on their rails, and reading heeling angle off a pendulum at the mast. Less than 2° difference was found between boats.

In the Small Point One Designs a plank was wedged across each cockpit and under the far rail, so that a hundred and sixty pound man might sit out exactly fifteen inches beyond the sides. This canted the boats and showed heeling angle on the same pendulum gauge. Varying keel weights, estimated at 475 pounds down to 350, now told a different story. Five older boats, known to place well only in strong winds, heeled less than 11°. Fourteen average boats, some fast, some slow, heeled 14°–16°. One round bilged Sonia hull, outstanding in light air, but poor above twelve knots, and thought to have a light keel, heeled 22½°!

Stability Test B. Do Boats Slow Down Under Heeling?

Sailing prams and Small Point One Designs were towed without leeway at three speeds, and heeled from 0° to 50° in 10° steps. It was necessary to steer them as pull readings were taken.

In prams, lifting the windward chine at first gave better speed. This occurred at 10°. With the lee chine splitting the water, no rudder was needed until 20°. At any heel beyond 25° prams grew hard to steer, and those with broad catboat rudders dug in their bows. Response to helm was poor at high speeds and high heeling angles.

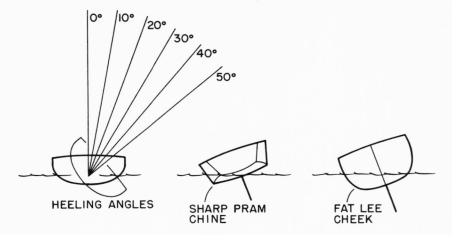

The round bilged Small Point One Design hulls barely slowed down at angles up to 10°, but towed harder above this. As heel increased their fat lee cheeks met the water. Tiller angle and pull both climbed. At 20° of heel rudders would brake and burble. It seems a waste of time to race these boats at more than 30°. They lift, snake and wallow. Speed fall-off can reach one foot in four against a level boat.

Stability Test C. Does Heavier Ballast Pay?

The Small Point One Design that heeled excessively is a rabbit in very light air, but asks constant hiking to windward, and can be seen to roll more than other boats at her mooring. Two hundred pounds of lead were placed under her floorboards, where, at one foot below the hull's center of balance, it exercised a righting arm of 200 foot pounds. The boat was sailed in ten races, half of them in gentle winds. She proved a hair slower off the wind, perhaps 50 feet a mile, but far better to windward, where she required less rail balancing by her crew. The inside lead was then removed and only 150 pounds set into a slot in her deadwood atop the iron keel, where, at two feet beneath the center of balance, it now exercised 300 foot pounds of righting arm. Improvement to windward in moderate airs was startling. The boat sat up like a sinner in church, ate high into the wind, and in gusts and stormy going improved as much as *Weatherly,* the cup defending 12 Metre, after her 1962 reballasting.

Fore and Aft Trim

Fore and aft trim failures show most dramatically in small catboats, which with their masts forward, can be sailed under in strong winds. Crews in short hulls can not shift about, yet transfer of only fifty pounds will raise or sink a bow. Medium sized racing boats are trimmed fore and aft on various systems. Some like to sail bow-down to windward, but will squat the stern running free to "keep it from sucking." Others lift the stern to avoid sucking. The widest fore and aft trim variations are seen under spinnakers.

Fore and Aft Trim Test A. Pull As the Bow Lifts or Sinks

Hulls were towed with and without leeway at several speeds, and were steered. Trim lines were painted on each bow and stern.

Mid trim averaged to be fastest on both prams and Small Point One Designs, with no pronounced slow-down until bows or sterns were clearly high. Before strong winds in the prams rigs could depress the bow and force crew weight aft as a safety measure. It was easy to exaggerate this attitude. The Small Point One Designs threw less spray in breaking waves with their bows lifted. Maximum loss attributed to poor fore and aft trim was 200 feet a mile.

Centering Weight to Minimize Pitching

Once the best fore and aft trim level had been achieved, there remained the refinement of hull control against pitching. Some feel that racing boats must be kept light in the ends by centering ballast so they will pass more easily through lifting swells.

Columbia was credited with an advantage over *Sceptre* in that she climbed and fell without hobbyhorsing in a seaway. On the other hand, *Ranger,* the non-pareil of J boats, was said to ride absolutely level through the lumpiest seas when others were bobbing and slatting. Rough tests were made to determine whether hulls weighted in their ends sat more level in a bobbly seaway than their sisters with everything amidships, plus several tests on whether the center-ballasted hulls eased with less spray and fuss through breaking wave tops. It was difficult to achieve weight spreading in the prams, where ballast centers three inches behind the belt buckle of the skipper, but two sixty pound children, one forward and one aft were used. In the Small Point One Designs water ballast was substituted.

In both types there was increased drag as heavily weighted ends splashed into seas. When waves were merely lumpy and winds were light, sails seemed to slat less actively with weight dispersed and the hull kept level. It seems, therefore, that each type of seaway asks its special treatment, according to whether the problem is one of easy hull movement, or of holding draft in the rig. Maximum loss through worst centering of weight appeared in the nature of 100 feet a mile.

Weight Shifts to Reduce Helm Pressures

The skipper who sails with twenty pounds of tiller pull would certainly go faster with three. Value of a trailing rudder is shown in Jack Wood's technique of heeling Tech Dinghies to windward before the wind. The luffing couple generated in catboats with their full sail plan to leeward is then equalized by an unbalanced underwater hull form; zero rudder pressure results and the windward tilted boat runs by others heeling normally and needing firm tiller pull to stay on course. When close hauled, those who wish to inch into the wind commonly move crew weight forward. This gives the small, but pronounced weather helm that skippers believe helps them to feel the boat and eat out into the puffs. When the purpose is to *reduce* weather helm, weight is moved aft, a useful application of this principle being on leaving a mooring, when if all hands step aft the lifted bow will fall off on the side to which the tiller points.

Helm Pressure Test A. Can Helm Pressures Be Changed by Weight Shifts?

Hulls were towed at several speeds and pulled askew by lines until steady tiller pressures were needed to make them run straight. Weight was then shifted: forward to increase weather helm, aft to lighten it. Pounds needed to tow the boats were constantly checked. Tests under sail were also run. Ounces of tiller pull on a straight heading were established, and efforts made to vary these by weight shifts in either direction.

The tests indicated that tiller forces can be changed by shifting weight, but not to any startling degree. Hull shapes differed in permitting it. Prams with long catboat rudders were less sensitive than those with high aspect ratio dinghy rudders. In the Small Point One Designs tiller pressures were far more affected by sheet setting than by weight placement.

A Handicap for Over-Heeling and Bad Trim

Since these faults are caused (and cured) more by tactical sailing methods than by matters within a hull, we here assign them only the moderate penalty of—

100 FEET A MILE

Tests on Leeway and Lateral Resistance

Because the forward power from a close hauled sail is largely at right angles to the boom, sailboats move crabwise to windward, and still slightly so on reaches.

If sailboats had no keels they would slide directly out in line with the pressure from their sails. Being shaped underwater to restrict lateral movement, their hulls translate sidewise wind forces into motion ahead. Keels vary in efficiency from the

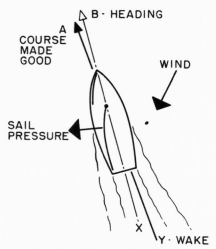

fine drift-limiters of 12 Metres to the relatively ineffective dag-gerboards of prams. Since leeway is always produced by wind-ward working sailboats, its angle can generally be seen by sight-ing aft along the boat's center-line. In the diagram, Y represents the visible wake, and X the straight line aft.

The close hauled boat in this instance is heading above her course made good. The angle between her heading and track over the ground (between A and B) is likewise the amount of leeway. In Small Point One Designs such drift-down to windward is about 4°; in sailing prams, nearer 6°.

Leeway Test A. Does Leeway Increase Hull Drag?

In the towing procedure Leeway was simulated by running a line out to the stern of the sailboat and pulling it slightly askew. How this twist to a course slightly off the lee bow affected pounds-pulled was examined.

Results varied with hull shape, but it was found that once a sailboat was turned in her passage through the water by over 3° of leeway, her towing force rose in the nature of 10%. In the leeway position she is therefore slower.

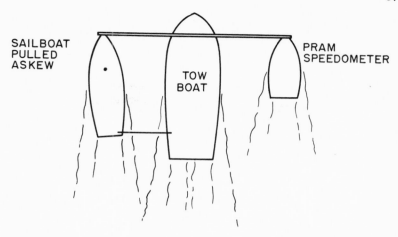

SAILBOAT
PULLED
ASKEW

TOW
BOAT

PRAM
SPEEDOMETER

Leeway Test B. Does Some Weather Helm Reduce Leeway?

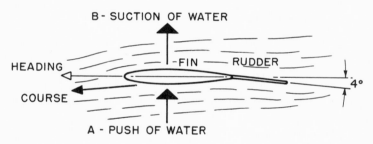

B- SUCTION OF WATER

HEADING
COURSE

-FIN —— RUDDER

4°

A - PUSH OF WATER

A keel or centerboard inclined to the passing water during
leeway is said to act as an underwater airfoil that can nudge its
hull out to windward. Positive pressure works at point A, and
suction at point B. It is further believed by some that such
hydraulic lift is most effective when the rudder, instead of
trailing aft, is held in the weather helm position of about 4°
shown above.

Hulls were towed in simulated leeway, and when given a
small amount of weather helm (3″–4″ at the end of a three foot
tiller) *did* seem to ease out and away from the towboat as if
lifting upwind. Accompanying this effect was a slight reduction in pull needed to tow that hull. Efforts to increase hydraulic lift by widening the angle of weather helm to make an

underwater wing composed of deadwood and rudder of even higher power, soon failed. The rudder began to burble, and pull readings climbed sharply.

Two aspects of hydraulic lift stood out:

1) It varied according to keel-rudder combinations; prams with wide rudder-to-daggerboard gaps, giving less than deep keels with rudders attached.

2) Just as with airplane wings, it increased with the *square* of hull speed, not in simple proportion. So it is most beneficial to the fast moving boat and constitutes an argument for Footing as against Pinching.

Leeway Test C. Underwater Profiles That Restrict Slipping

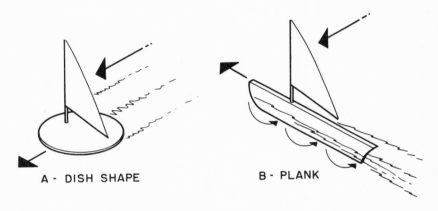

A - DISH SHAPE   B - PLANK

Because it is the side profile presented by a hull to water that blocks leeway, a number of plywood shapes of the same area were towed to see which could restrict sideways movement the most. Sails placed upon the round and shallow dish A, could not even make it reach broadside to the wind. Instead, it slid squarely off to leeward. B, the long flat plank can be made to reach. But it is a poor upwind profile, compared to a thin, deep fin, since it suffers "end losses" as water eases up and under its long flat keel to relieve such high leeward water pressures as might have exerted force to windward.

U VS. FLAT PLATE

SLIPPAGE IN HEELING

Round ended sections when pulled sidewise as keels, did not restrict slippage as well as sharp ones. If the bottom edges of a keel curve off, greater leeway results. Again, because heeling reduces the effective area and depth of a keel, any flat plate at right angles to the water limits drift better than one that is slanted.

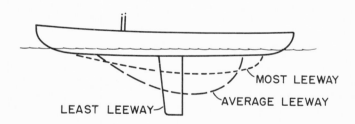

LEAST LEEWAY

MOST LEEWAY

AVERAGE LEEWAY

On an identical canoe hull, the keel shape that best prevented leeway resembled one that produces high lift as an airplane wing. It was deep and thin; that is, of high aspect ratio. Although most efficient to windward, such a sailboat keel has the practical disadvantages of extreme draft, and so asks compromise.

Leeway Test D. Gains Through Underwater Fairings

Few changes can be made to the keel profiles of class boats, but inspection of the underbodies of persistent losers at Small Point showed that these do not conform 100% to class plans and lack some lateral resistance. Such lack was obvious on Sonia hulls, which came from the builder without forward extension of their deadwood.

As delivered in A, the deadwood joined the hull at a sharp angle, leaving only rounded bottom ahead. As modified in B, one Sonia hull now has her deadwood curve up into a fairing eighteen inches long that merges into the stem and adds a hundred square inches of lateral resistance area after the manner of the Gomes "Y" stems, which were supplied to let them "hold onto the water better to windward." That Charley Gomes' system works, is shown by the fact that unchanged Sonia hulls have never beaten his on this point of sailing.

Leeway Test E. Improvements to Hull Balance

Sailboat balance can be importantly changed by underwater fairings; so in the Small Point One Designs, where these vary, widely different tiller pressures are found. Boats in this fleet that need minimum rudder pressure to stay on course are faster than those that need much. The Sonia hull with added fairing, now asks only the shadow of tiller pull to windward, where without it she steered heavily.

Efforts were made on a number of hard steering boats to reduce helm pressures. To lighten weather helm the sail plan was raked or shifted forward, or underwater lateral resistance furnished aft. To reduce lee helm the sail plan was raked or moved aft, while underwater resistance was supplied forward. Such adjustments amounted to accommodations of the center of effort of the rig to the hull's underwater center of lateral resistance. One or both were shifted until the boat held steady to windward with little rudder. Since underwater profile is hard to change, first resort was always to moving the mast. But hull profile was not accepted as fixed, since existing centers of lateral resistance often proved incorrect. A clear example may be seen on five of the early sailing prams, which had deep skegs running from their sterns to amidships. So much lateral area, if centrally placed, might have removed the need for a daggerboard. The boats would have tacked poorly, but would in effect have been keel-prams, drawing only a foot. But set so far aft, the skegs served only to produce lee helm. All sailed faster when they were removed.

On two Small Point One Designs movable fairings of 3/4" plywood, 300 square inches in area, were set first ahead, then aft of the deadwood. Skin friction was surely increased, but the fairings changed tiller pressures completely. Placed forward, weather helm up to ten pounds was created in a moderate breeze to windward. Placed aft, lee helm of a pound.

HANDICAP FOR EXTRA LEEWAY

Poor underwater form can cause losses up to—
75 FEET A MILE

TESTS ON RUDDERS

How rudders turn sailboats at all is a complicated matter. Some naval architects include rudder area with underwater profile in their computations for centers of lateral resistance, some half of it, and some omit the rudder. A good rudder allows its hull to be tacked smoothly and kept on course with ease, while transmitting to the helmsman's fingers vibrations precisely descriptive of current sail balance and speed.

Rudder Test A. Do Class Rudders Differ in Shape and Turning Power?

The first Small Point sailing prams had wide catboat rudders, variously shaped, but averaging about as shown here:

They tacked the little boats slowly, could be used to scull them about, and gave a heavy feel. Being shallow, they rarely grounded. Wide, equally shallow daggerboards were used with them, which to counterbalance the aft-extending rudder blades, were set well forward. Skegs were unnecessary. When the beamy El Toro hull became popular, its deep, dinghy type rudder came too.

Both rudder and daggerboard were now quite thin, with their centers close together.

These dinghy rudders tack the prams so quickly that a released tiller flips out of a child's hand. They send almost no pressure to his fingers, being virtually balanced under sail. And they ground hard in shallow water.

In the Small Point One Design Class the first Gomes rudders A, were only thirteen inches long, as against a dimension of twenty-three inches specified in the Burgess plan B.

The small rudders seemed adequate, and when a few longer ones appeared on new boats, the original owners boasted: "Our rudders feel lighter than yours, and have less skin friction, so they're faster." In time, as class leaders began to prefer the long rudders, one or two checked to discover: the long rudders gave a steadier feel, they used less tiller arc, steering and tacking; when pressed down in a seaway their response was surer.

Tests on rudder efficiency were run on broad reaches in twenty knot winds, which showed that when a long rudder blade needed 8° of tiller to hold course, the short blade took 15°, and that whenever 20° was exceeded, a burble sounded under the boat, accompanied by a feeling that the short rudder had released its grip on the water. As the small rudder lost effectiveness, all competing boats appeared to speed up. This was diagnosed as "water stall," a product of high rudder drag. Local fishermen advised that when their motorboats had been equipped with short rudders they too were ineffective when the helm was put over hard in a seaway, and that consequently wider blades had been fitted. This posed the question of whether the small rudders had enough area to absorb the sail power generated on these boats in fresh winds.

Best Rudder Shapes in Theory

In comparing the efficiencies of rudders, textbooks on naval architecture show that rudders of aspect ratio 2 must swing fifty per cent further to equal the turning power of rudders of similar area, but aspect ratio 6. "Aspect ratio" here means a

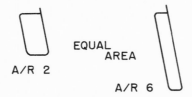

dividing of a rudder's depth by its breadth. In this turning operation the rudder of aspect ratio 2 will produce 2½ times more harmful drag than the paddle-shaped aspect ratio 6 model.

The class-boat racer will observe that an aspect ratio 2 rudder is of itself deep and narrow, that one of aspect ratio 6 is exaggerated, even for dinghies, and that his freedom to use more efficient rudder shapes is almost nil under class rules. We therefore examine a few rudders purely to determine whether it *would* be advantageous to use a new shape, providing it were allowable.

Rudder Test B. Rudder Efficiencies with a Class

Using a single pram and its sails, first with a catboat rudder, then with a dinghy type, tiller pull was compared in a ten knot wind on reaches and to windward. A two foot tiller was used with both blades. Arc of tiller needed to hold course and tack was measured, and speed of tack compared.

The El Toro, dinghy type rudder, took half the pull of the catboat rudder. It also tacked the pram more quickly. Feel of the catboat rudder was steadier and preferred by beginners. The El Toro rudder was so closely balanced that it took only a fraction of the arc needed by the catboat type.

Long and short rudders in the Small Point Class were also compared for pounds pulled and tiller arc. Tiller angle for the small rudder was double, sometimes triple that of the longer. When the long rudder averaged 4°–5°, the short needed 12°. When forced down hard, the small rudder burbled and slowed the boat. The long one produced a smoother turn. General response to the long rudder was better, particularly in high seas. A comparison to windward found the long rudder conveying a feel of superior control. In light air the small blade grew better able to direct its hull. Here the small rudder, in spite of a theoretical superiority in aspect ratio, appears to lack the square inches to do its job. Its drag by skin friction is less, but in fifteen knots of wind its total drag becomes far more when it burbles and stalls out.

Rudder Test C. Are Very High Aspect Ratio Rudders Faster?

Very thin, deep rudders were tried on sailing prams with little improvement over the standard El Toro type. On a Small Point One Design a thin aspect ratio 2 rudder was tested for amusement by bolting a deepening piece to one of the first small rudders, which then extended it well below the keel.

A/R 2 RUDDER   STANDARD A/R 1/2 RUDDER

The boat certainly responded more quickly with this rudder than was her wont, above all in tacking, and her feel improved. But the rudder was not used in competition, the feeling being that it must strike all rocks and snag countless yards of seaweed.

Rudder Test D. Closed Gap Between Rudder and Hull

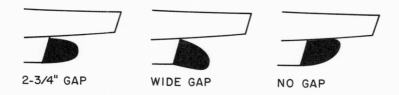

2-3/4" GAP   WIDE GAP   NO GAP

Some skippers believe it important to close the gap between the top of a rudder blade and the hull. The Burgess plan for Small Point One Designs calls for 2¾″ separation. One fast boat first sloped her rudder far down, as in the second drawing, but the following season, lifted it to almost no gap, as in the third. The slanted rudder post made it difficult to snug this rudder hard up to its hull and still retain full swing width. In any case, her order of finish was the same with the lifted blade as it had been with the drooping one.

Rudder Test E. Sharp Trailing Edges to Reduce Drag?

Experts agree that knife-like trailing edges make a rudder faster. This is not done on the ¾″ plywood rudders of the sailing prams, but the Small Point One Designs that win all have thin rudder edges.

It was not difficult to tow both square edged and knife edged planks upright through the water at speeds between one and six knots, and to observe how much fatter the ripples are behind the square edges, and that these ask more power to tow. Pull measurements were accurate enough to show that at medium speeds a blunt edged rudder can deliver itself of enough ripples to consume a pound of valuable sail power.

Handicap for Best vs Worst Rudders

50 FEET A MILE

9
A RATING PLAN FOR SAILS

Sails are the racing boat's motor. Beginners see little difference between them. They simply buy sails, hoist them, and use them. Yet Cornelius Shields thinks they contribute 70% of boat speed and vary tremendously within a class.

To show how sails drive hulls we first trace briefly their development up through the centuries from simple wind pushers running free, into deflectors close hauled that convert part of the wind's energy into boat motion. Sail history is one of creeping progress over the ages, with results limited by poor materials and the paramount need for reliability upon a stormy ocean. As a vital commercial force, propulsion by sails went out with the ruffled pantalette.

Chapter 12 offers a theoretical background on power production from cloth sails by placing model rigs in a small wind tunnel and asking controversial questions. In Chapter 13 we compare many full sized sails in the Small Point racing classes to see which win and why. The slow ones are assigned handicaps in feet per mile. Finally, Chapter 14 combs from this material a few ways of upping efficiency in modern racing rigs.

10 HOW SAILS DRIVE BOATS

It is interesting to follow the slow evolution of sails up through the dimness of maritime history. In all probability the grandparents of modern racing sails were simply bushes or palm fronds, set in the bows of primitive dugouts to assist human paddlers. Even today a large bag or pair of pants with the legs knotted will speed a canoe to leeward. Such clumsy wind catchers, when aided by steering oars, will help the most inefficient dish of a hull to drift downwind into a quarter of the horizon's arc. During the thousands of years of Mediterranean pre-history sails of plaited palm leaves or rough hides snared fair winds to this end; when breezes turned contrary, oars were used, or the craft lay at anchor until some god could be entreated to provide a change.

PRIMITIVE SAILS WENT DOWNWIND ONLY

Ability to sail across the wind on beam reaches was developed by the Arabs for commercial or warlike purposes when they slanted up and down the Red Sea broadside to seasonal winds. Egyptians also reached along the Nile. Reaching progress was slow, for it was necessary to combine a flatter adjustable sail with enough hull extension below the waterline to limit leeway. Early reachers had to head well above course

98

made good, but in so doing could move into half the horizon like crabs. By Roman days reaching passages of three months were common in proper season. Ships developed deep hulls, sails were slung on broad yards that could be veered to the wind, and there were still captives to row dead to windward, and enough prayers to assure favoring slants.

EARLY BEAM REACHING

For ships to make good any heading tighter than side-on to the wind, took improved design. Sails had to become arched and better placed upon hulls. As experience showed one particular sail-to-hull marriage to balance more docilely than another, it was copied, although mistrustfully, for seamen are conservative. The ability of Viking galleys to stand off lee shores during winter gales under their low rigs and leeboards, kept many Norse pirates alive for further depredations. Exhausted oarsmen who otherwise would have been chewed to bits in the Iceland surf, praised ships that limited downwind drift. Each rig that evolved in the early North Atlantic meant victory in a war for survival, from which vessels unable to hold courses fairly high upon the wind never came home. They simply foundered.

It was after the Middle Ages before sails were refined to a point where seafarers could rely upon steady progress upwind. Prince Henry the Navigator is credited with finalizing this achievement in the Portuguese merchant fleets. But he had countless forgotten assistants, each of whom contributed his small improvement to the crude rigs of that day. The Chinese were struggling to windward by the year 1000 with their fully battened junks, and the lug and gunter rigs that spread from Turkey to Holland served, when placed in suitable hulls, as steps toward our modern jib-headed rigs.

For early sails to drive hulls upwind it was necessary that they be changed from wind-absorbing bags to be pushed along, into flatter expanses curved something like a bird's wing that could be trimmed in toward the boat's centerline, there to redirect the wind's energy while accepting some of its force.

The windward working ship also had to have a keel that would reduce leeway by holding onto the water until the largely sidewise forces from its sails might be resolved into forward motion. Even with suitable sails and hull, it was still necessary for the center of effort of each rig to be properly located fore and aft relative to the center of lateral resistance of the hull. Through the years countless promising rig/hull combinations must have failed due to poor accommodation of these centers. Even today we find badly balanced racing boats.

How Sailboats Get Upwind

MODERN SAILING TO WINDWARD

The average sailboat makes good a course only 45° on either side of the wind, leaving 90° of the horizon-pie into which she must proceed by zig-zagging. When running free any baggy umbrella can be tugged along; to hold close onto the wind a sail must be more of a Wind Diverter, a Deflector that chops

into air much as a curved propeller blade slices the oncoming
water.

The flowing air mass as it strikes a sail has weight and kinetic
energy. The sail produces power by turning this mass and
absorbing some of its push. At whatever angle a sail is opposed
to the wind, it bends the air mass aft, at which instant part of
the wind's energy is transferred down through the mast and
stays into the hull. Forces developed in a sail, as a result of
wind sliding across it, have components that may be dia-
grammed into Lift, Drag and Heeling, similarly to those of an
airplane wing. But the useful, or resultant force from a sail is a
pressure moving out at approximately right angles to the
boom.

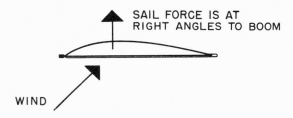

This resultant force urges the hull straight out to the side.
But the flat plate of the keel has been placed beneath the hull
to oppose side motion. So long as the sail force points even
slightly forward of amidships, the whole craft will pause, heel a
bit, then begin to slide forward in the direction least opposed;
at the same time making some leeway.

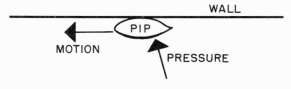

The process is similar to that occurring when an orange pip
is squeezed against a wall. If pressure is just a little from behind, the pip will skip out and ahead. If it is squarely against

the wall there will be no motion. While if it points backwards, the pip will start aft.

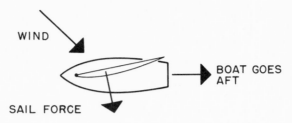

This explains why we cannot keep pulling in our main booms until they are over the windward rail in the hope of heading straight into the wind's eye. As soon as a boom passes the boat's centerline, sail force acting out at right angles, points aft of amidships. So the boat starts to move that way too.

Recent Sail Developments

Once sailing vessels began making windward passages, further generations refined rig and hull combinations for specific purposes. The square rigger, a form suited to long runs in favoring trade winds, but not close winded, reached its peak in the *Flying Cloud* and other fast clipper ships. Commercial fore and afters like the seven-masted *Thomas W. Lawson* had many small sails that could be set with winches and run by limited crews. The racing fishermen *Bluenose* and *Columbia* were smart and seaworthy with fine speed upwind. Improvements upon the open sea always take years: a new rig must not only be clearly superior, but safe under the worst weather and most inept handling. Many old time sailing maxims were inaccurate and showed admiration for manly virtues rather than efficient boat driving. In 1920 fishermen still boasted: "The best man carries the most sail," or "No power except in a fat, lifting jib." Sails in the western world have always been cloth, for it is light and cheap. The stiffened Chinese fully-battened sails were conceded to be efficient in strong winds and to point high; but they were adjudged dangerously heavy and pesky to trim and reef.

Before aeronautical techniques that might have improved sails were developed, wind propulsion, except for amateur sailboat racing, had gone with the carrier pigeon. Some sail research was done at Massachusetts Institute of Technology in the 1920s. And shortly thereafter the interest of sailors was stimulated by the work of Manfred Curry. The racing cognoscenti avidly embraced the similarity of cloth sails to airplane wings, and identified their rigs with low speed glider wings mounted on end. Shatswell Ober showed that when a cloth sail is trimmed well in for windward work it produces more useful force, or lift, as a result of suction along its lee side rather than from push or positive pressure against its windward one. This captured the racing imagination and sailboats were seen as sucked, not pushed along.

Further tests indicated the value of the jib as a flow-smoother for the lee side of the larger mainsail. With the coming of genoa jibs the Slot Effect was emphasized and jib overlap thought so vital that some provided it, even at the cost of jib area. The Bembridge Redwings, however, proved that with a given jib area, a boat sails fastest when all of this is exposed as sail in its own right, and that overlap at the expense of area does not pay.

The tendency to "go aeronautical" proceeded to such extremes that today there is revulsion from the idea that sails are simply low speed glider wings set upon end. Several modern writers even *reject* the evidence that suction along the lee side of a cloth sail contributes the major part of drive.

Undoubtedly there has been overstatement of the similarity between sails and airplane wings. Most early experiments were made on tin wings, shaped like sails, not upon sails at all. A tin "sail" placed in a wind tunnel will hold its curves at far closer angles to the wind than anything cut from floppy, flexible sailcloth, and so give deceptive readings. No airplane wing, even one from the highest lift glider, operates at anything approximating the broad angle at which a cloth sail sits when working its very closest to windward. Of course, when running before the wind or on broad reaches sails are not used for wing purposes at all: they are pushed along and do not generate lift from air passage across them.

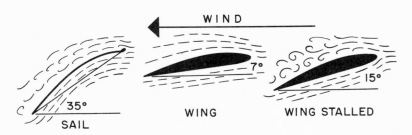

When a cloth sail is pulled in to the very tightest angle at which it will draw, it is still some 35° off the wind, and is operating "fully stalled" from a wing standpoint. By comparison, the slowest glider wing cannot produce lift when opposed at more than 7° to oncoming air. If placed at 15°, not even half way to the closest angle used by sails to windward, it will burble and stall; large eddies form on its curved upper surface, and any glider it might be supporting would drop like a stone.

Basic Shortcomings in Cloth Sails

Another difference between wings and cloth sails lies in the major losses to sails through Twist. In a wing this is called: "Excessive Washout of the Tips." Some writers feel that the twist so noticeable in sails (the wider angle at the headboard than at the boom, which may reach 45°) is necessary to compensate for generally stronger winds aloft. But Maj. Gen. Parham, writing for the Amateur Yacht Research Society in Britain, shows through tests of both twisted and untwisted cloth glider wings that this curve-off is excessive in sails, and that where close-windedness is desired it should be reduced by vangs to hold the boom down, or by battens, or by bending spars. Other experiments seeking to cure twist through use of stiff

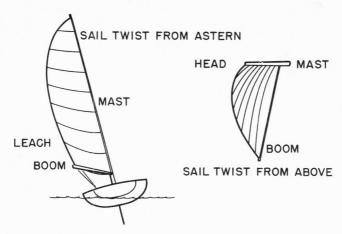

Chinese bamboo sails, prove that such devices allow boats to head extremely high to windward in strong breezes, and are useful on iceboats, but that the old European prejudice against them had validity in that they cannot compete with cloth sails in light to moderate airs.

Cloth sails stiffened by full length battens, however, such as are used on racing catamarans, have been found to improve performance, if one accepts their awkwardness and occasional breaking. They give a firm light sail that does not flog, allow a huge roach, and will hold a luff out to designed curves in light air at which standard sails collapse. It has sometimes been possible to hold out an unsupported cloth luff by starch, or by cutting light weather sails of extra heavy cloth; but full length battens do it more easily.

CONSTRUCTING AN AMATEUR WIND TUNNEL
TO TEST MODEL SAILS

The Psalms state: "Two things are too wonderful for understanding—The Way of a Ship on the Sea, and the Way of a Man with a Maid."

Now as to the "Way of a Man with a Maid," there is enough enthusiastic research always under way so that by middle age most of us come to understand Nature's aim in this delightful enterprise. By contrast, the "Way of a Ship on the Sea" remains mysterious. How a hull plunging in a seaway adjusts her stability centers for equilibrium, and how the pressures from her sails balance under water resistance and give forward motion, can frustrate long haired specialists. Small Point sailors believe that they win more races with their brains clear of such chaff. But those who learn how cloth sails produce their power are able to work out gains, not only through better direction of sail forces, but by increasing them at need.

A Schoolboy's Wind Tunnel

The simple wind tunnel shown was set up for $50 to the high amusement of local racers. It is based upon a two foot ventilation fan, and is a blower type that will test model sailboat rigs up to its own height. While the scoffers were right in that it is no precision instrument capable of coefficients from which the power of full sized sails may be predicted, nevertheless it yielded duplicate results on repeated tests, and opened a few eyes as to how wind drives cloth sails, how these may best

Wind tunnel and sail testing rig

be trimmed, and the general sail shapes that give most speed.

A quarter horse-power motor drives the fan and generates wind currents up to 15 miles an hour, which may be slowed to 10 or 5 by interposing one or two thicknesses of window screen. Theoretically, a model sail with a one foot boom span will perform in a fifteen mile breeze like a ten foot boom in a one and a half mile wind—boom width times wind speed equalling fifteen in both cases. But this fine point of scale was ignored by the writer, to whom the fifteen miles of wind blasting from the fan felt precisely like fifteen miles out upon the course, and whose model sails thrashed and fluttered in it and asked materials stout enough to withstand that velocity. A more accurate wind tunnel can be built that sucks air across the model, rather than blows air by it. But this requires an expensive closed throat and so much allowance for wall eddies that the height of rigs tested must be reduced.

A grid was placed before the fan to straighten the air flow and reduce propeller whorls, and an anemometer was used to

check the flow pattern for uniformity. The sail under test sits
at the center of a turntable in a steady stream of air, where it
may be swung to desired angles. Examples are: 45° and less
for windward work; 67½° for close reaching; 90° for beam
reaching; 135° for broad reaching; 180° for running free. It
was only necessary to test upon one tack, and here the port
is used.

The rig sits in water on a float that can move freely ahead
and to leeward. Wind forces acting against the sail pass down
and become angular pressures working to move the float, which
is held in place by three strings: that to the stern measuring
Forward Pull, those to the upwind rail, Side or Heeling Force.
The strings in turn attach to scales.

Heeling sail with battens installed

The tank shown is the bottom tray of an icebox. It might appear simpler to mount the rig upon a cart sliding on castors and dispense with water. But when sail force is applied, even when castors slide over glass, there is much friction, which is compounded when the model heels and needs a restraining flange on its upper windward side to hold it down. By contrast, a one foot by three inch block of styrofoam easily floats the rig illustrated and positions itself during readings with little friction. Placing the mast on the upwind side will limit heeling.

Three scales are provided to measure: Forward Pull, Side Force Forward, and Side Force Aft—the single reading for Forward Pull being the heart of sailboat speed. It is quite possible to link both Side Force strings for a single reading. But this does not allow precise location of a sail's center of effort, which slides aft as its boom goes out. By using two side scales their combined readings equal Heeling Force, which is assumed to act as a moment through the center of effort half way up the sail. The proportionate reading between the scales fixes the fore and aft position of this Heeling Force. For example, if the scales are separated by ten inches and both read 3 ounces, the Heeling Force centers between them; while if the after scale reads 4 ounces and the forward one 2 ounces, it rests two-thirds of the way toward the after scale.

The scales are pendulums weighing a bit more than a pound and hanging into water. Each has a wide piece of tin fixed crosswise beneath the surface to provide damping, without which they jiggle wildly and give erratic readings. While small extension springs are easy to fit as scales, they are almost impossible to damp. The pendulums can be calibrated by a letter scale. A sail two feet high with a one foot boom (one square foot in area) will produce Forward Pull on a broad reach in the nature of 20 ounces, so they must read that high.

Model Sails

Doubters were quick to point out that sails provided on model boats in stores have no arch and so are useless for tests.

But it proved easy to make arched sails, once proper dacron or nylon material was obtained of about two ounce weight, or approximately what goes into a woman's dress.

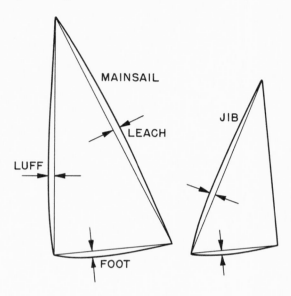

Step 1) With the material laid out flat on a table, pencil in the straight (interior) lines, representing the sail's base dimensions.

Step 2) Provide for sail shape by drawing the curved (outside) lines. For a mainsail of average draft, suitable edge curves are:

> Luff —1″ in 60″, maxin.um depth ⅓ up
> Foot —1″ in 42″, maximum depth ⅓ back
> Leach—1″ in 25″, maximum depth ½ up

For an average jib:

> Luff —1″ in 60″, maximum depth ⅓ up
> Foot —1″ in 30″, maximum depth ⅓ back
> Leach—straight

Step 3) Cut out the whole affair with scissors, carefully leaving half an inch of material *outside* the curved draft lines. Hem the leaches lightly on a sewing machine.

The sail is now ready for mounting in its spars, which is the final trick in making good arched sails. For a mainsail, obtain soft white pine half-round in sizes half an inch in diameter or less, to be used as masts and booms. Place the sail material between them and tack mast and boom ends together with brads. Now pull the central material gently inward, until the curved draft lines lie exactly along the insides of the half-round. This puts belly into the sail. When everything looks right, the central part of each spar receives enough additional brads to secure the desired sail shape. Finish by sticking cardboard battens along the leach with Duco cement. In this way a good mainsail of any desired draft with its own mast and boom can be made in thirty minutes; and one that may be fattened or flattened later.

It is more difficult to turn out a fine jib. The easiest way is with a luff pole and jib boom, obtaining draft exactly as in a mainsail. However, by carefully gluing thin wire along the luff and foot curves with Duco cement, then ironing these edges flat, the desired wing shape can be obtained.

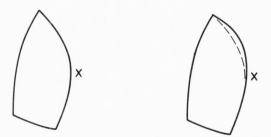

A fair parachute spinnaker is easy to make by cutting out two pieces of light material shaped similar to the first sketch above. Lay one over the other, sew them together along the curve x, then hem the other edges and open out the resulting bag. By fattening the top of the curve x, as in the second sketch, wider shoulders are obtained. A bit of good guessing, and you are in business with a spinnaker that lifts nicely.

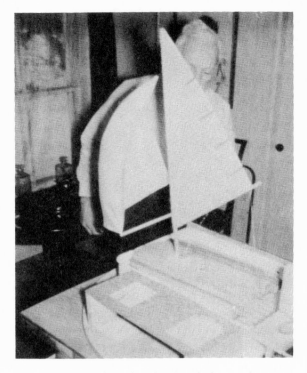

Testing the spinnaker in wind tunnel

First Use of a Small Wind Tunnel

Perhaps one reader in fifty will decide to make for himself a wind tunnel of the type shown. This he can surely do. And it is in the first ten seconds after switching it on in his living room that he will learn the most. The normal result is to blow all house lighting fuses, and bring screeches from adolescents who are honing their rapier brains upon television. Even more dramatic is a ripping off of curtains by the air blast, and the crash of old Uncle Eph's ashes down from the mantlepiece across the hearth. All this is a pity, to be welcomed in the interests of science. In reality it is a sacred moment, with the experimenter standing upon the threshold of knowledge. Soon he will examine sail forces, their directions, amounts, and learn how to control them in racing.

For the less ambitious the condensed results of twenty examinations into sail theory now follow.

Warning Against the Sin of Pride

The experimenter who earns wisdom by testing sails should not expect fleet admiration in addition. His unskilled opponents will put him down as a crank who is somehow trying to take advantage of them, while veterans who respect only the rewards of their own experience, will growl: "Come on out and learn racing the hard way, son. Just like *we* had to."

12

WIND TUNNEL ANSWERS TO 20 DISPUTED POINTS ON SAIL POWER

During the winter of 1961 the two foot wind tunnel was asked its opinion on a number of sail matters about which racers sharply disagree.

In these tests air speed was variable between 1–15 mph, with ability to check forces produced on all headings by scales, and airflow over the model rigs by smoke and streamers. Sails of different shape and draft were examined. Sheets were trimmable, and masts able to rake or cant. Standard mainsails were one square foot in area, jibs of one-third a square foot, and spinnakers of different types.

Confirmation Off a Dock, Full Size

Many of the tests were duplicated, full size, in the summer of 1961, using class sailboats attached to three scales, an anemometer, and ability to control rig angle to the natural wind by a stern line. No significant disagreements appeared with the wind tunnel's findings on model sails, which now follow.

SAIL TEST #1. WIND FLOW OVER A MAINSAIL AND FORCES THEN DEVELOPED

Although the fuses blew three times when your correspondent first turned on the wind current, after several days of examining what occurs when air strikes, passes over, then leaves a sail, it was clear that—

114

1) A close hauled fabric sail can draw well to within about 35° of the oncoming wind. Since the sail's boom is normally out 10° from the center line of the boat, the boat herself moves at an angle of 45° off the wind, and tacks through 90°.

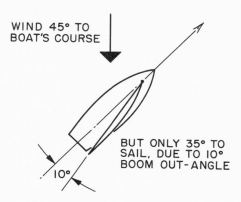

WIND 45° TO
BOAT'S COURSE

BUT ONLY 35° TO
SAIL, DUE TO 10°
BOOM OUT-ANGLE

10°

2) If a well cut sail is pinched 5°, one-third of its forward thrust drops away. Pinched 10°, more than 50% is lost.

3) In its close hauled aspect a sail acts as a bender of wind. It is through such turning of a mass of moving air that sails extract kinetic power to move boats.

4) A worsted streamer on the end of a stick shows that after air leaves a close hauled sail it continues in a direction roughly parallel to the boom for several boat lengths, then swings back into line with the prevailing wind, terminating the bend.

5) Dead before the wind the sail becomes a parachute that does not turn an air mass at all. Any bag that can be pushed along is an acceptable down wind shape.

6) On reaches the sail partakes both of a wind bender and a parachute. The closer the reach, the more it turns passing air; the broader, the more it is simply pushed along.

7) In no case does a cloth sail operate as close to the line of incoming air as a wing, to which 7° of offset can be excessive and cause stalling. Cloth sails operate "stalled" at all times.

8) No cloth sail can hold courses as tight to the wind as the tin "sails" that are sometimes used to duplicate them in wind tunnels for accuracy of shape and general convenience. Tunnel tests with metal sails are unrepresentative of sailboat rigs.

9) Major differences between airplane wings and sails are—
The Wing is first driven through the air by a propeller. Being stiff, when held to a narrow angle of attack and moved at relatively high speed, it produces Lift at right angles to its line of motion. *It generates no forward power of its own.*
The Sail contrives its own forward push. Since the resultant of all forces acting through it points approximately at right angles to the boom, so long as this resultant remains slightly ahead of abeam, any close hauled boat that is restricted in sideways motion by her keel, will slide out ahead.

10) Smoke blown through the wind tunnel shows as eddies that curl and bubble away like a wake as they leave the sail. This wind shadow, three to five boom lengths long, will slow other boats that encounter it. The shadow of a close hauled boat at first follows the direction to which it has been bent, then flops off to leeward with the general wind. That of a sail running free tumbles straight out ahead of the boat.

11) Air curving past the two sides of an arched sail moves faster and closer to the lee side than to the windward.

12) On the windward side, and particularly near the mast, a yarn streamer shows pockets of stagnation.

13) As wind slides aft over the windward side of a sail it tends to swing to the nearest edge, rather than to flow back horizontally.

14) Near the boom there is a major effort by air to duck down and escape to leeward into an area of lower pressure. A wide fence along the boom can limit this curve-away, but without apparent increase in forward drive.

15) Just below the narrowing head of a sail the air veers sharply upward. Airplanes sometimes use fences and end plates

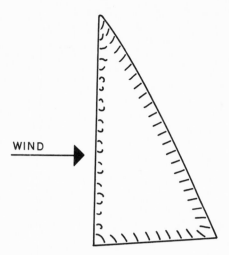

to reduce what they call "tip vortices." But such dams across a low speed cloth sail do not increase thrust.

16) Tests on numerous mainsails show that the ratio of forward thrust to side force (heeling) on various headings is approximately as factors of:

	Forward	Aside
To windward	3	6
Close reach	7	9
Beam reach	11	8
Broad reach	14	3
Running free	12	1

17) The fact that forward thrust on a broad reach climbs to a factor of 14, as against only 3 to windward, does not mean that the reaching boat will go almost five times faster. To double the speed of a displacement hull normally requires *three* times more power; to triple it, *nine* times.

18) Heeling force may climb so high on close and beam reaches as to exceed ability of hull and crew to counter-balance. It may then be necessary to "feather"—to free the mainsheet slightly while maintaining the same heading, and take drive only from the sail's after batten area as its forward part luffs.

19) As wind moves aft, heeling forces merge into forward thrust. The same wind power works to overturn the rig, but instead of pressing across a narrow boat, it now blows the long way and meets far greater stability.

20) The center of effort of a sail shifts aft as its boom goes out. On a sail ten feet wide this slide aft can reach several feet. With the sail generating force out to the side of the boat, a turning couple is formed that fights to swing it into the wind. Tiller pressures increase. If it were possible simply to slide the whole rig forward, balance with the hull could be restored; but since it is not, other methods of equating the rig to hull pressures may be necessary, such as heeling to windward to create a lop-sided underwater form, or moving crew weight aft.

21) The mainsheet trim that gives maximum forward thrust on each sail angle was found to be with the sail *just hard.*

22) When a sheet was eased until its sail barely luffed, both forward thrust and heeling fell sharply.

23) When the boom was trimmed in too far, forward thrust dropped as much as 50%, while heeling climbed 70%.

24) The effects of overtrimming were shown by blowing smoke past the sail. Large burbles then formed along the lee side, and instead of sliding smoothly aft, tore away early.

25) Full cut sails experienced this lee side air separation more violently than flat ones.

26) Standard mast placement relative to the mainsail's leading edge was with the mast directly ahead, as in (A).
But when the mast was turned to windward so that it lay above the leading edge as in (B), forward thrust improved by as much as 20% with no increase in heeling.

27) This improved forward thrust with the mast upwind of the mainsail's leading edge was most marked on close hauled courses, but still evident on broad reaches.

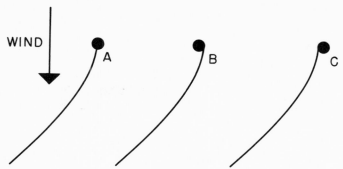

28) When the mast was turned so as to lie to *leeward* of the sail's leading edge, as in (C) above, forward thrust fell 10% below what it had been with the mast in its normal straight ahead, or (A) position.

29) The improved thrust to windward with the mast upwind of the leading edge was greater with flat sails than with full ones. On a flat sail the twisted mast seemed to arch the luff area more effectively; whereas with a full sail the arching became excessive and backwinded the luff.

30) All forward thrusts were 10% to 15% higher when the boom was held down by a wire vang so that the sail could not lift. This improvement held even to windward, but was most pronounced on free courses.

SAIL TEST #II. HIGHEST EFFECTIVE HEADINGS WITH CLOTH SAILS

Ability to point 5° higher to windward than one's opponents, while still holding the same speed, produces a nine yard gain in every hundred sailed, or enough to win each race easily. The joker lies in "holding the same speed," for we have already seen that a sail's forward thrust drops when it is pointed too high. Since we should all like to hold as high upwind as the great A. Knapp, let us examine the limits through which it may pay to imitate him.

If we place a mainsail of normal draft in the wind stream,

offset it 35°, adjust the sheet for maximum forward thrust, then slowly narrow the sail's angle to the oncoming air, we find:

1) At 5° closer than the best preliminary setting forward thrust falls off 30%.

2) At 10° too close it drops 55%–60%.

3) At 15° it has lost 75%–80%.

4) When the sail is pinched to a heading 20° above normal it may still seem to draw, but without any forward pull at all.

5) With a full cut sail (1 in 7 arch) the best original pull, in the neighborhood of 35° offset, is at a 3° wider angle than with a standard sail (1 in 10 arch). But this full sail's pull is some 10% higher than that from one of standard draft. Unhappily, the baggy sail's heeling force will be 15% higher than standard, which appears to limit its usefulness to light airs.

6) A very flat sail (arch 1 in 15) will head 3° to 5° higher at its best early setting than the standard draft. But here both forward thrust and heeling are 10% less. So the flat sail, while preferable in high winds, is a low power producer in moderate going.

7) An absolutely flat sail will point 15° higher than one with fair arch. But it gives almost no forward thrust.

8) If the mast can be turned to lie upwind of the sail's leading edge, forward thrust is improved 15%–20%, and maximum readings are retained some 3° closer to the wind than with the mast sitting normally ahead of the luff.

9) Careful adjustment of a vang to hold the boom down and the sail in one plane, lets most sails point 1°–2° higher without loss of forward thrust or increase in heeling.

10) After the experimenter locates what appears the best sheet adjustment for his sail at 35° off the wind, he will often find that its forward thrust can be improved by freeing the sheet 3°,

or even 5°, which implies a tendency toward over-trimming of mainsheets.

11) The beginner's scheme for heading straight upwind by pulling the boom in across the boat to the windward rail is worth examining. With the boom to windward an extremely tight heading *does* become possible. But the sail's resultant force, which still acts out at right angles to the boom, now points aft of amidships and stops the boat dead.

Limitations upon Embryo Knapps

Should the reader see in this information rewards for extremely high headings, these demands of practical sailing make the skill a delicate one:

A) For the 9% shorter distance sailed by heading 5° higher to stand up as a gain, the boat must go no more than 9% slower in the process. Yet a 5° tighter heading was seen to cost 30% in forward thrust.

B) A sailboat that is pinched only a little loses much of her hydraulic lift. This windward acting force is produced by sliding a well-shaped keel through water at a slight angle of attack, as when making leeway, and at its best can nudge a hull up toward the mark one full boat length a minute. Hydraulic lift has a built-in reward for fast footers over pinchers, in that it develops not in proportion to boat speed, but to the *square* of that speed. Whenever a boat climbs up to four knots from three, the lift of her keel rises not as a ratio of four against three, but of four times four, or *sixteen,* against three times three, or *nine.*

C) Many hull forms, perhaps the reader's, do not permit tight windward courses without exaggerated leeway. Boats with deep fins average to point high and not slide off, but fat prams and scows, particularly those with inefficient centerboards, crab away badly when pinched.

D) Rough seas and breaking waves often command a boat to be driven if she is to force through at all. In heavy going a tendency to pinch can bring stubbing and fast drift down to leeward. Strong adverse currents can also nullify distance gained by high pointing, since the lower speed will hold the boat too long in unfavorable conditions. Of course, when the set is fair there may be a bonus in pointing high and simply riding along upstream.

E) Even when sailors *know,* from some such device as a mast-head fly, the precise angle at which it should pay to oppose their sails to changing winds, few are capable of locking onto that heading without such slavish attention that they lose more by omissions elsewhere. The average skipper who holds within 3° of a chosen course is doing well.

Conclusion on High Heading

Since the helmsman steering to windward must sin either toward pointing or fast footing, it is the opinion of this corner that he sins the least when he *keeps his boat moving.* Pinched boats suffer the very worst losses, for they go dead and send no data to their helmsmen's fingers. Driven boats are at least alive and forever begging for more skillful direction.

SAIL TEST #III. IS MOST DRIVE FROM THE LEE OR WINDWARD SIDE OF A SAIL?

Even the early converts to Darwinism who flocked to applaud our descent from apes were not more convinced of their teacher's wisdom than yachtsmen of the 1930s who adopted the thesis of Dr. Manfred Curry that sails are simply wings placed upon end. In this conception a sail's lee side is glorified far above its windward one, and racers are seen as sucked, not blown to victory. Over the past decade guerilla articles have begun to snipe at rigid application of the sail/wing principle, until today one responsible sailing book flatly terms Dr. Curry's lee side theory of air flow as a large load that Farmer Gray will shortly take away.

In the South Sea Islander's phrase, let us now determine who is "saying the thing that is not," by placing a mainsail of standard draft in a fifteen knot windstream and restricting air passage across it by a spoiler in these ways:

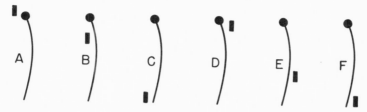

Close hauled, as in A) with the spoiler beside and ahead of the mast, there is a spot where it cuts forward thrust by half, and heeling even more. The sail shakes back to its leach and the rig sits up.

For a short distance aft of the mast and across the belly of the sail, B), the spoiler does little harm.

Near the windward leach, C), the spoiler can actually improve forward thrust by 15%. Yet it increases heeling even more, and seems to act like a flap at the trailing edge of a wing. Such configurations might aid sailboats in very light air when they could stand up against the excess heeling.

Any positioning of the spoiler to leeward near the mast, when still on windward courses, as in D), drops forward thrust and heeling by as much as 75%.

For two-thirds of the leeward cheek of the sail, E), forward thrust can be cut almost to zero by the spoiler.

Finally, there is an area near the lee side leach, F), where first it does little, then no harm.

On close reaches the same general results applied as to windward, although less dramatically. On both windward and leeward sides of the mast the spoiler did much harm, and serious harm over two-thirds of the sail's lee side. Again, near the windward leach it raised both forward thrust and heeling.

From a beam reach and wider the damage of restricting air passage by the spoiler lessens on both sides of the sail, and especially along the lee side where it becomes negligible. Upon the windward side before the wind, it is easy to set up spoiler angles that seem to improve performance as if by an artificial increase of bagginess.

We conclude: The critical areas of a sail lie near the mast and for two-thirds of the curve aft along its lee side. Interference losses here to windward can climb to 50% of available thrust if the blocking extends far up the sail. And Dr. Curry appears to have known whereof he spoke.

SAIL TEST #IV. SAIL POWER LOST IN HEELING

Beginners like to roll a sailboat over on her ear, where, with water splashing all about, they feel they are going fast. Under Hull Tests we saw that to heel far over presents a slower hull profile to the water, asks more helm to stay on course, and relaxes keel grip on the water so the boat slips off to leeward. It is now worth determining whether a canted sail plan causes further loss.

The sail used was average draft, and could be sloped off progressively to 50°. Wind speed was fifteen knots.

Offset 35°, as if to windward, forward pull remained steady from upright to 10° heel. It then began to weaken. Heeled 20°, it fell 11%; heeled 30°, 42%; heeled 40°, 62%; heeled the full 50°, 90%. Side force, which started upright at approximately double the amount of forward pull, fell just a bit more slowly as heeling progressed, and moved aft in the process.

On a close reach, 67½° off the wind, forward thrust fell with heel, but less sharply than to windward. At 40° it retained half its upright value, and at 50°, 40%. Side force started a bit higher than to windward, and dropped slowly with heel. Again it moved strongly aft with heel.

Squarely across the wind on a beam reach, forward thrust fell more gently with heel, losing only 35% at an angle of 40°, and slightly more at the full 50°. Side force changed little, but still crawled aft.

On a broad reach 135° off the wind, forward thrust lost only 15% at extreme heel. Side force actually climbed a hair, moving as usual well aft.

Dead before the wind forward thrust did not change at all as the boat heeled. With the entire rig far out to one side and setting up a strong windward turning couple, side force increased 50% at extreme heel and moved strongly aft.

On all points of sailing and at all heeling angles, when a properly adjusted vang held the boom down, forward thrust was improved and side force slightly reduced over the no-vang condition.

We conclude: It is only to windward and on close reaches that forward thrust falls away badly with heeling. On broad reaches and before the wind there was little loss. This seems due to the materially different angle at which the heeled sail offers itself to horizontal wind. When close hauled, any increased heeling presses the mast and rig down wind, lowering its profile and accepting wind pressure as an increasingly glancing blow. Running free, so far as the following wind sees, a heeled rig presents its full face and has only dipped its boom out to the side without changing that angle. For this to sharpen, the bow would have to plummet and slant the mast far ahead.

Side forces always move aft with heeling, and at extreme angles can generate bitter weather helm. Their amount climbs or falls with forward thrust, but more gradually.

Sail Test #V. Rise in Sail Power When: Wind Freshens. Sail Area Is Increased

If the wind across a sail doubles, does forward thrust increase by less than 100%, by exactly 100%, or by more than 100%? If a sail is enlarged by 10%, does thrust in a steady wind improve by less than 10%, or by something more? And does it make any difference what part of the sail is enlarged? Sailors entertain firm opinions on these questions. And, oddly enough, so does the wind tunnel.

Three wind speeds were used: 10, 13⅓, and 17 miles an hour. Two sails: the area of the first being a third larger than the second. It was possible to add a wide cardboard roach to each of them.

As wind speed increased, forward thrust and side force of both sails increased roughly as the *square of wind velocity*. This means that doubling the wind speed upped sail force *four* times.

In the matter of area, the two sails tested were of like cut, but one measured 126 square inches, the smaller 93 square inches, an approximate size ratio of 4 to 3. Comparative forward thrusts for these sails on all points of sailing and in different wind strengths were almost in accord with their sizes— or as 4 to 3.

In theory a small sail is less efficient than a larger one; so this small sail performed better than expected. In its *heeling*, however, the small sail justified the experts, in that under all conditions it gave readings *under* three-quarters of those produced by the larger. It is possible that this small sail was better cut—a fact not apparent to the eye.

The last test was to determine the extent to which added roach increased sailpower. One design classes commonly limit sail dimensions along foot and luff, but not always the width of roaches. Occasionally we see light weather sails with roaches so wide they can scarcely stand. The extent to which it pays to pile on this extra roach was examined by stapling skirts of heavy paper to the sails already tested, area increase being one-tenth that of the original sails, or more than is seen on full sized roaches.

Close hauled, the greatly enlarged roach gave almost identical forward thrust and heeling as without it. There was an impression of $\frac{1}{8}$ ounce better forward thrust; but no more. On a close reach, forward thrust improved 8%, and heeling *diminished* by that much, moving aft as in the standard sail. On beam reaches, broad reaches, and before the wind, forward thrust was some 12% better than with the unaltered sail. But heeling fell off steadily, until before the wind it was less by 30%. Here the surprising item is not that forward thrust improved on off-wind courses with the wider roach, but why heeling did not keep step? It is possible that the generally flatter leach area, a result of stapling stiff paper to the sail, gave a freer air flow.

We conclude: In the interests of winning races it is more important to obtain wind of higher velocity than to add a few extra feet of sail area. Doubling wind speed will increase sail force *four times,* doubling sail area, only once. A wide roach, although of little aid to windward, does improve speed running free.

Sail Test #VI. The Value of Aspect Ratio

Sailors construe "Aspect Ratio" as the ratio between a sail's height and its breadth. By this concept, which is only partly in accord with the aeronautical meaning, they rate a mainsail twenty-five feet tall and ten wide at the boom as "2.5 Aspect Ratio"; such abstract value being obtained by the unabstract process of dividing ten into twenty-five.

In the 1920s, when jib-headed rigs supplanted the low and broader gaffs, some Bermudan mainsails had luffs only a little longer than their booms. But, as race results soon demonstrated that the taller and thinner a rig, the faster it went to windward, masts grew to unstayable heights and brought in class restrictions, whereby small racing boats were limited to masts between two, and two and a half times their boom lengths. These common sense 2–2½ Aspect Ratios prevail today.

Average racers believe that while a "pencil" rig is faster to windward, a squatty sail will reach or run even faster, and being lower, will heel less. This, however, is only the unsophisticated view, for a few theoreticians contend that the high aspect ratio sail is always superior, even in the matter of heeling. It is interesting now to feed this question into our unbiased wind tunnel, and while it grinds out its wisdom to wait with eyes closed and hands extended like true modern scientists, asking our machines to drop us the answers to life's great problems on neatly printed cards.

Two sails were used in a wind stream of 17 miles an hour.

The ridiculously low aspect ratio of ½ was contrasted to a normal AR 2 by using the same sail, its leach serving as such in both cases, but the old head becoming the new clew, and vice versa. This gave the AR 2 sail a luff of twenty-two inches and a foot of eleven, the AR ½ sail, the same dimensions in reverse. Draft was excellent in each case.

Air flow across the windward side of the close hauled AR 2 sail showed the normal effort to escape to leeward at the boom, and in a lesser upward swirl toward the head. When the long footed AR ½ sail was trimmed in for best results close hauled, its boom sat out 5° beyond normal, and only along a pathway at its very center did airflow proceed straight aft. Elsewhere the air sought to escape under the full length of the long boom, as well as up from the top third of the sail. Worsted on a stick showed that a short distance aft of this low sail the air mass resumed its path with the general flow and was not bent as effectively as by the taller one.

| | High Aspect Sail | | Low Aspect Sail | |
	F. Thrust	Heeling	F. Thrust	Heeling
To windward	3¼	11	1⅓	11
Close reach	9	13	7¼	12½
Beam reach	17½	11	17½	11
Broad reach	19	7	20	10
Running free	20	6	21	9

In both sails the center of effort slid aft as boom angle widened.

The Wind Tunnel shows in this table that forward thrust to windward of a high aspect ratio sail is far superior, and to a lesser extent so on close reaches. Flow patterns of the low aspect sail confirm it as a poor *wind bender* that does not extract as much kinetic energy from passing air. On a beam reach neither sail had a thrust advantage. But broad to the wind or before it, the low sail was narrowly superior.

Heeling pressures shown above in ounces, require one adjustment. The heeling force that tips a boat is in reality a moment, acting as a lever from the sail's center of effort. And in the high aspect sail this center is two inches higher than in the low, or up 25%. Above-deck centers of effort for these model rigs were eight inches as against ten. So multiplying this distance times ounces of heeling, gives a new heeling table.

	High aspect sail	Low aspect sail
To windward	110 in/oz	88 in/oz
Close reach	130 in/oz	100 in/oz
Beam reach	110 in/oz	88 in/oz
Broad reach	70 in/oz	80 in/oz
Running free	60 in/oz	72 in/oz

Here we have evidence of *more* heeling in the high aspect ratio sail than in the low—to windward, on close and on beam reaches. But on broad reaches and before the wind, the low aspect sail will heel its hull further and ask more corrective rudder.

Sail Test #VII. Hard Spots, Hooked and Fluttering Leaches

Surface irregularities can distort a sail's surfaces in many ways, the most common being: lumps at inner ends of batten pockets; a tightness running upward from the clew just before the battens, often with flop-over of the roach to leeward; a loose, fluttering leach; hooking to windward of a leach, which can bend as narrow an area as the tabling of a jib, or one as wide as the entire roach of a mainsail, including its battens. For each lump, strain-line, or wrinkle a sailor can be found who insists: a) It is harmless. b) It is disastrous.

After thrust and heeling of an average draft sail had been established to windward, on a beam reach, and running free in 13⅓ knots of wind, the following flow disturbers were placed upon it, and new readings taken:
1) Seven hard spots on the windward side ahead of the battens.
2) The same hard spots shifted to the lee side.
3) A loose and flapping leach stapled to the true leach.
4) The entire roach-plus-battens hooked to windward.
5) The same roach twisted away to leeward.

	Unaltered sail Th. H.	Hard Spots wind. Th. H.	Hard Spots lee. Th. H.	Loose leach Th. H.	Roach to windward Th. H.	Roach to leeward Th. H.
Windward	2 6	1¼ 7½	1 6½	2 6	1 7½	1 5
Beam R.	10½ 6½	9 7	9 7	10½ 6½	9 7	6 5
Running	14½ 3½	15½ 4	14½ 3½	14½ 3½	12½ 3½	13 3

Losses in forward thrust through these sail disfigurements were most serious to windward. Thrust was also low on beam reaches when the roach was bent away to leeward. Flow checks with worsted showed that whenever the windstream could not slide smoothly aft, eddies formed. That these turbulences caused drag was shown by higher heeling readings. On full sized sails hard spots often deform the inner ends of batten pockets where these are too short, or the battens too stiff. In these tests such lumps caused high drag. When moved ahead into the windward belly of the sail, they caused less.

Hard spots on the sail's lee surface made less heeling than to windward, but were even more harmful to forward thrust, and especially when cluttering the curved cheek of the sail in the fastest wind flow. The fluttering leach did no apparent harm, except to cut forward thrust to windward *very* slightly. In this test the flapping area was additional, whereas on an actual sail it might run its tremors well inboard. Lower thrust readings were obtained as the roach area was hooked progressively to windward. Heeling on close hauled courses now rose very high. On beam reaches heeling was only slightly above that with an unaltered sail; before the wind it was the same.

Bending the entire roach away to *leeward* produced much stronger effects. Now all readings fell away, but forward thrust the most. Even on a beam reach thrust losses were serious. Running free, they were noticeable.

Sail Test #VIII. Porosity, Smoothness and Weight of Sail Materials

Before the availability of tightly woven dacron sail cloth, racers worried about the power lost as air seeped through their porous mainsails into the low pressure air stream to leeward. Whether a slick surface made a sail faster than a rough one, was also disputed. It has long been agreed that in very light air a filmy sail will lift and come alive when one of heavy material hangs dead. But now some light weather working sails are cut of heavy dacron in narrow panels, for the same reason that Paris dressmakers mould their curvaceous clients into gowns of full bodied fabric tailored from many parts—they hold their shape and produce more *power*.

A standard draft sail was constructed of wide mesh nylon netting. After it had been tested in a $13\frac{1}{3}$ knot wind stream, enough clear varnish was sprayed on to half seal all gaps. More readings were taken. Additional spraying then filled all gaps and produced a surface through which air could not leak.

	Mesh sail		Half filled		Solid surface	
	F. Th.	H.	F. Th.	H.	F. Th.	H.
To windward	$\frac{1}{4}$	1	1	$2\frac{1}{2}$	2	5
Beam reach	1	3	$3\frac{1}{2}$	$4\frac{1}{2}$	8	6
Running free	7	1	$9\frac{1}{2}$	3	11	4

In its full mesh condition the sail was useless to windward. It bent no air at all. On a beam reach it was almost useless. Before the wind, it had $\frac{2}{3}$ of normal power, but only $\frac{1}{3}$ normal heeling.

As varnish was sprayed on, sail forces improved. When no leakage was possible, they equaled those of a standard sail.

To examine the effects of slick surface versus rough surface, a standard sail was first roughened with starch, tested, then ironed, waxed and polished for a re-test.

	Rough sail		Waxed sail	
	Fw. Th.	H.	Fw. Th.	H.
To windward	1	3	$1\frac{3}{4}$	$5\frac{1}{2}$
Beam reach	$10\frac{1}{2}$	6	12	6
Running free	$15\frac{1}{2}$	3	$14\frac{1}{2}$	3

To windward the slick sail was surprisingly improved. But as a price for efficiency, its heeling was also high. On a beam reach the waxed sail was still superior. Heeling was identical.

Before the wind the rough sail actually pulled more, with heeling still the same.

To determine the advantages, if any, of heavy over light materials, three light cotton sails were checked against three of heavy satin taffeta. One of the light cotton sails was then made heavy with starch, and retested.

The heavy sails proved in all cases as good or better than the light. At their best they were 25% better. Clearest superiority of the heavy sails was close hauled. The three light sails gave more changeable readings that were sensitive to minor sheet adjustments. As wind speed dropped, the heavy sails retained some advantage, seemingly through holding their designed shape. Gauge accuracy was poor on any test below seven miles an hour.

When enough starch was added to the light cotton sail to give it increased bulk, instead of the improved readings that had been expected in view of the superiority of taffeta over thin cotton sails, forces were all just a hair lower. The sail was heavier and stiffer; but it also seemed to have shrunk, and to perform as a flat model does against one of normal draft. It pointed higher and heeled less, but with perceptibly less forward thrust. Surfaces had been roughened by the starch, so they were smoothed with an electric iron. Readings now improved. This was not considered an accurate test of the virtues of heavy versus light sail materials, in that body alone had not been added.

We conclude: A sail with wide pores is clearly useless to windward. But today this is an academic conclusion, since zero air can seep through stabilized dacron sail cloth. The greased sail was faster than expected. Modern sails are all slick when new; so perhaps it was not only dacron's ability to hold shape that let it oust cotton so promptly from racing boats. After several years the sizing wears off a dacron sail and it shines less. Should it then be re-sized or waxed? Also, if extreme slickness improves forward thrust 5%, no racing sail should be stuffed into a sailbag to form a million wrinkles. Instead, it should be ironed weekly, then rolled upon a long stick, or flaked reverently into wide folds.

Presuming a sail is beautifully cut, Hard's use of five ounce dacron and twelve inch panels seems to promise some light weather advantage over the more common three ounce and eighteen inch panels, through better retention of shape. These tests showed no gains through stiffening a sail whose shape was indifferent to begin with. Perhaps tremors from a shivering leach might be eliminated by starch, or a luff held out to permit very tight headings, if the absence of sail-shake did not lure the helmsman into pointing too high.

Sail Test #IX. Value of Extremely Full Sails in Light Air

Racers are in general agreement that very full sails are faster in winds below five knots, and particularly down wind. At Nonquitt we children knew this was so, for we had all heard of the fair maiden who saved her virtue from a raffish steam yacht owner on the New York Yacht Club cruise when she fled in past Cuttyhunk in a dinghy with only her billowing nightgown as a sail. Experience says that in drifting conditions a full cut jib lifts and draws better than one very flat; while in mainsails, Corny Shields, perhaps the best light weather skipper of his generation, always ordered maximum draft just above the boom. The deep curvature problem grows complicated in spinnakers, for late research suggests that an exaggerated central bag traps air, instead of easing it off both leaches and encouraging their spread.

Readings were taken on a very full sail of 1 in 7 arch, which was then flattened back to a normal 1 in 10 arch and rechecked.

The 1 in 7 baggy sail proved less efficient than the standard 1 in 10. It produced only 50% the forward thrust to windward, with little reduction in heeling. At all wind speeds the baggy sail was worse, even at the lowest. Its pointing ability was less by several degrees. When set at 5° closer to the wind than its best close-hauled reading, forward thrust fell 90%. When pinched in this manner the standard sail lost only 50%. On a beam reach the baggy sail was still 10% inferior to the 1 in 10. Before the wind there was little difference. The very full sail could not be strapped in hard; its best forward thrust coming with sheets well started. Air flow about the fat sail broke away from its lee cheek earlier, except in a near calm.

We conclude: A very full sail is a slow sail—unless the skipper knows he will meet no wind strong enough to blow out a match.

SAIL TEST #X. VALUE OF EXTRA FLAT SAILS IN HIGH WINDS

Any helmsman caught with full sails in a gale to windward knows how his boat must stub, wallow and drop back. What a joy it is to shift to a flat mainsail that allows effortless high heading and eases tiller work to comparative child's play.

After high wind readings were taken on a very flat sail of arch 1 in 15, normal belly of 1 in 10 was restored, and the sail re-tested.

The average draft sail, arch 1 in 10, developed approximately 10% more thrust to windward in all wind speeds. Heeling forces close-hauled differed little between the sails. But those on the flat sail, arch 1 in 15, were definitely further forward, which meant it required less helm. The flat sail could be pinched 5° above its best heading and still retain 60% power; the average sail held only 50%. So, luffing through puffs would be simpler with the flat sail. On a beam reach the average sail still produced 3%–5% more thrust and heeling. But again there was pronounced shift aft of the normal sail's center of effort, where the flat sail's center stayed forward. Before the wind there was little difference between the two.

We conclude: The advantage of a flat sail in heavy winds seems to lie only in ease of handling. The flat sail can be headed higher with less helm, and subjects spars, stays, and hull to less punishment. It gives less drive, but all of that can be steadily used.

SAIL TEST #XI. BEST SPOT FOR MAXIMUM ARCH

Sailmakers are likely to cut maximum arch into their products about a third of the way back. But for specific purposes they will shift these deepest curves with all the abandon of a fashion editor moving the eternal masses of the female form divine to conform them to his mode of the day. Mr. Thomas Sopwith, before his *America's* Cup challenge in *Endeavour,* is said to have run tests on the best spot for mainsail arch that showed it made little difference. American sailmakers place the deepest bag in a catboat mainsail almost at the mast; but when a jib sits out ahead, bending its own air in toward the boat's center line, they flatten the luff and cut its depth further aft to prevent backwinding. When a masthead genoa overlaps the forward half of a mainsail, this section may even be quite flat with fullest draft toward the leach.

A mainsail was tested in four arch positions: a quarter aft, a third aft, centrally, and three-quarters aft. After each check the boom was opened and foot curves changed to shift the arch position, whose depth was held the same in each case.

To windward, forward thrust was virtually the same with any arch location. Side forces were 15% higher with the arch dead center. With it well ahead, or well aft, they were similar. The sail's center of effort moved aft with its arch.

On a beam reach, forward thrust was unaffected by arch position. Heeling was only 3% higher with arch dead center. On this point of sailing center of effort also shifted aft less strongly with arch movement.

Before the wind, forward thrust, heeling, and center of effort all stayed relatively put with arch movement.

We conclude: Except for mainsails used over genoa jibs, a forward arch in the neighborhood of one-third aft of the mast combines the best factors; and particularly the lowest heeling.

But sails with widely different arch locations are not inter-
changeable, and may even need mast movement to hold rudder
pressures low.

Sail Test #XII. Fat, Bendy and Raked Masts

A mast that stands firm as the Pope in squally weather is like
a fine moral character—we all think we have one, until someone snoops around with a camera to prove us wrong. Ninety-
five per cent of modern racing sails are cut for straight spars.
But the problem of insuring that sails never deform is not
solved by erecting telephone poles, since even the presence of
a mast upon a mainsail's leading edge can cut thrust 15%.

Now we ask these questions:
1) How much sail power is lost by a very fat mast?
2) Does a bendy mast lose sail power?
3) What are the effects of mast raking?

To answer 1), a standard mainsail was tested behind an extremely fat mast. The mast was then planed down to about
normal proportions without touching the sail, and the tests
repeated. Finally, the same sail was re-checked with the very
thinnest mast it was possible to get.

To windward, forward thrust proved lowest for the very fat
mast, 5% higher for the intermediate, and 25% higher still for
the thin. Side forces were lowest for the fat mast and centered
well aft. They were 5% higher for the intermediate and a bit
more forward. They were 10% higher for the thin, and still
more forward, as a reflection of its higher thrust.

On a beam reach, thrust was least again for the fat mast, and
5% higher for the intermediate and the thin. Heeling was
slightly less for the fat mast and centered aft of the others.

Before the wind there was little improvement in either
thrust or heeling as the mast was slimmed. We therefore conclude: The smaller a mast, the less it deforms leading edge airflow. Thrust gains with a thin mast are most notable close
hauled.

In answering question 2), "Does a bendy mast lose sail
power?" it was necessary to identify the primary ways in which

a mast bends, and how these deform a sail. At first glance there seem to be four—

a) Mast center bowed out ahead, with the top aft. This is the common high wind curve when skippers set up their permanent backstays to "flatten the sail."

b) Mast center bowed out to windward, top to leeward. Also common.

c) Mast center bowed aft, top hooked ahead. Rarely seen in exaggerated form and thought dangerous.

d) Center bowed off to leeward, top hooked to windward. Reverse of b), and often accompanying it on the opposite tack.

The important thing to a racer is the extent to which a curved mast alters the shape of his mainsail. And fortunately there are only two basic sail disfigurements that stand out in practice: when the mast center bows away from the boom and takes belly from the sail; when it bows back toward the boom and adds belly. Many effects duplicate. For example, a sail is similarly distorted close hauled with its mast bowing out ahead, as when running free with it bowing out to windward. In both cases draft is removed.

Mast Bow Ahead

Sailors often set up their permanent backstays in a breeze and bow their masts out ahead on the theory that by reducing mainsail draft they can point higher and limit heeling. "See how flat that sail is, son," they cry. Maybe so, maybe so. But what about that hard ridge that now extends all the way up ahead of the battens from the end of the boom to the mast near the jibstay intersection?

When A, the masthead, draws aft under backstay tension, the mast center bows ahead below a fulcrum at point B, where it is held by the jibstay, and draft is removed from the lower luff at X by this mast curve. Simultaneously the leach, line Z, slackens. The boom end (clew) at point C, drops. But since point B is unyielding, a taut line rises across the sail to support the boom. This hard ridge ahead of the battens is, in company with a flapping leach, the trademark of a sail distorted by a

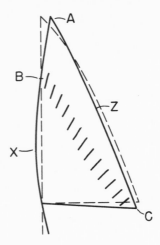

mast bowed forward in this way. With no provision built into the sail to withstand such diagonal strain, permanent stretching of the sail cloth is likely.

Mast Bowed Aft, Masthead Hooked Forward

The second basic distortion—bowing the mast center aft toward the boom on close hauled courses, while the masthead

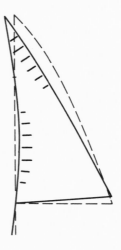

hooks over the bow, or in its commoner form, bowing the mast center to leeward when running free, brings a simpler sail change. The entire leach area is tightened, while extra draft is forced into the luff. Principal strain causes a hook-over of the upper leach, a section better able to withstand it without yielding.

What It All Costs

To gauge the cost in forward thrust and heeling of each type of mast bend, a standard draft model rig was first tested upright, then deformed in four different ways, and retested in each.

To windward, forward thrust was best with the straight mast. Center bowed to leeward lost 21% power. Bowed ahead lost 25%. Bowed aft lost 35%. Bowed to windward lost 38%. There was much less variation in side forces close hauled. Heeling was 10% *under* straight mast condition with the mast center bowed to windward, no doubt in reflection of the low forward forces here. It was 10% above standard with the mast bowed aft, which put belly into the sail and moved its center of effort aft. Heeling was similar in the other conditions, the straight mast still showing slightly the lowest.

On a beam reach the straight mast pulled best by 5%. Bowed to windward with top to leeward pulled 10% under average. All other bends pulled equally. In the matter of side forces, the straight mast heeled the least by 10%, with its forces slightly forward in the sail. All others were equal.

Running free, the straight mast pulled 10% more than any bent mast, all these being equal. The straight mast heeled 10% less than any other. Bowed to windward with top to leeward heeled 10% more than any other bent mast, and 20% more than the straight.

We conclude: The straight mast was always superior, its thrust advantage often exceeding 20%.

To answer question 3), the Effects of Mast Raking, the same sail was used on a straight mast, but with ability to rake it up to 30° in any direction.

When sailing to windward, mast upright and raked aft gave identical thrust readings. Raked to windward pulled 17% less. Raked ahead and to leeward pulled 25% less. In the matter of side forces, lowest heeling proved to be with the mast raked ahead. This shifted the center of effort well forward. Raked to windward also gave low and forward heeling. Raked aft was in the middle with forces centered aft. Mast upright, and raked to leeward gave similar heeling, just above that of raked aft. When raked to leeward, forces centered well aft.

On a beam reach, thrust readings were all similar, except that raked aft was 5% low. In side forces, raked ahead heeled the least by 10%, with others equal. Raked to windward had forces centered farthest ahead, with upright the next most forward.

When running free, mast raked upwind gave 10% less forward drive than the others. In heeling, raked to windward was a surprising 50% lower than the others, and raked downwind 15% higher.

We conclude: Mast upright and raked aft were clearly superior close hauled, while before the wind, mast upright was slightly superior.

Mast Facts in Practical Racing

Study of these tests shows: thin masts are faster than fat ones; stiff masts are faster than bendy ones; a mast should stand straight, or rake slightly aft.

To the extent that mast thinness and stiffness are incompatible, how far should we thin ours down to reduce interference, if a wriggly spar may result? Logic supplies this answer:

We have seen that extreme mast fatness costs at most 25% of thrust; while in a normal racing class the loss of a plumpish mast to one beautifully thin will hardly exceed 5%.

The maximum penalty for mast flexibility can be 38%, and even a mild shimmy loses 10%.

Since flexibility costs twice as much as bulk, we settle for: *the smallest mast that will stand straight.*

Sail Test #XIII. Loss through Jib Curve-Off

In his book Enterprise, Harold Vanderbilt details the hours he and Starling Burgess worked to cure slackness in the headstays of that cup defender when close hauled. They were convinced that compression bends in the mast, or any lean that encouraged jib and staysail luffs to bag away to leeward, greatly diminished pointing ability. In summer racing we note many saggy jib luffs on windward legs, particularly when it blows. This curve-away is so common that it becomes an emblem of second flight boats.

To determine its cost, a standard draft mainsail of 140 square inches in area was placed in the wind stream behind a jib one fifth its size, and without overlap. After the rig had been adjusted, the jib luff was progressively slackened, and readings taken to establish any harmful effects of the practice.

To windward with the jib luff tight and all sheets properly adjusted, forward thrust for jib and mainsail together were 33% higher than for mainsail alone. Yet only 20% in jib area had been added. Addition of the jib raised heeling force 10% over that of the mainsail alone, and moved the rig's center of effort definitely ahead.

When the jib luff was slackened, almost all jib force fell away. The jib went baggy and would not draw on so close a heading. However, inability to point was less marked than loss of thrust. Sitting like a hammock well to leeward of the mainsail luff, the jib could easily be made to produce no forward thrust at all. Yet in its bagged shape the jib still produced nearly the same heeling as when flat.

Forward thrust and side forces on a beam reach with the jib luff tight were greater than without the jib by 20%, which is approximately the same as the jib's added area. Center of effort was moved forward. Loosening the jib luff on a reach made no change in these readings. The baggy jib lifted and drew very well off to leeward.

Thrust readings running free with the jib were slightly more than without it, even when it was largely blanketed by the mainsail. Winging the jib out, sent these higher in proportion to the added area, or at most by 20%. Slackening the jib luff had no effect here, either upon thrust or heeling.

We conclude: A jib luff bags because rope halyards stretch and are not swayed up. Pulling the masthead aft with the permanent backstay can also bow the mast center ahead and squat both side stay and jibstay attachments a few inches lower, loosening them perceptibly. Jib luffs may be tightened by runners (on large boats) to hold the mast back firmly against the jibstay; by leading the main shrouds twelve to fifteen inches aft (on small boats) to hold similar jibstay tension; by using a wire jib halyard and a tack down-haul/camcleat combination that permits instant re-tensioning; or by an adequately stiff mast.

These tests show that it is important to maintain a firm jib luff to windward. A baggy jib can sacrifice 20% of available forward thrust with ease. But on beam reaches or running free the sagging jib costs little.

Sail Test #XIV. Springing the Rig Downwind?

Since Admiral Nelson's day sailors have felt that they can pursue the enemy faster down the wind by "springing the rig." In addition to such freeing of stays and spars, they will bag their mainsails by casting off their permanent backstay, slackening the clew outhaul and main halyard, or locking up the main gooseneck. In case any of us actually do run faster with our belts and buckles all cut loose, let us try to establish the gains.

A standard rig of jib, mainsail and spinnaker was set up before a ten knot wind. Readings were taken with stays and halyards all set up hard, as if just after turning off a tough windward leg. Shrouds and other mast controls were then slackened, and the sails progressively adapted to fuller shapes.

The rig ran fastest with its mast dead erect, and did not seem to care whether stays were loose or tight when it found this position. Because the mast top had at first been bowed well aft, freeing the backstay placed more draft in the mainsail luff and gave 12% better thrust. It was always necessary to hold the boom down with a vang, otherwise thrust fell away 15% to 20% and heeling rose.

The jib drew slightly better under the lee of the mainsail, or when held out to windward by whiskerpole, when its down-haul, halyard, and sheet were not dead firm. Trimming the spinnaker was an art in itself. It was necessary to encourage lift in the leaches so that air would pass away freely to either side. Thrust dropped with any attempt to hold this sail in a stiff, flat triangle.

We conclude: The moderate thrust gains achieved here do not appear to result from freeing, or even cutting away stays as Admiral Nelson is credited with doing, but from conforming the sails to more suitable downwind drafts.

Sail Test #XV. Best Jib Winging and Spinnaker Pole Positions

Tenets and dogma for the location of jibs and spinnakers running free vary with the hair color of the expounder. All have opinions, but few can support them with figures.

To shed light upon the jib and whiskerpole matter, a jib and mainsail of average draft were set before a ten knot wind. The jib could be bagged or flattened, and the up-down setting of its whiskerpole shifted upon the mast. To extend the same service to spinnaker poles, the same jib and mainsail were tested, plus a spinnaker of the same area as the mainsail, but only 80% its hoist.

Jib and Whiskerpole Findings

1) With the jib fully bagged, its extension to windward was less by a third. Although the jib now seemed in a more efficient cup for wind entrapment, it intercepted fewer lines of force and gave 10% lower thrust than when pushed straight out to its maximum.

2) Best whiskerpole trim was approximately in line with the main boom. Lifting the inner end a few inches on the mast stopped skying, which when excessive, reduced thrust.

3) Hoisting the jib an equivalent of four feet above deck gave before-the-wind readings just a bit higher than with it lower.

4) At 30° wider than a beam reach, jib forces fell as this sail was progressively shielded by the mainsail. Best trim on a broadening reach was with the jibsheet leading wide to the tip of the main boom, which preserved the parallel gap between sails.

5) At the same point where jib thrust fell off with the jib trimmed conventionally to leeward, it rose sharply with the jib pushed out *ahead* of the forestay on a very long whiskerpole. On anything approaching a broad reach (135° off the wind), forces with this pre-winging out of the jib well beyond the forstay reduced weather helm. Either an extra long whiskerpole was needed, or a club on the jib foot.

6) With the main boom held down by a vang, it was possible to sail as much as 25° by the lee without jibing. Such broad reaching by the lee with the whiskerpole trimmed far aft, produced 5% higher thrust than that dead before the wind, but still 10% under what was obtainable by jibing over and resetting the jib on the new windward side. Momentary bearing away to something not too far from the downwind course may not be so harmful as thought.

Spinnaker Pole Findings

1) The jib was required on anything tighter than a broad reach. Wider than that, and when dead before the wind, the rig drew a hair better with no jib.

2) Comparative pull between mainsail alone dead before the wind, and spinnaker alone, was as 14 to 11 in favor of the spinnaker. Being centered, the spinnaker produced no weather helm. In diminishing winds the light spinnaker definitely outdrew the mainsail and became the sail to watch.

3) Although the spinnaker is cut round and designed to pull straight ahead of the boat, the further it could be eased out to windward into clear air of its own, the harder it drew. This means that subject to class rules, the longer the pole, the more spinnaker power.

4) It had been the writer's belief that spinnakers should be encouraged to assume a lifting golf-ball shape by raising the pole at the mast. But here the spinnaker pulled best when it was set to cut the broadest slice of following air without hardening its leaches.

5) To the extent that cocking the inner end of the pole high on the mast stopped the outer end from lifting, which made the spinnaker small and round, it was worth adjustment. But a level pole was more easily controlled by the down-guy.

6) There was no evident gain in freeing the spinnaker halyard, so that the sail moved forward into freer air ahead of the mainsail. When this was done the spinnaker became baggy and hard to adjust for spread.

7) Being off just a hair from best spinnaker trim can cost 25% in pull. A spinnaker sheet and guy, actively coordinated to shifts of apparent wind as signalled by the masthead fly, seemed more important than fancy positioning of the pole or halyard.

8) All fittings, such as toppinglift and down-guy, were necessary for spinnaker pole adjustment. Often 25% more pull was realized by trimming the sheet out to the end of the main boom, which encouraged spread of the leaches.

9) Apparent wind abeam was the closest these tests showed it pays to carry a parachute spinnaker. With the pole against the forestay and the spinnaker sheet trimmed to the end of the main boom, a gap between spinnaker and mainsail equivalent to three or four feet could be maintained that prevented backwinding the mainsail and let the spinnaker ride out full and

strong to leeward. But side forces now rose and forward thrust barely improved over that of jib and mainsail alone.

10) If the jib was dropped and the spinnaker pole trimmed out through the jib's normal position to leeward, it was possible to carry a well cut spinnaker whose sheet ran to the tip of the main boom even up to a close reach. The spinnaker appeared to tug, but contributed a forward drive to the boat that was little over that of jib and mainsail. Conceivably in winds barely strong enough to fill a nylon spinnaker, but not enough to stimulate working sails, such close reaching under a spinnaker might gain. But its heeling would be dangerous in gusts, and without the jib, maneuverability would be low.

11) When running dead before the wind, up to 10% more thrust can be had by sailing just a hair by the lee, and pulling the spinnaker aft as far as possible into clear air of its own to windward of the mainsail. Mainsail thrust is penalized, but in zephyrs the spinnaker is the more powerful sail. It is possible to swing 25° beyond the straight downwind course without jibing and to realize a thrust gain of 10% over the straight run. This tactic might have short lived value as part of a starboard tack versus port tack gambit, although, by jibing over, forward thrust would be even higher.

12) Running free, it was found possible to carry both the jib with its whiskerpole and the spinnaker simultaneously. When trimming was exactly right, this combination gave a thrust increase of 4%–5%. It was more apparent in strong winds with the spinnaker surging well out ahead; in light air the jib made the spinnaker flutter and there was no gain. The foot of a jib may be cut at such an angle that its sheet will lead to the spinnaker pole. This eliminates need for the whiskerpole.

SAIL TEST #XVI. VALUE OF THE JIB SLOT

Nautical theory sixty years ago said that each sail worked for itself and that the degree to which it lifted was a measure of its power. Before World War II Dr. Manfred Curry converted the heathen to his Slot Doctrine, whereby the jib of a sloop wields supernatural power as a speeder-upper of low pressure air along the mainsail's lee side. Any racer who refused to view his mainsail as a low speed airplane wing set upon end, and his jib as a leading edge slat, was credited with a skull of solid bone, plus offensive obstinacy. Today a few writers deny to the jib/mainsail slot any validity, nautical or historical, and would gladly erect a galley smoke-stack in it or hang their wife's washing there.

To search out the facts, a jib and mainsail of average draft were set in a ten knot wind stream, and airflow across them checked at various spots by smoke and streamers.

Close Hauled Findings

1) Marriage of jib to mainsail produces a more potent mix than the total of their separate powers. Adding 20% in jib area increases a mainsail's forward thrust 33%.
2) Smoke, and worsted on a stick, show that air is speeded up and bent in by a jib toward a yacht's center line. Such off-the-jib air on a sloop strikes the mainsail luff more from ahead than does unbent air on a catboat, and requires flatter forward mainsail curves.
3) Worsted, moved across the lee sides of sloop and catboat mainsails, shows that re-directed air from the sloop's jib acts as a flow-smoother and delayer of separation in the area ahead of the battens, which cuts down eddies and their drag.
4) If as little as a third of the slot is blocked, thrust from the complete rig drops 25%.
5) Maximum forward thrust accompanies a jib in-trim in which the jib leach sits parallel to the nearby mainsail luff throughout its entire height, without hook-over to windward or loose fluttering off to leeward. As the boat's heading changes, jib sheet leads upon the deck must change to maintain this steady air nozzle, much as a hose directs a stream of water. Thrust peaks sharply at the best setting and can fall 20% when this is lost.
6) With a working jib of given area it does not pay to forfeit any of this as mainsail overlap. Maximum close-hauled thrust

was obtained when the entire jib received air of its own. Overlapping a quarter of the jib lessened thrust 10%.

7) An examination was made into whether the jib tack should
sit squarely on the deck, as in the Snipe Class, even though this
placed much of the jib below the level of the main boom, or
whether the jib should be at maximum height. Height as such
did not prove as important as placing the entire jib so that it
directed air over a part of the mainsail luff, in which case 5%
thrust improvement was noted.

8) Class rules limit the fore and aft position of the jib tack, but
a check was made into thrust with the jib perched far ahead, as
on a bowsprit, against what was obtainable by shortening the
fore triangle back to the mast. Best thrust was with the jib
leach approximately as far aft as the mast, or a few inches ahead
of it. It dropped when the jib clearly overlapped the mainsail.
It also dropped in the order of 10% when the jib tack was
pushed so far ahead that jib and mainsail became separate en-
tities.

9) Athwartship setting of the jib tack is limited by bows coming to sharp points. But these tests showed that the close-hauled
jib draws 10% better with its tack well to *windward* of the
boat's center line, than when it sits at the stem or anywhere to
leeward. Highest jib thrust was with the tack in line with an
extension of the main boom. This is where it sits on the improved rig considered in SECTION III of these SAIL TESTS.
By implication, a blunt nosed scow might go faster upwind if
her jib tack could be shifted 12″–15″ to windward on a track.

Findings on Reaches

1) On close and beam reaches, smoke and worsted showed the
jib/mainsail gap to lose some of its ability to speed air flow
past the mainsail's lee side. Thrust was improved 10% by widening out the jib sheets, or by running them to a suitable block
on the main boom, when the angle of the jib foot permitted.

2) Reaching thrust was highest with the jib tack pulled definitely *aft* from its best windward setting. Sliding the reaching

jib out upon a bowsprit quite destroyed its slot effect, although it counter-balanced weather helm.

3) Again it helped to move the jib tack to windward and into line with an extension of the main boom. Since the jib now sat well to windward, it reduced heeling. Moving the tack to leeward gave 10% *less* thrust.

4) At about 90° off the wind (beam reach) the slot effect as shown by smoke, grew weak. Thrust could still be improved by shifting the jib tack to windward, and also by placing it further *aft*.

5) At 135° off the wind (broad reach) the slot effect was hardly noticeable and eddies broke away from the lee side of the mainsail near its center. Ten per cent more thrust was gained by winging the jib out ahead on a very long whiskerpole. This also reduced tiller forces.

Findings Before the Wind

1) Smoke and worsted streamers now showed no slot effect whatever. A jib winging out acts only as a parachute with eddies twisting ahead from its lee side.

2) If the spinnaker is set and the jib left standing and not poled out, there is little in the way of jib sheet trim that gives thrust improvement. In light air it appears best to douse or brail up the jib. An effort is almost never seen to use both jib and spinnaker on the same pole, or the jib on its whiskerpole in addition to the spinnaker poled out normally. But the wind tunnel showed that in strong winds very careful trimming gave this configuration minor possibilities.

We conclude: Dr. Curry's Slot Doctrine is more than just curry powder.

Sail Test #XVII. Jib Sheet Settings

Doctrine for the placement of jib sheet leads varies widely for: sailors, sails, and weather. Standard practice in this regard is—

In-out

From 7°–16° depending on whether the hull can point high, or must be driven.

Ahead-aft

Forward to tighten the leach. Aft to tighten the foot. If the jib has a mitre, the jib sheet deck-block is generally placed several inches forward of a continuation of the mitre line.

For jib draft

With a flat jib, well in. With a baggy one, well out. In light air, well out to stimulate full draft. In fresh winds and smooth water, well inboard. In strong winds and rough seas, well out for drive.

For point of sailing

To windward, farthest inboard. Reaching and running, progressively farther out, and aft.

To evaluate these settings, jib and mainsail combinations were tested at all angles in winds of varying strength.

1) Best to worst jib trim cost 20% of thrust. Maximum thrust peaked sharply. Average to indifferent trim cost 10% of this.

2) An effort to use one setting for jib sheet leads on all points of sailing, as is common on racing boats, reduced maximum forward drive on average *10%*. Even constant retrimming did not regain this loss.

3) Best jib sheet tension, once the leads were in place, was with the jib luff just hard. A minor trembling was preferable to rigidity, and advertised itself as the too-taut sail did not.

4) A jib working independently was simple to trim. But trouble arose in that then it was no longer a pre-flow adjuster for the mainsail and did not conform to the mainsail luff for that job.

5) The entire expanse of a perfect jib that directs slot air smoothly across the mainsail luff must move in precise step with shifts in main boom angle. Such coordination is impossible with a fixed jib tack and one-position jib sheet leads.

6) For 10% higher thrust, the jib tack should move to windward as the main boom goes out, remaining directly before it.

7) There is an additional 5%–8% in thrust available through locating the jib tack farthest forward when close hauled, and easing it back toward the stern on a reach.

8) When nearing 125° off the wind (broad reach) with the jib tack fixed at the stem, the jib should be whiskerpoled out ahead to clear it from the lee of the mainsail. It now pulls 10% more, and somewhat lessens heeling and helm pressures.

9) An easy way to escape the losses of a fixed jib tack, and one-position jib sheet leads, is to extend the main boom ahead and mount the jib tack upon it, as is described later in SOME IM-PROVED RIGS. The jib now moves automatically in step with the mainsail as a fixed slat upon its leading edge. The result is: 10% more thrust with the jib always in new air of its own; no need to wing out the jib; less heeling and weather helm on reaches; greatly simplified sheeting and lower sheet tensions.

10) When restricted to conventional jib placement, adjustable deck track, snatchblocks, or other means of widening out sheet leads, such as running them to the boom, are necessary if more than 90% of potential thrust is desired.

Sail Test #XVIII. Losses through Twist

Forty years ago no one bothered to reduce Twist in the gaff mainsails of racing boats. Booms were long and heavy enough to hold a short leach straight, and if one did kick high before a gale it was thought exciting. The shift to Bermudan rigs brought in tall, unsupported leaches and stubby booms. Let such a boom lift twelve inches, its upper sail then curved away until the headboard swung out 45°–50° past boom angle, or to where we see headboards today on second flight boats.

As better racers turned to boom vangs to hold their main-sails in one flat plane, old timers, who hate anything artificial, rose to insist that sail twist was not only proper, but beneficial, in that it was a sail's natural adjustment to the "stronger wind aloft." They even exhumed photographs of square riggers with their upper yards all braced to this freer wind angle.

Pro or Anti-Twist?

As we move to check the cost of sail twist in the wind tunnel, let us briefly examine the old timers' love of it. They say three things:

a) The wind blows stronger at the top of a sail than at its bottom.

b) On a moving boat, any stronger top-wind comes into the sail more from astern.

c) Twist, with its out-curving leach and headboard to leeward, is necessary to face the upper sail into this freer wind.

The more skilful sailors, who work to reduce twist, answer these arguments only by winning. A twisted sail is a slow sail, they say; and Ted Wells will flatten his mainsail by vang after rounding a windward mark before raising his daggerboard.

Is the Wind Stronger Aloft?

Sailors do not need to pass completely through the whale, as Jonah swore he did, to find where wind blows the fastest. All that is needed is to weight two shingles, hang them on pins out an automobile window, and calibrate them up to "20 mph" by how far they blow back from the horizontal. Next find a tall exposed dock, set one shingle at water level, the other at the top, and watch for half an hour. It will be discovered that what scientists call a "wind gradient" exists, and that air clear of surface friction *does* blow approximately a third faster at twenty-five feet than at six. This difference between what strikes the tops and bottoms of our racing sails is about what Dr. Curry and others quote in their tables; and of course aviators take it for granted that winds at a thousand feet will blow stronger than on the runway. Up to this point the old timers seem correct.

But How Much Twist Is Required?

A simple vector for a moving sailboat shows that whenever wind strikes the top of its sail at a third higher speed than the bottom, old timers are again correct in that the effect is as if the upper wind came in a bit more from astern, or *freer* than the lower wind.

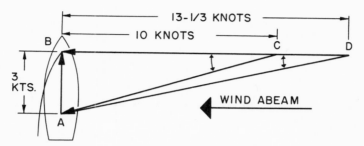

Here is the vector of a sailboat making 3 knots in the direction AB, while wind blows in from abeam at 10 knots, BC, to the bottom of her sail, but 13⅓ knots, BD, to its top. Comparison of the angles BCA and BDA shows that the upper wind is *6° further aft.* This is the maximum freeing of the upper wind, because vectors for the same boat going to windward or on a broad reach, show the fast upper wind as only 3° and 5° freer.

Since twist that old timers wish in their sails is only necessary for a maximum out-angle of 6°, how much swing-down does this justify in the five inch headboard of a Lightning Class sailboat?

Answer: Only *HALF AN INCH*

Here is the rub. Far from justifying the lifted boom and 45° mainsail twist of a losing sailboat, correct adjustment to the stronger wind aloft demands that mainsails be strapped flatter by boom vangs or adjustable mainsheet travellers.

What Sail Twist Costs in Power

A standard jib and mainsail were set in the wind tunnel, and air flow adjusted by screens to strike the bottom at ten miles an hour, but the top at thirteen and a third in a 6° freer angle. The rig was tested with the main boom held down by a vang, which was then removed and the boom allowed to lift.

As twist developed its upper leach would soften and require in-trim of the boom.

With Vang-on the rig pulled *more* than with Vang-off by:

    15% to windward
    15%   close reach
    18%   beam reach
    25%   broad reach
    18%   running free

Heeling with the Vang-on was *less* than with Vang-off by:

    20% to windward, with forces shifted ahead
    12%   close reach, with forces slightly ahead

No difference on other points of sailing.

We conclude: The vang's ability to hold a mainsail in one relatively flat plane is, after proper sheet trim, the single most important sail adjustment. No other correction, except perhaps the cure of a very limber mast, can raise thrust 20%.

SAIL TEST #XIX. PARASITIC DRAG OF MASTS, STAYS AND CREWS

An old Nonquitt sailorman who hated drag, would warn: "Boys, drag slows a boat so much, you can't let a man with big ears on deck. And always get a bald headed lady to trim your jib sheets: she'll really smooth out those eddies." He was a perfectionist. But Star class crewmen still drape over their rails to lessen wind resistance, and anyone who has towed an unrigged sailboat across a boatyard knows how easily she comes along without her mast.

Whenever a boat moves ahead, or heels to a breeze, her hull, rigging, and crew produce eddies to hold her back. The reader may wish to undertake a rough drag computation for a twenty foot sailboat in order to learn how much speed is gained when masts are slimmed or stays eliminated.

The first step is to total the flat plate area of rig items affected by wind, while ignoring the hull whose resistance is fixed. We have a mast, twenty-four feet long by three inches thick, with a frontal area of six square feet; stays, jumper struts, sheets and halyards, all corrected for interference effects as they join larger bodies, of approximately three more square feet; and lastly, the heads and shoulders of the crew, at another three square feet. Total flat plate area = 12 square feet, or about the size of a card table.

How much this costs in drag may be seen by setting up flat cardboard shapes in the wind tunnel, where we find that in a ten mile wind, one square foot pushes back, or drags, *ten ounces.* As wind speed changes, this drag lifts or falls in proportion to the square of the new wind speed. But at ten miles an hour our flat plate of twelve square feet drags *120 ounces.*

This seems a high penalty, and fortunately eddy producers on sailboats, such as masts and stays, are largely curved on their edges, and only in Scandinavia are crew heads square. A useful rule of thumb is that the drag penalty of round-edged shapes is only *half* that of a flat plate. So we halve our 120 ounces down to 60 ounces.

Now we face the complication that drag-producing elements on sailboats move slantwise across the wind, not squarely against it, as if in a wind tunnel. This lowers their drag; but at the same time the boat has forward speed that tends to restore air flow velocity. It would be easy to fill a page with vectors showing how wind forces combine on the various courses. But we may condense them by saying that a sailboat slanting to windward into a ten mile breeze makes drag at the same rate as if she sat in the wind tunnel at eleven miles an hour; that when reaching, her drag falls to what it would be in the tunnel at three miles an hour; while before the wind her now favorable drag is what she would produce at seven miles an hour. Correct these drags according to the ratio of their squares, multiply the results times our 60 ounce drag figure, and we come up with an estimated total drag on the basic points of sailing of:

> To windward—72.6 oz (4.5 lbs), adverse
> Reaching   — 5.4 oz (.34 lbs), adverse
> Running free + 29.4 oz (1.8 lbs), favorable

The reader will now wish to see how much this total drag affects the speed of his sailboat. It will vary between hulls; but its effect upon a conventional Small Point One Design is shown on the chart.

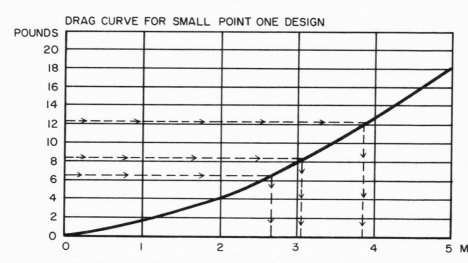

DRAG CURVE FOR SMALL POINT ONE DESIGN

Starting on the lower line at the normal speed of 3 mph, work up to the pull curve, then left to the pounds line, where we find that to tow this fast, 8 pounds of propulsion was needed. Now, we have estimated the power lost by drag to such a sailboat to be: 4.5 pounds to windward, .34 pounds on a beam reach, and 1.8 pounds (gain) before the wind. This represents the *total* drag penalty of rig and crew, only a small part of which could ever be eliminated, unless the boat were to sail around the course without her mast and crew. But what does so much drag cost in speed? We can visualize it by assuming that to windward and reaching the boat had that much more sail power, while before the wind, that much less. Instead of 8 pounds driving her, she would now have:

	Lbs Pull	New chart speed	Gain/loss per mile
To windward	12.5 lbs	3.8 mph	1408 feet, gain
Reaching	8.34 lbs	3.1 mph	176 feet, gain
Running free	6.2 lbs	2.75 mph	440 feet, loss

These considerable figures are the product of *all* drag, so as practical sailors we must determine how much we can possibly eliminate. Put another way: What is the widest percentagewise difference in drag seen on racing boats of one class?

The reader may guess for himself; the author only suggesting that in unrestricted classes, drag inequality due to bulky, as against very slim frontal areas, might reach 25%; but that in a well regulated one design class it would be nearer *10%*. This means curable losses of 140.8 feet and 17.6 feet a mile to windward and reaching, at the price of 44 feet a mile now assisting the draggy boat before the wind.

Composite Drag Handicap

Those who prefer an inclusive drag penalty, applicable over an entire race, face a last hurdle—how to weight their penalty for the extra importance of windward legs? An easily remembered figure that seems fair is that a very draggy boat can drop to a slippery one—

50 FEET EVERY MILE

Sail Test #XX. Heeling Through Excess Weight Aloft

When the Maine cocktail sailors heard that *Weatherly*, by removing a two pound wind direction indicator from her masthead, *saved 150 pounds of heeling moment at the deck,* it was good for an hour's convivial discussion. But no one hurried down to his own sailboat and shinnied up the mast to pare off a few ounces. We have seen that canted hulls are always slow, and that any sail plan heeled beyond 25° loses a quarter of its thrust. Whether the reader should initiate a weight saving campaign upon his rig depends on how he answers these two questions:

What is the widest weight-aloft difference in my class?

Do boats that are bulky up there win races?

All masts with their rigging, even very light ones, contribute to heeling as they support sails. Heeling force is measured as a moment in foot pounds, the weight of a rig being seen as acting to leeward from the top of a lever arm half way up the mast. One pound centered a foot high heels the boat only one foot pound, but raise it to fifteen feet, the approximate balance point of a Small Point One Design, and the damage is fifteen times as great. Small boat rigs are necessarily tall, if not spectacular poles like that on *Weatherly,* so four ounces at the top of a Lightning mast needs six pounds of counterpoise down in the cockpit.

An easy way to discover the heeling penalty of obese rigs is to go to the boatyard in the spring, pick up a number of class masts with their stays and halyards, find how high up they balance, then weigh them. The Small Point One Designs with conventional double jumper rigs show differences of:

> Heaviest mast with all rigging — 75 pounds
> Very lightest mast with rigging — 38 pounds
> Greatest weight difference $\overline{37}$ pounds, or almost 100%

This 37 pounds centered fifteen feet high exerts *555 foot-pounds* of heeling moment to leeward (37 × 15 = 555). Any boat so burdened must dedicate 185 pounds in the loins of someone hiked three feet out to windward simply to stay level. It was found possible to pare away this entire excess load as follows:

Mast materials	Sitka spruce is far lighter than fir	10	lbs
Mast materials	A beefy mast can be shaved	15	lbs
Stays	1/8″ stainless steel will hold 2200 pounds, 3/16″, 3700 lbs	2	lbs
End fittings	Swagings are smaller and stronger than bronze sockets loaded with zinc	2	lbs
Jumpers and crosstrees	Aluminum tubing gives less weight and windage than wood	2	lbs
Halyards	Rope and cleats are bulky compared to flexible wire cable and halyard hooks	1½	lbs
Mast track and screws	Nylon or aluminum are 50% lighter than brass	3	lbs
Masthead fly	Plastic should replace metal up where ounces count	½	lb
Working sails	4 pounds difference can be noted between sails of different sailcloth. Unless heft contributes to shape, some of this is waste	1	lb
	Total savings possible	37	lbs

Now as the reader reflects back over his own fleet for an answer to: "Do boats that are very heavy aloft win our races?" Small Point experience may be stated as entirely in the negative. Any skipper who loads down his boat with a new mast and fittings so strong that he will never have to worry about them, always does poorly next year. Just as surely, any boat given a trimmer (but still straight) mast, finishes noticeably higher. It is easy to see why, when paring away only five pounds fifteen feet overhead will save the balancing efforts of a child out on the rail.

The basic problem, therefore—whether the reader will gain through instituting a weight saving program in his rig— can be answered with an unqualified, *"Yes!"* Cutting down heeling moment is one of the few tasks on a racing boat that, once well done, may be forgotten.

13

POWER DIFFERENCES IN FULL SIZE SAILS

Those racers who hate theory will now be pleased to embrace the Facts of Sails, full size. Here are the differences between sails actually used on a fleet of nineteen eight-foot prams and twenty Small Point One Designs. Information was obtained by:

Examining sails individually

Measuring their thrust in captive tests off a dock

Sailing two boats side by side to establish no-interference pull rates

Checking long term race results

The first three tests cover Size, Draft and Thrust differences between sails ostensibly equal. The second three show the extent to which rig balance and trim methods differ throughout a fleet. The last gives a percentage of thrust lost between poor, average, and very best rig adjustments. All are furnished to make a boat's eventual Race-Rating more accurate.

PRACTICAL SAIL TEST #1. VARIATIONS IN MATERIALS AND SIZE OF ONE DESIGN SAILS

Because sail plans for both eight foot prams and Small Point One Designs are freely available, it might seem that sailmakers would supply uniform products to these fleets. Such, however is not the case.

Pram Sails

Nineteen boats comprise this class, a majority having homemade dacron mainsails, and a few, professionally made

160

sails by Hard of Long Island. When the first prams were built
their sails were of transparent Mylar film, cut over a form,
and with draft one foot in twelve, located a third aft of the
mast. These sails were fast and equal. Being able to see through
them helped beginners and compensated for the fiendish rattle
when they luffed. Unfortunately, although the Mylar was tried
in two thicknesses, it cracked and became useless after a season.

Fourteen homemade sails were then made of 3.8 ounce Bain-
bridge dacron. Some were shaped over a form, others cut in
normal fashion on the floor. Panels were a full thirty-six inches
wide, and sewing by dacron thread. A few had luffs of plastic
tape, but the majority were reinforced with dacron. Each
sail had three plastic battens and a plastic head-board, some of
which were boomerang-shaped to lift the head as much as four
inches above the mast-top. There was little difference between
any of these homemade sails, except for crude early stitching.

As competition tightened five owners bought dacron sails
from Hard. These were beautiful little loose-footed mitre-cut
mainsails of exactly the same size as the homemade ones, and
of average draft.

Except for the very first homemade dacron sails, which grew
baggy, none showed any advantage. The racing skill of children is so variable that the more experienced won with any
equipment. Of the two winningest sails over three years, one
is by Hard, and the other the last of the homemade floor-cut
affairs, which came out with beautifully even draft.

Small Point One Design Sails

Starling Burgess' sail plan for this class shows a loosefooted
mitre-cut mainsail of 120 square feet, a jib of 40 square feet,
or a larger overlapping jib of 60 square feet. In 1961 spinnakers were purchased on a fleet order, with dimensions similar
to those of the Lightning Class.

The first cotton working sails were cut in 1937 by Prescott
Wilson. Before World War II sets were also bought from Ratsey and a local sailmaker. Sails in those days varied from 10%

undersize, to 5% above the sail plan, or by as much as 20 square feet on a 160 square foot rig. Some of colored material were so light that they stretched badly. A majority of the winners were from Ratsey, all cut in narrow panels. Postwar cottons, again from Ratsey, were handsome and narrow clothed with few individual differences. The change to dacron started in 1956. For years one cotton sail remained with an owner who declared that "Sails are all the same." So was his record: always dead last. One boat with Ratsey cottons continued to win over the first dacrons through 1958. Makers of the dacron sails used by this fleet then were:

	No. of sails
Ratsey	11
Hard	11
Hood	1
Boston	1

All these Small Point dacron working sails measured within an inch or two on hoist and foot, except that one year three Ratsey mainsails arrived nine inches short in the hoist, a deficiency that did not trouble their owners who were all heavy weather sailors. Weight of sailcloth and width of panels are:

Ratsey 4 oz. dacron sailcloth. Wide panels.
Hard   5 oz. dacron. 12" panels on the premise that heavy, much-tailored sails hold truer shape in light air.
Hood   Thin, beautifully white sailcloth of his own production. Wide panels.
Boston Stiff, white dacron of moderate weight. Panels of average width.

Headboards and batten lengths were similar, except that Hood's battens were extra long. Although the sail plan calls for four mainsail battens, Ratsey for some years supplied only three. Hard added a short foot-batten to this loose-footed mainsail. Roach on Ratsey and Hood mainsails was only five inches; about eight for Boston; and twelve for Hard. Few Ratsey owners specify a preferred wind-speed for their sails. Hard, Hood, and Boston sails were all ordered for winds "on average 10–12 mph," which predominate locally.

Spinnakers were supplied by Hard on a fleet order and do

not differ, except in color. Two antique spinnakers are still being used against them: one an outsized flattish sail with an
illegally long pole that the owner refuses to discard; another of
only 60% the present class area.

A sailmaker is at the mercy of his customers. For five years
the keener Small Point skippers have been ordering from
Hard, so his six sails win 90% of the races, except that when it
blows over thirty one accomplished heavy weather Ratsey man
commonly wins. Because three-quarters of the fleet's racing is
in winds between ten and twenty miles an hour, it would seem
that an owner planning to use a single set of working sails
should specify that they be cut for that wind range. But this
is by no means always done. Since 1970 a number of Lowell
North's sails have been used, as well as some from Rockell
of England.

PRACTICAL SAIL TEST #2. DRAFT, AND ITS LOCATION IN ONE
DESIGN SAILS

Prams

All homemade sails, built over a frame or cut upon the
floor, were arched one foot in twelve, with maximum dept a
third aft. Hard's pram sails have like draft.

Children at Small Point compete in average weather, and
since their skills are not sufficiently developed so that one
wins in light, another in heavy, the best racers seem able to
win with any sail. Their courses are short, with so many reaching legs that the benefits of a fine sail are obscured.

Small Point One Designs

All the Ratsey dacron mainsails at Small Point are flat with
draft well forward, arch about one in fifteen, and little roach.
In half a gale these sails heel noticeably less than others, and
it is then that they win their races. In light air such flat Ratsey
mainsails rarely ghost out ahead. Ratsey jibs are fuller than
their mainsails and will draw well with slackened sheets in a
near calm.

Hard owners in the Small Point Class all requested "light weather sails" and limited top wind speed to fifteen miles an hour. The first three sets showed fully rounded curves that would have pleased the painter Reubens and won consistently in their designed conditions. But in winds above fifteen knots they heeled badly unless both main and jib sheet leads were widened to the rail. Later sails under Hard's new "Delta Series," while not quite so lively when drifting, are clearly superior above twelve miles an hour and heel far less. "Delta series" jibs are outstanding.

The single order from Hood was for "light weather," but both jib and mainsail arrived very flat, particularly the jib. Mainsail arch is in the order of one in fourteen, with deepest draft in the center as if for a genoa jib, which is not used in this class. Although there is little roach, the battens are long. It is a handsome sail, taped, not roped along the luff. There is always some leach flutter on both jib and mainsail.

The one set of Boston working sails has been used less than a season and not in every race. Both jib and mainsail are smoothly cut, arched less than is Hard's practice, and very good in a breeze, if not quite so successful in light weather.

Results in competition attributable to draft are: Hard's full cut early sails have the best record in winds under ten knots. Hard's "Delta Series" averages to be fastest near twenty knots. Ratsey's flat sails win in heavy winds. Because only a few Small Point skippers have the fittings to adjust sails built for one wind strength for an acceptable job in another, sails, hulls, and even sailors become typed as "light" or "heavy weather."

PRACTICAL SAIL TEST #3. BEST VS WORST PULLS

Prams and Small Point One Designs were checked for forward thrust in three ways:

Pivoting Off a Dock

Two side ropes absorbed heeling forces as shown. A third ran from the stern to a scale, which measured forward thrust.

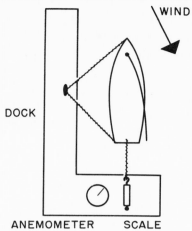

Tests required a steady wind and willingness to shift the boat's heading by the stern line (with scale attached) as wind direction changed. A direct reading anemometer stood near the scale so that, once thrust readings steadied, the wind force producing them could be noted. The whole procedure took patience and some guesswork to draw in a complete pull curve.

Sailing Side by Side Without Interference

This method required that two skippers spend a morning in similar hulls, using like trim and tiller movements, to come up in time with a "60 second Gain or Loss Ratio" for one sail over another. After several points of sailing had been checked, sails were shifted between boats, and the tests re-run so far as possible in the same wind and water.

Results in Competition

A notebook kept over three seasons of results obtained on certain points of sailing, in winds of certain strength, against certain opponents, gave highlights on the comparative speed potentials of sails. Most significance was accorded to results found when clear of tactical interference. Whenever one hull, thought equal to another, persistently gained 10% in distance, a check of her Towing Chart was made to determine what additional power she was receiving to move at the higher speed.

Findings

Pram sails were tested in the three ways described, with good cross-confirmation. Best-to-worst forward thrust on various points of sailing in no case differed by more than 10%. Widest thrust differences were on close-hauled courses. Here the five Hard sails were superior to many of the homemade and equal to the best. Before the wind no advantage was held by any sail.

For background in the Small Point One Design Class the very smallest and worst suit of the old cotton sails was dug out of storage and tested against the best cotton set still on hand, and also against the fastest of the new dacrons. Between it and the best cotton set, a thrust difference was found of 25%. There was an additional 10% difference, or 35% in all, between it and the new dacrons.

When tested off the dock, dacron mainsails best adapted to a certain wind strength pulled 20% more than others worse adapted. Dacron jibs showed as much as 30% pull difference. Two very flat jibs needed careful sheet adjustment to yield any power at all under unfavorable conditions. Spinnakers were tested by fastening a boat stern-about to her mooring, then reading thrust from a small scale, and wind speed from an anemometer. When similarly trimmed, none of the spinnakers ordered at the same time showed any advantage. The large pre-war spinnaker drew well before the wind, but poorly on reaches. The small pre-war spinnaker gave 55% less thrust than all others.

These off-the-dock tests consumed several days. Wind was seldom steady, or sufficiently strong. Using the natural wind can in time give good discrimination between sails. But the procedure needs refinement by some sort of large vane to keep the hull firmly opposed to the wind at a selected angle. A means of computing "total thrust produced" over a minute, against "total wind force used," would make drawing up an accurate power curve easier.

Several days of side by side sailing, without interference at distances up to seventy feet, largely confirmed off-the-dock thrust differences between best and worst sails. The fastest light weather sails delivered approximately 20% more thrust under their favored conditions than those poorly suited to that air. The best high wind sails were similarly superior to those with full draft in heavy going. But the advantage of "best" over "average" sails ran far less. Often in the nature of 3%–5%. The trick in establishing one-minute rates lay in sailing both boats through equal wind. It was necessary to ignore puffs or gusts that struck only one boat, and still to insure minimum interference. It was not a race, but a thrust comparison under a wind supply kept identical to the extent possible. Reversing sails between boats, once a rate was established, did not work so well as using one boat as the trial horse and changing sails only upon the other; for in this way sheet settings on the trial horse could be marked for future tests against other sails.

The single sail characteristic most clearly noted was the pronounced heeling of full cut sails in winds barely too strong for them, and the tiller skill then required to keep them footing. In light air it was equally plain that trimming a flat mainsail in hard simply strangled it, and, even more so, a flat cut jib.

Over a season's competition small, flat sails always finished higher than normal when it blew hard, just as full cut sails slid up through the fleet in zephyrs. But sail power as a measurable speed determinant was much clouded by skipper's skill. Helmsmen who sail their best in one type of weather seldom get the most out of sails cut for another. After allowing for such factors, it would seem that the *20 per cent* maximum thrust difference noted in captive tests off a dock and when sailing alongside, stand up. "20% thrust difference" is not the equivalent of so much in speed, as the towing chart for any displacement hull will show. Rather, it is in the order of 7%–8% in speed. We conclude on the basis of these first three practical sail tests:

There is wider intra-class difference between best and worst sails than is popularly imagined. And 20% thrust difference at speeds of 3 mph might yield a Sail Handicap toward a Race-Rating of .3 KNOTS, or 300 FEET A MILE.

Fine helmsmen extend the wind range under which a sail performs well, while poor ones narrow it drastically.

For top results a racing boat must have two, and preferably three sets of working sails. Number 1 should be cut for known average weather and will be used 70% of the time. Whether #2 should be flat or full depends upon the frequency of storms as against drifting weather. As a rule it should be flat.

PRACTICAL SAIL TEST #4. DIFFERENCES IN RIG BALANCE

A poorly balanced sailboat is slow, no matter what power her rig provides, for the cross rudder repeatedly needed to bring her back to course will act as a brake.

Pram Balance

A dozen sailing prams were examined for tiller balance:

All showed at least 1 foot pound of weather helm to windward in a 5 knot breeze. None had any lee helm. They had been designed to tack quickly and to seek the wind when roughly handled by beginners. Differences in helm pressure between boats were in the nature of ounces. Strongest weather helm was on one whose forestay had slacked off, producing an extra foot of mast rake aft.

Balance in the Small Point One Designs

Boats of this class with a jib and mainsail rig showed greater variation in tiller pressures needed to hold them on course. Their balance figures were taken close-hauled in winds below 10 knots and are given in foot-pounds. The scale was attached to each tiller at a point two feet ahead of the rudder post, so a reading of $\frac{1}{2}$ pound represented one foot-pound. $2' \times \frac{1}{2}$ lb. = 1 ft. lb.)

Number of boats	Helm	Foot-pounds
1	Lee	1.5
1	Lee	.9
5	Weather	.5 average
5	Weather	2.1 average
5	Weather	3.4 average
3	Weather	4.5 average

Fore and aft placement of masts differed by as much as eight inches. Mast tops raked as much as 18 inches fore and aft, or were bowed aft through backstay tension. Depth and location of mainsail draft affected balance importantly.

Judged by their racing records: The top five boats all had very small weather helm. Both boats with lee helm were in the bottom third. Those with worst weather helm were all in the last quarter.

PRACTICAL SAIL TEST #5. VARIATION IN SHEET SETTINGS

Sheet leads permanently fixed upon a deck cannot produce maximum drive and minimum heeling upon all points of sailing. How sheets are fixed in two fleets, and which type wins, was examined.

Prams

The main sheet rig on each of these small catboats is composed of a wire traveller across the whole broad stern with one end of the sheet slipping across it on a ring. The boom at its tightest is over the quarter, and since these beamy little hulls are not close winded, that is about proper trim. It is possible to draw the sail in further by hand, but not to any advantage.

Small Point One Designs

The mainsheets of most boats now have full width tracks and sliding deck blocks. To wind ward in light airs the block is permitted to slip 12″ outboard, and all the way to the rail on reaches. Close hauled in a blow, it is positioned directly below the boom so that down-pull on the main sheet flattens the leach and reduces heeling. One boat uses the Lightning Class or Crosby main sheet rig with two deck blocks 18″ apart. A close-hauled boom position outboard of center is so provided and the leach held straight under main sheet tension.   A few others trim their mainsheets to a central deck block, which is satisfactory in light going, but a leach-curver on reaches or close-hauled in anything over 15 knots.

Since traveller equipped boats win most of the races, their main sheet methods appear superior. They hold a mainsail flatter and supplement the vang in controlling twist.

As to jibs, Small Point skippers often complain of inability to "Go to windward on the port tack," or "She's logy in light air." A check of all jib sheet leads showed them to vary in-and-out from 10° to 18°, that several varied by 5° on opposite sides of the boat, and that fore and aft settings were not planned to give a jib luff that would break evenly throughout its entire length as the boat swung into the wind. Only six boats used outboard jib sheet leads when reaching. Most now have freely adjustable jib sheet leads on tracks.

The top five finishers in the class all do more jib sheet moving than those below them, particularly in using new lead positions for different jibs, and progressively wider leads off the wind.

In the matter of spinnakers, only one boat makes a practice of varying spinnaker sheet angle, using the end of the main boom in preference to a deck lead well aft. She is one of the two leaders.

PRACTICAL SAIL TEST #6. CONTROL OF SAIL DRAFT?

Prams

Although skilful bagging or flattening under way can extend a sail's useful range by 50%, there is no means of changing draft at the foot of any pram sail. Clews simply hook into brass boat-snaps at the end of each boom. It is possible to harden luffs by halyard tension. But this is little done and would not long be effective with the manilla and nylon halyards in use.

Small Point One Designs

Two thirds of the boats use wire main halyards, and the rest dacron. Five are able to change draft of the loose-footed mainsail by small clew outhaul winches mounted near the mast; but only two use them actively. Other outhauls are at best semi-fixed. Half the main downhauls are adjustable; but only one or two are conveniently set for use under way. Almost all have vangs. One ex-International 14 helmsman uses his constantly to windward; others largely on reaches and running free.

Three quarters have wire jib halyards, the rest dacron. These rope halyards stretch during each windward leg and are fine promoters of sagging jib luffs. Fourteen have jib tack downhauls running to camcleats for quick luff tensioning, and all use them.

All can change their spinnaker's contour in time by raising the pole, freeing the halyard, or by easing out sheet, guy and down-guy. But only five run such controls through camcleats where they may be freely manipulated.

Do Draft Changes Affect Race Standings?

Order of finish in this fleet plainly justifies the adjusters. They win the close races.

PRACTICAL SAIL TEST #7. COST OF FAILURES IN FEET PER MILE

The following test illustrates the cost of bad rig balance, poor sheet location, and no draft control.

A good boat with good sails and all necessary fittings was

sailed about close-hauled in light air while fore and aft setting of her mast and its rake were adjusted until tiller pull measured on a scale read between 6 and 8 ounces. Draft was controlled under way and sheet leads given preliminary location.

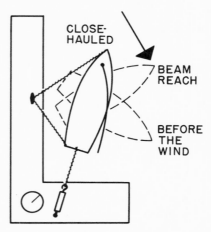

The boat was now pivoted off a dock in the fashion shown, and through careful trim her very best thrust readings obtained close-hauled, on a beam reach, and before the wind. Sheets were marked, wind speed noted on an anemometer, and the beginnings of a pull curve traced in. These steps consumed the greater part of a morning, and when completed, gave a fair picture of that rig's maximum potential.

All shrouds were then loosened, the mast moved out of place, sheet marks erased, and the lead of all sheets changed. Six skippers of varying skill were given the boat in turn, with this statement: "She's yours. Take your time and set her up just the way you would like her. Mark your sheets. Then we'll take new readings."

After each skipper finished, the boat was sailed to windward long enough to discover the tiller forces she now required; she was then returned to the dock, put back into her pivot rig and checked for thrust on three points of sailing at the sheet settings chosen by that man.

Findings

The most skilful of the six skippers took 45 minutes to set the boat up to his liking; another good sailor took 30 minutes; the rest simply screwed everything together and went by sight, consuming on average 15 minutes, but one barely 10 minutes.

In the matter of reducing tiller pull through rig balance, both better sailors brought these forces down to within a few ounces of what had been more carefully obtained. But none of the others were within 10 ounces, and one was 1.3 pounds high.

The best thrust figures were within 5% of maximum potential. Average thrust close-hauled was 10%–15% low. One man was 20% low on reaches. Another was 18% low before the wind.

The Cost of 15% Lower Thrust?

Towing charts show that anyone unable to balance or trim his sailboat to within 15% of her potential can, without knowing it, lose—

200 FEET A MILE

14 SOME IMPROVED RIGS

Only a bushleague Mahomet would lead his Faithful through so many tests without offering a few miracles by which they might improve their own equipment. Exotic fully-battened mainsails or A frame masts are not meant, nor are expensive sail plans such as mast-head genoas. Rather, we limit our wonder-working to hopes of increasing speed in the many thousand sloop and catboat rigs already on hand.

The following suggestions have speeding-up capability for both Beetlecats and 12 Metres.

RIG IMPROVEMENT #1. TURNING THE MAST

In the wind tunnel we saw that a close-hauled sail whose round mast sat in conventional fashion squarely ahead of the

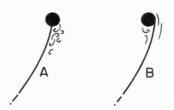

mainsail luff, as in A, lost thrust through blocked air flow and lee side ripples. Pivoting the mast to a position upwind of the luff, as in B, improved performance. Part of such gains persisted upon broad reaches, but fell to nothing off the wind.

Masts are turned in a few dinghy classes, notably the Penguins. In Finn Monotypes both mast and boom are pegged together so that the full rig wheels as the sail pays out; although

174

here the mast remains fixed at the sail's leading edge. Masts are turned even more effectively in sophisticated iceboat rigs and on inland scows. A paddle- or pear-shaped spar often supplants the round one, both producing a streamlined leading edge for the luff and increasing sail area. A related improvement in modern aluminum masts is the luff slot that replaces sail track and shuts the gap between mast and sail, which is otherwise a mother of pressure-loss and eddies.

If mast turning is desired, a problem on even small rigs is how to attach shrouds and stays without their winding up tightly and shearing off tangs as the boat tacks. Simply to pivot a mast over from the port to starboard tack on windward legs means passing it through 30°, while swinging over from one jibe to the other involves the 180° of a full about-face. A simple way to permit this is by a mast pendant of the type developed on iceboats. Shrouds and jibstay merge just before joining the mast, and a small tail attaches to the leading edge four inches higher, leaving the mast free to pivot. The joined stays form in effect a stout triangle that supports the mast while they are held aloft by its stiffness. Standing behind the pendant, the mast can swing freely into line with the sail's leading edge.

A tall mast with backstays and out-angled jumpers offers obstructions to pivoting. It is simple enough to swivel a permanent backstay at the mast top on a pin, but the lower halves of jumper stays turned beyond 45° will scrape a jibstay. Masts under thirty-five feet solve this problem by building up fore and aft dimensions until jumpers are unnecessary. It might be argued that classes like the 12 Metres that require masts of healthy minimum weight, incorporate enough safety factor now for a streamlined pivoting spar. Elimination of many stays and their windage would be helpful, but modern engineering has yet to produce anything in the eighty foot range that will turn.

Arch Control

Smoother air flow over a mainsail's lee side is not the only advantage of a pivoting mast. It makes possible an increase of arch over a sail's forward sections. We saw in the wind tunnel that turning a mast brought more thrust improvement to a flat mainsail than to a full one. It seems, therefore, that the control and adjustment facilities of this method might make it worth the while for a skillful sailmaker to design new sails for it from scratch.

Thrust Gains Through Mast Swiveling

Even a round mast expertly turned, improves mainsail thrust by—

20%	— to windward
5%–10%	— reaching
Very little	— running free

Rig Improvement #2. Pocket Luff Sails

An easier way to gain the advantages of rotation than by re-building a mast is through the pocket luff sail. The pocket luff was used successfully in Germany in 1912 and lately revived in racing prams.

Sail attached to mast with a sleeve   Sail attached to aluminum mast
                                                        with tapes

The luff of the pocket sail extends around the mast as a flap, which fastens back to the sail's body on the far side some six mast diameters aft. Dot fasteners hold it, but lacing eyes or a strong zipper work as well. The foot of the German sail also encased its boom, whereas on this Clamshell the rig is loose footed. The second photograph shows the difference between a standard pram sail and the pocket luff. The standard model (right) is held to its aluminum tube mast by nylon straps, which do away with sail track but leave an air gap between sail and mast.

Double, or wrap-around luffs offer these advantages:
1) Mast track and sail slot are eliminated.
2) There is no leakage between sail and mast.
3) When drawing, the sail sits automatically to leeward of the mast, which is then in a position of least resistance.
4) Draft can be changed by a cord.
5) Masts of common aluminum tubing may be used at a third the cost of specialized extrusions.
6) Since the mast offers low resistance, it may be fattened in small craft until it needs no stays.

Shrouds in the double luffed pram rig shown, fasten to the mast three feet below the top. Above their intersection the sail is not held to the mast except by halyard tension. No problem is presented on so small a sail, for the luff is held taut by a shockcord downhaul. On twenty foot masts and taller, stay attachments would block upward passage of the double luff. Yet five or six feet of the sail up to the headboard could not be left unsupported. The easy answer is to fit a revolving fiberglas fairing above the shroud tangs with both halyard and mainsail luff running up inside it. This holds the sail to the mast with zero gap, and turns freely with it as a streamlined leading edge.

Superiority of the Double Luff

The two identical prams shown in the photograph were raced against each other for a week. Rigs and sailors were interchanged, with these results:

1) Close-hauled, the double luff was clearly superior in that it pointed 3°–5° higher at the same speed.

2) Thrust advantage on tight courses was in the nature of 10%.

3) On broader points of sailing there was no evident difference.

Rig Improvement #3. A Pivoting Sloop Rig

The wind tunnel shows that while a jib is fundamentally more efficient than a mainsail because no mast blocks its leading edge, the jib of a sloop or cutter is penalized in that it should be operating further up to windward. The close-hauled jib with its tack fixed at the stem does not direct air back along the mainsail's lee side to full advantage. On reaches the jib is progressively shielded by the mainsail, until dead before the wind it is quite covered. It is not difficult to contrive a rig that overcomes these defects and still uses present sails and gear.

The single basic change is a new main boom. It is now a split wishboom, passing on either side of the mast, and extending far enough ahead to take the jib tack. Both jib and mainsail swivel in step as the main sheet goes in or out, the jib end of the lengthened boom edging out to windward as the mainsail drops off, and vice versa.

The jib may be hoisted along a wire from the forward end of the new boom to the mast, or its hanks dispensed with and the luff wire used as a stay. The mainsail clew fastens to the after end of the boom. When both jib and mainsail are hoisted, short vangs on either side of the mast hold down-pressure on the boom, although a lock on the mast can supplant them on small boats. It is necessary to rig a single jib sheet that swings across a narrow traveller on the boom. Once adjusted, this sheet is forgotten and jib and mainsail controlled simultaneously by the main sheet.

Starting from scratch it is best to use a pocket luff mainsail that slides about a fixed mast. Next best is a rotating spar. But even an unchanged mast with sail track is no handicap, except that small in-out adjustments of the boom may be necessary when sailing dead before the wind due to eccentricity of the boom's rotation in respect to the fixed sail track on the mast that does not wheel with it.

Advantages of the Pivoting Sloop Rig

1) The jib, moving in step with the mainsail, always funnels air through the jib/mainsail slot at precisely the determined angle.

2) Even dead before the wind the jib receives clear air of its own.

3) The pivoting rig develops more thrust than the standard sloop.

4) Sheeting is simplified. Once set, the jib needs little change. All boom control is through the main sheet. But since the jib counterbalances 30% of mainsail forces, there is less than normal main sheet tension and all its parts may be smaller.

5) On reaches with so much jib area to windward, heeling forces are smaller.

6) Since the jib balances out much of the mainsail's windward turning couple on broad reaches, weather helm is less and the boat moves faster.

7) A pivoting rig whose jib almost equals the mainsail might

be placed half way aft where the hull is broadest and shrouds
have the most effective lead.

8) Before the wind, the jib stands vertically opposed to following air, not askew and half inverted as upon a whiskerpole.

9) Even with a parachute spinnaker lifting out ahead there is
no need to drop the jib. The wind tunnel shows that jib, mainsail and spinnaker now produce more thrust than mainsail and
spinnaker formerly did.

10) Mainsail draft can be changed by easing the boom fore
and aft against the mast, particularly with a loose footed sail.

Disadvantages

1) Small vang adjustments are often needed.

2) The new boom costs $12–$15 on a small boat.

3) Some class rules specify that the jib tack must fasten to the
stem.

Superiority of Pivoting Over Standard Sloop Rig

The wind tunnel shows that with identical sails and masts
the pivoting boom can give thrust increases up to—25 percent.

RIG IMPROVEMENT #4. A CHESAPEAKE BAY BALANCED JIB

The owner who simply wishes more jib drive can get it by
the old Chesapeake Bay device of mounting the jib on a club,
hoisting it free of the forestay, and applying down-tension by a
flexible wire fastened a third aft on the club and running down
through a deck block to a tackle and camcleat. Such a jib sits
better and gives more thrust than one on a stay. It was formerly
used by sand-baggers who wished to crowd on more sail and
to push jib area far out ahead without interference of a forestay. It is popular today on small over-canvassed racing boats in
Sydney Harbor.

A number of improvements on this type of headsail are
available:

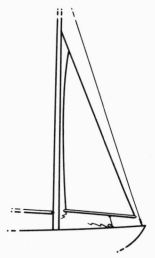

A) The full battened balanced jib that scarcely flogs when eye to the wind.

B) The convex luff with battens that is extremely efficient.

C) Even the scalloped leach that permits flattening in a breeze when the downhaul is set up hard.

Balanced jibs give more thrust than those on a stay because:

1) Close hauled, a part of the jib luff sits out to windward and more in line with the main boom, as the wind tunnel says it should.

2) On a wide bowed boat (scow) its downhaul may slide on a track, allowing windward adjustment that will hold the luff in

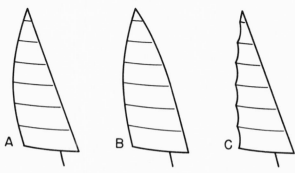

clear air on broad reaches, and remove the need for a whiskerpole running free.

3) Having a third of the jib out to windward reduces heeling
and helm pressures.

4) Closely balanced on its club, the jib exerts so little sheet
pull that a child can trim it.

5) Jib draft is responsive to downhaul tension.

Superiority of This Jib in Thrust

Compared to the standard hanked jib on a forestay, the
wind tunnel finds a Chesapeake Bay balanced jib superior by
5%–10%.

RIG IMPROVEMENT #5. JIB AHEAD OF FORESTAY ON REACHES

The skipper who does not wish to undertake any major rigging change can still get more drive on broad reaches by forc-

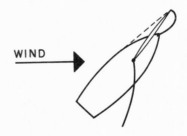

WIND

ing his jib well out ahead of the forestay on a long whiskerpole.
Pulling there as if in reverse, it cuts new air that has not been
slowed by the mainsail.

To hold a jib well ahead of the forestay asks something up to
three feet longer than the standard whiskerpole. Even a spinnaker pole does not give the ability to telescope out to a precise length. There is a sudden pressure as the jib first passes
the stay. A flap off to leeward is succeeded by skying, both of
which may be controlled by holding jib sheets and quickly
hooking the inner end of the pole high on the mast. It may be

necessary to run a light wire back from the pole's outer end to the deck near the main shrouds to protect against bending or breaking off the pole against the jibstay.

Advantages

1) Once past a beam reach more thrust is developed by a jib well out ahead in wind of its own.

2) Such a jib, pulling to leeward at the end of its long leverage arm, opposes the mainsail's windward-turning couple and reduces the need for cross rudder, so the boat goes faster.

3) Broad reaching across a finish line, the boat with her jib poled four feet out ahead, still has a one foot lead over a sister whose stem leads her by three.

Disadvantages

1) A telescoping pole is required. A long, solid pole stows unhandily, and is incapable of the length adjustments that give best jib trim under this method.

2) To work the jib out ahead in fresh winds takes strength. In over 25 knots it also takes skill, for the pole may snap against the forestay.

Gains Under This Method

On reaches wider than 110° the wind tunnel says that jib thrust improves with the jib forced out ahead by 5%–10%. At the same time tiller forces drop by more than 10%.

RIG IMPROVEMENT #6. HEADBOARD CONTROL

One day at the Boat Show, Jack Sutphen, the frostbite dinghy champion, was discussing the extraordinary ability of Arthur Knapp to point these little boats high to windward. Mr. Knapp, he observed, habitually set up his halyard so tightly that it cocked his mainsail headboard hard up against a pulley on the mast top. Where the Knapp headboard tilted stiffly out, all others hung lower and could flop from side to side. Jack Sutphen believed that Mr. Knapp attached importance to this tilt, for he always maintained it, in spite of the deep groove it cut down the head of his sail running free.

A similar phenomenon has been observed in the Small Point One Designs, which have permanent backstays. When a careless skipper over-hoists his mainsail, the headboard will not pass under the backstay between tacks, but remains blocked on one upwind side. If this happens on a light air windward leg, the boat seems to hold higher than others nearby, while footing at equal speed. Such tighter heading is in spite of a deformed upper roach, which is held up by the backstay. When tacking frees the headboard to its normal position, the boat falls off to her regular heading.

After observing several gains through this crude miscarriage of justice, the author concluded that: It could only be the result of twist limitation in the upper sail. And if so, it should be possible to achieve the same gain on both tacks.

To this end a flexible stainless steel cable, $\frac{1}{16}''$ in diameter, was run up the backstay, passed through a leader behind the headboard, and hooked to its after edge. The deck end of the cable ran down to a baby camcleat, convenient to the helmsmen. Once the sail had been hoisted and slack taken from the control cable, a tug would limit side to side angle of the headboard or bring it to almost nothing.

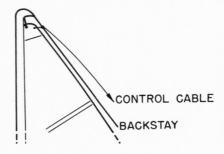

CONTROL CABLE

BACKSTAY

Pros and Cons

On the plus side, the device fills a control gap by offering exact adjustment of the head of a racing sail. It is always possible to align the lower sail by mainsheet, and the central leach to some extent by vang or placement of the mainsheet deck block. But enough down-pull on sheet or vang to swing the headboard into line means a tight leach and sacrifice of the flowing sail curves so desirable in light going.

On the minus side, there is one more long wire to stow and to make windage, and another control that must not be forgotten, for to jibe with the mainsail headboard locked may strain or tear the leach.

The device can clearly be improved. Perhaps it should be part of the masthead crane, a spring loaded affair that would drop at the pull of a cord. Again, it may point to some similar control attempt upon the upper leach of jibs, which are natural "twisters," but whose slot effect upon the mainsail needs constant adjustment. *Weetamoe* of the old J boats did something of this sort with double clewed jib.

Results in Racing

Working to windward in various winds the device gave headings tighter than normal of approximately 3°, with no apparent loss in speed.

15

FITTINGS AND TRIMMING DEVICES

Devices that help a skipper and crew balance their hull, trim sails instantly, and spot each wind shift, are in a sense Convenience Items. They allow better tactical use of a racing boat. Many proud veterans scorn light, quick acting fittings, and worship at the altar of heavy cleats and blocks. But today a boat lacking camcleats and like aids, finishes poorly. When sail adjustments are impossible underway, when ladies with small hands can not hold tugging sheets, then what should be teamwork becomes simply work. The slow and obstinate win few races from the quick and eager.

As a further step toward Race-Rating sailboats, this chapter indicates the advantage held by one with all modern fittings over others equipped only for day sailing and a "good time."

GROUP I. HULL CONTROLLING DEVICES

Heeling Indicators

In Hull Test #4 we found that heeling over 10° slowed a boat badly. It is common practice to hold about 5° of leeward heel in light air to fill the sails, and when running free about the same in windward heel to cancel rudder drag.

A good crew maintain these angles without order by easing sheet, or by hiking out as the lee rail dips. But a simple pendulum indicator or airplane ball-bank will warn them when to take action. When the pendulum hits its red line all hands hike to bring it back. In so doing they may expect to gain over

186

crews that only balance when their lee rail rolls under—50 feet a mile.

Fore and Aft Levels

Pendulums pitch too much in a seaway to show fore and aft trim, but a slow acting bubble level can do this well, once it has been calibrated with full crew aboard. There is pronounced nose-down trim when someone climbs onto the fore deck to jibe the spinnaker. A bubble level will show the helmsman how far aft he must slide to compensate. Possible gain through holding the fastest fore and aft balance is at least 25 feet a mile.

Tiller Deficiencies

Tiller lengths vary widely within a class: from two feet, to three feet six inches in the Small Point One Designs. Good skippers like to steer with a light touch, and longish tillers supply leverage to this end. An extra foot of tiller permits the helmsman to center his weight near the crew's. It also brings him to "mast abeam" a foot sooner when passing an enemy to windward.

Tillers are often loose at the rudder post. Some at Small Point have six inches of play, which makes them difficult to "feel." Slop is normally removable by tightening the tiller bolt or inserting washers.

Two Small Point One Designs have rudders so stiff that once set, their helm stays put regardless of wind. Either these rudders pinch in their hangings, or the packing glands are too tight.

Because no helmsman can eat upwind with a sloppy or half-locked rudder, losses from bad adjustment here can reach 50 feet a mile.

Hiking Sticks

Hiking sticks are necessary on all small racing yachts. They allow a helmsman of 160 pounds to move that much lard 18

Hiking stick on rudder in use

inches outboard, a major aid in a breeze. When the class hull is tender, and the skipper a fat man, or lady of generous proportions, such resistance to heeling can be worth 50 feet a mile.

Hiking Straps and Trapezes

Many classes prohibit trapezes, but hiking straps are rarely prohibited and are even more useful than the hiking stick, since they encourage all hands to move out over the rail. Discarded firehose makes good hiking straps, but a gap between the outboard edge of the seats and the side of the boat is even better. In rough weather it is absolutely necessary for crew weight to sit outboard so that maximum sail drive may be used and feathering delayed as long as possible. If the skipper cannot hook his feet he will not even use the hiking stick confidently. If the crew fear to fall overboard they will balance the boat with less dedication. In stiff going, hiking straps are worth 75 feet a mile.

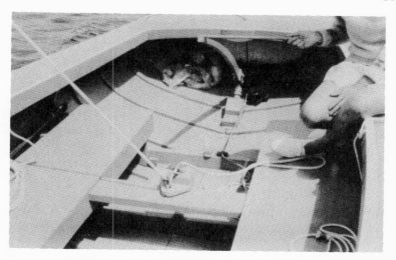

Space between seat and boat for hiking. Note mainsheet control

Bailing Equipment

A bucket of water weighs upwards of twenty pounds, and it is easy to ship 300 pounds of this damp material in one knockdown. Let the reader check our Hull Tests for how much 300 pounds slos-shing in the bilges will slow his boat; then let him add another 50% for lost stability.

Self-bailers are fine if boat speed is high enough to make them work, which it rarely is in displacement boats. Floor openings average to be poorly contrived for bailing. The entire bottom should sit open at the spot of deepest water. Cans, sponges and buckets must lie ready to hand. In extra rough going it pays to have some kind of pot on a stick that will permit bailing from the windward rail. It is possible to conceive ideal ways of freeing a sailboat of water, such as a liftable canvas bag inside the cockpit floor, able to remove five gallons at a throw. Splashboards, or partly covered cockpits, seem attractive when surf is filling the boat. But all such things are in the way a good part of the time and easily mislaid.

When it is needed, good bailing equipment is worth 200 feet a mile.

Hull Speedometer

Marine speedometers work well on large sailing yachts, but nothing has yet been devised for the small racing types that is more than an aid for comparative sail trimming.

GROUP II. SAIL TRIMMING DEVICES

Control of Twist by the Vang

We have already considered the power losses due to twist and its curving away of the mainsail's upper leach. Almost all Small Point One Designs use vangs to hold their booms down and gain effective sail area. A further advantage of the vang is that with the mainsail in one flat plane, the bottom of the sail needs no over-trim to stop the top from luffing. Heeling and weather helm are reduced, and there is less braking rudder across the boat. At Small Point, losses up to a hundred yards a mile are suffered by boats without vangs, on broad reaches when the wind is puffy.

Inconveniences of the vang are:

A tight vang weakens the sail track at the gooseneck. Crew mobility is reduced unless the vang is held up by shockcord when not in use. It always seems to trap one haunch per jibe. It needs constant adjustment, and if too tight at the start of a run will prevent the boom's full extension.

But the vang is helpful even to windward. Some Small Point One Designs have their mainsheet deck block amidships, where even with the boom well in there is insufficient down-pull on the leach to prevent its curving. In a strong breeze to windward a vang will flatten such mainsails, much as bending the mast does, while in any lull it can be slackened to restore fullness. In anything approaching close competition the vang is worth 150 feet a mile.

Sheet Adjustability

Doctrine varies in each class for the placement of jib leads in winds of different strength, and with jibs of different draft. It is not only a question of in-and-out, but of up-and-back. On close reaches, settings both outboard and back generally prove faster; boats reaching in a seaway seem to stub, weave and stop if these are left far inboard.

International 14 Foot Dinghies vary the breadth of their main sheet travellers. To windward in a blow the deck block stays out at the rail where, once the boom comes in to that angle, further pull on the sheet flattens down the leach area and lessens the heeling force of a full cut sail. The Small Point One Designs, by contrast, trim to the center of the boat and need a vang to achieve leach flatness, greatly diminishing their ability to carry a light weather mainsail in a breeze.

For either jib or mainsail to develop full power, or minimum heeling, they must have variable sheet leads. Lack of adjustability can cost 150 feet a mile.

Camcleats

Quick action camcleats are indispensable on a modern racing boat. The skipper who steers with one hand, and holds forty pounds of main sheet strain with the other, has little energy left for tactics. When his old fashioned mainsheet cleat slips a turn or jams a half hitch, he can lose ten yards in a luff. But camcleats hold what slack has been taken in automatically, and eliminate so much need for strength that they place women upon nearly equal footing with ape-handed men. At Small Point the greybeards distrust them because: "They won't let go by themselves; they'll turn you over!" This is to assume a cleat as endowed with the magic power of self-release. It would be as fair to expect the tiller to dodge the next right-of-way boat.

For a sailor to appreciate the full value of camcleats he needs only to time fifty cleatings and uncleatings with one; then compare the seconds used by an old-fashioned teak deck cleat that requires two turns of the sheet, plus or minus a half hitch. No serious racer can afford the loss of two seconds per cleating, without handicapping himself 50 feet a mile.

Sheets

Dacron makes the best racing sheets, for it does not stretch. The braided types wear well in camcleats. A single part jib sheet is always preferable when the crew has enough strength to trim it. All sheets should be individually colored for quick identification as between main sheet, jib and spinnaker. Red and green plastic tape on the ends will distinguish port from starboard, and an inch or two of similar tape will show normal settings in the camcleats, which in turn allows the sheet handler to trim flat, full, or to feathering setting in an instant. In light air it may pay to have a super-light set of jib or spinnaker sheets of $1/8''$ dacron, and to be able to reduce the main sheet to a single part.

Having the very best in sheets is worth 10 feet a mile.

Bending and Straightening Spars for Rig Balance

Few classes encourage movement of spars under way, although some countenance mast rakers that put pressure on the mast butt to induce bending. Wedges at the partners are often used to straighten or bow a mast. Tightening the permanent backstay can bend the mast top area appreciably, when jumpers are set to permit it. All such efforts are designed to increase or diminish fullness in a mainsail. The normal sail is cut for use on a straight spar. Bowing the mast forward, or bending the boom down, draws material out from the center and flattens draft, which in turn reduces heeling.

To vary the curve of a mast by stay tension can be tricky, and something to be done differently for each mast. Simply to tighten down the shrouds, in the hope of holding a mast firm and straight, may have exactly the reverse effect by introducing compression. Many good sails are ineffective today because of "S" curves so produced. The best way to check a mast for straightness is to sail on various courses and sight repeatedly up along it as sheet tension is changed. A mast that is quite true on the starboard tack may bend in or out at its center on the port by as much as eight inches, and ruin a mainsail there.

Jib to mainsail balance is affected by sheet placement, by the height at which the jib is carried above the deck, and by curve-away of the jib luff. The standard height for the jib tack is assumed to be close to the stem, although each new jib may be tried at something higher. The jib luff must hold very close to straight if the boat is not to be penalized in pointing ability.

Adjustments to spar curvature that will spring a rig, or improve sail shape under way, offer gains in the order of 50 feet a mile.

Light Sail Equipment

Light sails need fittings especially adapted for fast hoisting and delicate adjustment. A minimum list is:
1) A Turtle, bag, or tray into which the spinnaker can be packed, from which it will emerge without twisting, and which will not blow overboard as the sail goes up.
2) A halyard—single or double ended, and preferably woven (not layed rope, which can spin); Brummel hooks, never ordinary boat snaps that snag on jumpers; a swivel in the head of the sail; the halyard marked to show "Full up" and "One foot out"; a small camcleat for rapid cleating.
3) A spinnaker pole of correct length, with reliable end fittings that can be engaged one-handed. The pole to be adjustable 15" up and down the mast, so that the spinnaker may be encouraged to spread its leaches. A toppinglift and forward guy.
4) Spinnaker sheet and guy of twice the overall length of the boat, marked with colored tape for preliminary camcleat settings and ending in Brummel hooks that cannot snag on shrouds. Fairleads to be well aft, with a boom-end snatch

block that can take them further outboard. Camcleats centrally located for all hands.

Gains possible through best over worst spinnaker gear are 50 feet a mile.

GROUP III. AIDS TO HELMSMAN AND CREWS

Wind Direction Indicators

Seventy-five per cent of the Small Point sailors use tell-tales five feet up their main shrouds, where they are inaccurate due to eddies and a tendency to foul. A few skippers fancy they need no visual indications of wind because they are "experienced." Cornelius Shields of the International One Designs used an oversized green masthead fly. Wind direction is steadier at that height, and exact knowledge of its fluctuations assists the windward working helmsman. From a mechanical viewpoint he has only to line up his headboard with the fly, then maintain this angle throughout shifts of the apparent wind. To do so for a minute at a time from the windward rail is a strain on the neck; it is almost impossible when steering below the mainsail on the lee side. What the masthead fly shows is human fallibility. After a week's practice, holding a steady fly-to-headboard angle becomes second nature, and rather less important than encouraging a sense of lift and speed in the hull. The need to watch the fly constantly then departs; an occasional glance being quite enough.

On reaches, where the mainsail is repeatedly adjusted to shifting winds, it becomes difficult to establish a set angle between masthead fly and headboard. The further the main boom swings outboard, the further the fly goes ahead of it, although this angular difference is less pronounced when the mainsail is held down flat by a vang. Dead before the wind, with the fly pointing straight out ahead and invisible from the cockpit, a colored plastic ball on the counterpoise will still warn whenever the wind crawls far enough off the end of the main boom to threaten a jibe.

There are many good masthead flies on the market. One can easily be made from a pheasant's tailfeather. Its counterpoise must be exact, otherwise when the boat heels the fly will drop to leeward and falsely signal a shift aft of apparent wind. Flies should be painted a color that stands out against the blue sky, and be fairly large or with a flat top that can be seen from below.

For racing to windward, an extremely accurate heading gauge can be set on the mainsail luff about two feet aft of the mast and some eight feet high. Whenever a mainsail is sheeted in, tests with a bit of fluff on a stick show that air currents reverse sharply at this spot whenever the apparent wind angle lifts ahead or falls aft of proper trim. Flow reversal is so sensitive here that a bit of yarn mounted far enough out so as not to stick to the sail can be a valuable racing tool.

In a half calm, cigarette smoke will show the direction of what air there is, as will inspection of the masthead flies on competing boats, particularly those at a distance.

Accurate knowledge of wind direction is vital in racing. Only a greenhorn expects it to be steady, or that he can predict its momentary shifts. Sailors of middling skill sometimes become slaves to wind indicators and steer by them mechanically. The very good skipper is *ahead* of his masthead fly. But if asked to sail a dud boat, the first thing he checks for, and installs if absent, is a good masthead fly. Average loss without one is 75 feet a mile.

A Large Compass

Say "Compass" to a racing helmsman and he will think "Fog." But Ted Wells mounts a small airplane model on the mast of his Snipe and with it checks the scope and frequency of wind shifts. A large floating card type is even easier to read.

A compass gives the crew interesting data. Once they note an average heading of 81°, let us say, on the starboard tack, they will needle their helmsman if he falls below that through carelessness; or if the drop-off is forced by a veering wind, they will sense the value of coming about and pointing higher on the opposite tack while that change lasts.

On shifty days the wind can move 10° with ease and hold its new direction for minutes. An alert crew armed with a compass will establish average life for these changes, and make possible wide gains upwind. Although to tack on every assumed header will not pay, 5° of higher heading on those that persist for a hundred yards gives almost a nine yards lift toward the mark. A large compass, well used in shifting winds, is worth 50 feet a mile.

Tacking Lines

Tacking, or Sighting Lines, may be laid out with tape on either deck in these directions: 45° ahead, squarely abeam, and 45° astern.

Whoever is designated to sight from the cockpit along the applicable line can give vital information on whether a mark is abeam, whether a competitor is gaining, and whether or not he can safely be crossed. In converging situations it may mean loss of 30 feet to be forced under an opponent's stern after an abortive effort to cross his bow, when, had it been known that such crossing was impossible, a lee bow position might have been assumed from which to poison him with backwind.

For all hands to have confidence in information from tacking lines means practice in their use. Corrective allowances are wise in puffy winds when it is possible that present course can not be maintained. In tideways, and when moving into lulls, like care is needed. The tacking line is simply another crew aid, which, when expertly used, is worth 25 feet a mile.

Special Gear for Heavy Weather and Repairs

Various convenience items are listed here that should be aboard so long as weight and stowage space are kept low.

An anchor line, usable for emergency towing.

Heavy weather clothing for the regular crew.

On cold days a thermos of hot coffee.

Two or three good life cushions.

A small sliding drawer under the after deck. In it, dry and ready to hand:

>pliers
>screwdriver
>cotterpins
>plastic sail-mending tape
>marlin
>copper wire
>knife
>oil can
>brass screws
>clevis pins
>lacing cord
>short lengths of ¼″ dacron line
>race circulars
>stopwatch when not in use

RACE-RATING BOATS THAT LACK FITTINGS AND TRIMMING DEVICES

While no one can predict that in a specific race the items here mentioned will carry the exact values specified, it seems fair to deduct from the Race-Rating of any boat that lacks them completely:

NO HULL CONTROLS	50 FEET
NO SAIL CONTROLS	125 FEET
NO CREW AIDS	50 FEET
TOTAL REDUCTION	225 FEET

16

Total *Losses Possible for:*
HULLS, SAILS AND TRIMMING DEVICES

The losses considered so far have been those of equipment. The boat either has, or lacks them before the start, so her Race-Rating will be penalized in accordance. Let us total what we have come up with so far, then turn to the matter of sailors' skills in order to assign unit ratings to boats and their crews.

HULL LOSSES	PER MILE
Heavy hull	150′
Poor hull shape	50′
Foul or rough bottom	300′
Bad stability and trim	100′
Excess leeway	75′
Poor rudder	50′
WORST HULL LOSS	725′

SAIL AND RIG LOSS	
Bad sails	300′
Imbalanced rig	200′
High drag	50′
WORST RIG LOSS	550′

FITTINGS LOSS	PER MILE
Hull fittings	50′
Sail fittings	125′
Crew aids	50′
WORST FITTINGS LOSS	225′

TOTAL POSSIBLE BOAT LOSS   1500′ A MILE

Of course "1500 feet a mile" is so huge a loss that the combination of bearded bottom and horrible sails needed to produce it could hardly be found on one boat.

198

SECTION IV

HELMSMEN AND CREWS RATED ON THEIR TACTICAL RACING SKILLS

17
TACTICS TAKE OVER:
THE RACE SEEN AS AN IMPURE SCIENCE

Up to this point a reader engaged in evaluating his boat has been able to view it with the leisurely calm of a "pure" scientist. Now, in moving out upon the course, he suddenly faces a hive of enemies, all eager to interfere with him, and whom he must treat as roughly. Competition is a very "impure science."

All matters here considered—wind, crews, and the separate parts of a race—are for the purpose of determining what each technique costs or gains in feet. Others may sail as they please: we only wish to know how successfully. For, given that knowledge, we may complete their, and our, Race-Ratings.

18

WIND, AND HOW RACERS
CORRECT TO ITS CHANGES

Wind is the racing boat's fuel. Winning skippers try to use not only a better grade than their opponents, but more of it, too, if they can. Novices are puzzled when told to point squarely into the wind's eye. But an expert helmsman dozing at a beer party can swing his nose into the wind and estimate its gustiness and velocity. In competition such a veteran is warned of wind shifts by changes in hull liveliness and by his masthead fly. The old racehorse has no black or blue magic. He simply reacts to a breeze.

Why Wind Blows

Aerologists say that wind blows as a result of uneven heating around the world. Air, when warmed by the sun over tropical and desert areas, expands and begins to move in vast parcels. Currents of cold, heavy air push down around the light, warmer masses. Air oceans cool as they are driven up over mountain ranges; absorption of water vapor and its return in the form of rain promotes heat exchange and instability. Such mixings proceed upon a globe-encircling scale and are explained in the Air Mass Theory of Weather developed by the Norwegians in World War I. Whenever a fresh southwester has blown for several days in our racing area, the wind we sail by is only one ripple of a great air river flowing up the coast.

If sailing winds could be changed into vari-colored smoke at each fifty foot level, we might see whorls and thickened branches gliding by overhead. Not all strata would move steadily, any more than all levels of a brook ease straight downstream. Bends, dips, and irregular skirtings would appear. We should observe our bottom smoke to be slowed by surface friction. Its passage over water would be smooth, however, compared to the dammings and diversions where it crossed tree-covered land or was ripped into eddies at rocky shores. We may visualize sailing wind as the lowest cut of a mighty air ocean that is sliding by above us. In calms it hardly stirs; during storms it is tattered and fast. We watch like snails from the very bottom as the great overhead mass rolls on and away forever.

The Illusion of a Steady Wind

Novice competitors like to imagine the wind as blowing steadily both in direction and force. If this were true, we might all race Bus Mosbacher to windward and see him gain less than fifty feet a mile. He would still beat us by superior boat handling, but his narrow margin would be exciting. Such closeness is approximated in fleets of twenty boats whenever the wind is extra steady. On tacking for shore, each skipper simply aims for Mrs. Jones' white outhouse, confident that he is about right. Steering for fixed objects is standard operating procedure for Class D and E racers. Even some with long experience cleat the main sheet when reaching on presumption of a steady wind.

Unfortunately the wind is not steady—either in force or direction. And a change in either demands some course or sail correction. A large part of the winning class boat skipper's lead comes from his skill in adjusting to wind variations, and particularly in anticipating their arrival a second before others do. To windward he will slant up into areas of favorable lift, or tack quickly to use the backs of those unfavorable. Off wind, he trims his main sheet or spinnaker pole to hold maximum drive. The expert will snake out ahead, easing up, down and back, while the greenhorn sees only steady wind.

Types of Wind Change Seen Along a Course

The stronger wind aloft—It is easy to discover that winds at twenty-five feet average to blow a third harder than at three feet. Just as the lowest water in a brook drags over the stones, so the lowest air is slowed by surface friction. As we climb to airplane altitudes winds speed up and tend to blow more from the west as a result of Coriolus Force, the turning of the globe from west to east. Racing sails are affected because their bottoms receive not only less wind than their tops, but what they get low down is eddied by hulls and crews.

Land masses that shift winds mechanically—Spots lie along each course where experience says we shall find favorable or unfavorable slants, plus more or less wind. Shifts here result from natural wind-benders, for example, the steep face of an island, or a flat, hot beach that sucks cold air off the water.

Wind streaks that come and go—Look out over the course on a clear day, and if the surface is smooth enough to allow study of surface markings, both dark and shiny sectors are seen. The dark reflect areas of stronger wind, the shiny, less of it. Such traces extend from 50 feet to several hundred yards, and while impermanent, may persist for as long as twenty minutes. After fading, they often reappear. As a rule they are wasp-waisted, rather than fat. Their curvings can lie 20° off the common wind. All of us have had the ill luck to be trapped between these air slots and to see lucky opponents sail by on either hand along the tails of brisker wind. If we struggle over to their accursed breeze, its ripples die as we reach them.

These air furrows are down-hooks from the great wind ocean overhead and result from mixing in the strata next above us. Aircraft carriers, which must steam straight upwind to catapult and land jet airplanes, watch all such curvings, and have a doctrine for them. The Air Officer, posted high above the surface, can observe wind patterns; and when all tails bend one way over a wide acreage of sea, a general shift to that direction is predicted and a course change prepared for the formation.

The airman's expectation is that an upper air mass has become dominant and will soon move down. In moderate winds a complete shift at the surface may take hours. Low down in our sailboats, we see only part of the process.

Freshenings and Lulls—Wind speed can climb or fade over intermediate areas, while its broad direction flows on unchanged. The racing skipper smiles when he sees dark surface shadows just ahead that mean stronger air. Flat spots indicate less wind, although he may hope that the calm exists only at the surface and a fine breeze is piping ten feet aloft. On crawling into any extended slick he will search uneasily for its oily limits. Such ups and downs in wind velocity are ceaseless, and the skill with which they are used separates the Racing Sheep from the Racing Goats.

Circular puffs and flaws—Offshore winds produce the many localized puffs that claw out and die all about us in what aviators call "turbulence." Northwest winds of autumn spread these flaws across the water. They strike down and blow outward, strike down and blow out, recurring like smallpox dots. Of cat's paw shape, and on average less than 50 yards apart, they are bursts of stronger wind accompanying the general flow, and result from mixing at lowest levels over rough land. When puffs first whirl away from their centers their velocity can be twice that of surrounding air. Unlike the Freshenings, just considered, which are stronger shelves of the common wind, Circular Puffs dart out at all angles and present favorable and unfavorable sides to racing boats.

Sailors Must Adjust to Each Type

Sailboat racers react to wind changes according to their experience. Beginners expect what is now blowing to keep blowing. They will head a bit higher to windward if everyone else does, but are less likely to trim the mainsheet on reaches, since sail angles on competing boats are not conspicuous. Those who sail woodenly by telltales or some device, will change course after these warn that they should. Veterans who have learned

that it pays to "luff in the puffs," will pinch up for a five foot
gain as the dark skirts of a fresher wind wrap all about them.
But the student of wind will do so more smoothly, besides improving upon the veteran's performance as the lift moves by.

Action Required by Each Wind Change

By the stronger wind aloft—We learned that wind strikes the
top of a sail approximately one-third faster than the bottom,
and so at a slightly freer angle. For a mainsail's headboard to
face this out-angle properly, which on a small boat is not more
than "half an inch out," the sail needs to be held down in one
plane, rather than allowed to curve away at the top. Vangs or
widened mainsheet leads are required, and need their most
active adjustment on reaches.

By mechanical bending of wind—Certain areas are known to
produce favoring slants and wind freshening up to 50%. Since
these will always be used by successful skippers, they should be
hunted out and studied by all. It is only necessary to recognize
that in given weather their effects repeat.

By transitory, but extended wind streaks—It is the racer's job
to detect and sail up such of these pathways as offer him more
or better wind, no matter how short their life. The Ted Wells
system of having one of the crew check course-made-good to
windward on a compass is helpful here, as is having a doctrine
for tacking on headers and into lifts. Often these slants can be
spotted well out ahead by those who practice watching and
singing out their approach angles. Whenever the compass shows
the boat to be knocked off by as much as 3°, it may pay to come
about and gain in tighter heading on the opposite tack what is
now being lost. Many lifts will be temporary, but to fight for
them is both interesting and improves a crew's tacking skill.
Quite obviously, it cannot pay to tack on each tiny header;
other boats may be in the way, or the course may lead into a
dead spot.

By Ups and Downs—We now approach the heartbeat of a helmsman's skill. Novices believe that if the wind freshens without

changing direction, their proper response is to plough straight ahead at pleasantly improved speed. But this is only true when running dead before the wind, at which time wind-direction and boat-course exactly coincide, and to steer straight along on any other course involves a small loss. The reason why a sailboat should luff slightly as wind freshens (to windward), or free her sheets on a reach, is because the breeze that drives her is always a two-part affair—Part One comes whispering straight aft over the bow as a result of forward motion, while Part Two is the natural wind. Their effects merge at the boat into an Apparent Wind, which is a poor term that might better be, "Inapparent Wind," or "Combination Wind."

The reader will easily picture the dual components of an Apparent Wind if he sees himself as driving straight ahead in an automobile at ten miles an hour through a calm. In this case he must feel "10 mph" of wind in his face, or the equivalent of over-the-bow wind in his sailboat. Let him now stop the car, and suppose that a twenty mile wind begins to blow from the right. This wind in brushing his right cheek corresponds to the true wind part of apparent wind when sailing. Lastly, he has only to restart the car and move again at ten miles an hour, with the twenty mile wind still blowing from his right, to have the two winds combine into a genuine apparent wind, which, as the vector shows, feels to him exactly like a wind coming in at 65° from his right, at 22½ miles an hour.

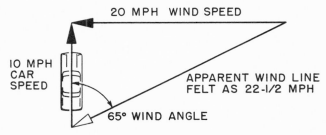

On a sailboat, the true wind part of apparent wind is always several times stronger than the boat motion part, for sailboats hardly exceed 3 miles an hour in a 10 knot breeze. Also, true wind velocity is more volatile than boat speed, rising or falling by as much as 50% with ease, or 100% in gusts. This faculty for wide change in the true wind's velocity is what repeatedly upsets the equation whereby a boat's apparent wind sets its direction, and which forces her to change course in a straight breeze. Since the sailboat moves to windward best by holding an angle of some 35° between her sails and the apparent wind, any improvement in apparent wind angle, however small, offers a chance to sail higher that the expert grasps with pleasure, but the beginner hardly at all. When the true wind rises from 10 to 20 miles an hour at a boat making 3 to windward, the shift is only *3° aft,* and barely 6° on a beam reach; both being helpful. But if the true wind diminishes, the shift is *ahead,* or unfavorable, and to this the expert again corrects, although perhaps not in the direction he would prefer.

We could construct many vectors to show the exact scope of course changes required by freeing or veering apparent winds. But all that the racer needs to know is that the chance for a small gain is open whenever he sails through wind of changing velocity, either up or down, even though it has blown from one compass bearing for twenty-four hours and will continue there for a century. Let the wind freshen momentarily, making its change favorable, and he can luff: let it slacken ever so little, and it will head him and all others nearby; so he must prepare to bear away.

The Normal Rise and Fall Sequence

How a helmsman reacts as he enters a shelf of stronger air *unchanged in direction* is the best proof of his skill. The beginner will feel and hear the freshening wind, but will steer straight on until he sees other boats heading higher. The mechanical sailor, eyes glued on the masthead fly, will respond to its warning according to his reflexes, *after* the new wind spins it above him. The veteran, who expects to luff in the puffs, will swing up the instant his boat heels. But a Wind Student starts

easing up seconds earlier, runs a smoother maneuver, and ends
several feet further ahead.

Now, is this all? Do we become top helmsmen simply by
luffing as wind strength climbs? By no means. For so far we
have faced only a quarter of a normal freshening sequence.
Here is the full pattern:

1) Wind strength climbing at the boat, as explained, draws apparent wind several degrees aft. So her helmsman can head
higher.

2) Boat speed picks up slowly under the new wind's urging,
and presently restores almost the first angular equation between wind over the bow and true wind. The effect is to swing
apparent wind back to its early position. So the helmsman must
ease off too.

3) Now the boat runs out of the stronger wind. But momentarily her speed endures. So apparent wind slides forward, forcing a course drop below that held at the start.

4) Boat speed drops down to its first level. With true wind
back at original strength, and both parts of apparent wind once
more in balance, the helmsman eases smoothly up to his first
heading.

This is the type of "S-ing" sailed through endlessly by good
helmsmen, without the slightest hitch or delay. The sharp eyed
reader will observe that exactly the opposite sequence must
apply upon entering a lull. For now as the boat slides into a
flat spot, her true wind falls away, while wind over the bow becomes a fatter fraction of apparent wind, and—

1) Apparent wind moves ahead. The helmsman groans, but
heads off with it. Above all, he does not tack; for until boat
speed drops, he would only meet the same header after struggling about.

2) Boat speed now slows, too. This allows apparent wind to
move aft to about its early position, and the helmsman eases up
with it.

3) As the boat glides clear of the slick and into wind of normal
strength, apparent wind goes several degrees freer. Again the
helmsman lifts gratefully with it.

4) Finally, boat speed returns to normal, upping wind over the bow and drawing apparent wind back to its original angle. The helmsman heads off too.

In all this "S-ing," which is by tiller to windward, but by sheet on reaches, the fine helmsman constantly repositions his sails to obtain maximum drive from apparent wind. It is this fractional extra drive that wins his races.

Action in circular puffs and flaws—On puffy days we witness the ultimate wind-demand upon a helmsman's skill. For with countless small wind-islands whirling down upon him, each presenting a favorable, and an unfavorable side, he can never feel that his art has been mastered. Because these darting patches are too small to allow him a choice as to the spot of his penetration, the fine helmsman can only use his eyes and correct as they strike, allowing first for lifts in wind velocity, then for shifts of angle that can reach 30° in an instant, for more shifts while he is inside the puff, and lastly for a slackening true wind speed as he leaves it.

Three Types of Circular Puff, and Their Treatment

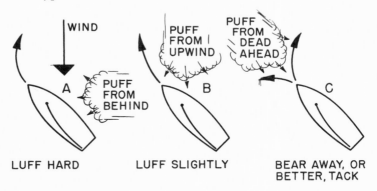

The circular puff that strikes from aft of abeam, as in A, is the simplest to counter. Its gustiness will slide apparent wind aft momentarily, and its approach is also favorable. A strong luff is indicated, plus a high course until quitting the puff, perhaps within a matter of seconds.

In B, when the puff comes straight down with the prevailing breeze, the effect should simply be that of a brief freeing of apparent wind due to higher velocity. Some luff is in order, with the expectation of bearing away as the puff drives by.

When, as in C, the wind circle blows in from ahead, there is complication in that the stronger gust will shift apparent wind aft, but the out-from-the-center direction is unfavorable and may more than counter-balance this. If the wind whirl is small and not squarely ahead, the helmsman may decide to bear off slightly and ride it out. But if it is extensive and he can tack smartly to run up its back, the possibility of a 50 foot gain looms.

Deductions on Racing Adjustments to Varying Winds

Old-timers believe that the ceaseless, delicate compensations necessary to sail fast in changing winds cannot be taught. Skill only comes, they opine, by developing over the years a highly educated "seat of the pants," a sort of Harvard Ph.D. of the sternpost. It may well be that ancient mariners do acquire supernataural talents in this area. But careful study of how wind behaves should greatly shorten the course.

19

CREW DUTIES AND EFFICIENCIES

If, as reward for a blameless life, we were permitted to choose the perfect crew for our racing sailboat, we might ask these virtues:

Physical — A rangy acrobat with strong hands, able to hike out 20 minutes at a time and to stand constant immersion in cold water.

Moral — Prompt, alert, 100% respectful of the skipper.

Character — Cheerful and forgiving.

Racing Knowledge — A master of racing rules and tactics. Able to advise under all conditions.

Such a paragon would be worth 200 yards in every race. Can we ever expect his like on a regular basis?

Of course not! There are perhaps a hundred such rare crewmen in the country. Generally they make up Damon and Pythias partnerships with the top skippers in international classes. They go about with them to championship regattas as vital cogs in their success. They may enjoy crewing because of the close knit team values, or they may simply not want the trouble and expense of their own boat.

Those Willing and Able to Crew

In summer racing we must use what is on hand. Anyone wishing a really fine crew must develop it himself. The field of crew candidates includes—

A sprinkling of men, seldom available except over weekends.

Quite a few ladies of all ages and sizes.

Teenagers. Generally unfocussed as to character.

Many children. Loud of voice, eager, but untaught.

Men on their vacations have so many family obligations as to make them poor bets for carefully worked out racing programs. If experienced, they will be asked to skipper other boats, and should be encouraged to do so to keep the level of competition high. If inexperienced, they enjoy strength advantages over women, but average to be harder to teach. The skipper who wants to develop a good crew should consider what crews hope to gain for their labor. This will commonly be:

Enough training so that eventually he or she may sail for himself.

The fun of being out on the water in competition.

The thrill of winning occasionally.

Pretty Women Make the Best Amateur Crews

Since your racing boat needs a steady crew, at the risk of sounding facetious one may be selected as follows:

A young, active woman with strong hands. For her ability to move quickly about the boat and to pull ropes.

A married woman. Married women have better understanding of complex operations.

The handsomest possible. Pretty women are more experienced than plain. They are also more intelligent. This is simple heredity; for successful men marry the prettiest women and soon pass brains down to their better looking offspring.

An advantage of using female crews in casual racing is that their presence improves racing manners. Their specific advantages over men and children are: they are more docile and willing to learn; they are more regularly available; when ladies compete, the base of racing is broadened.

At this point some will object: "But *we* sail as a family unit! We never take outsiders."

Exercises in domesticity are fine, *if* the skipper accepts the low order of racing efficiency that family crews entail. But here we are not considering whom we *have* to take, but whom we *should.* So if dear old Aunt Emily is with you for the weekend, by all means send her out on the committee boat to watch the race. She will not thank you for dowsing her with cold water or ordering her to pull ropes that lead she knows not where. Take her sailing on Sunday morning after church, or to a beach picnic.

Apostles of Togetherness will further suggest that the most closely knit racing unit is "Poppa and Momma," or "Father and his children against the world." There are many fine husband and wife teams, wholly unified in purpose, and, where winning is everything, their sharp edge can turn the trick. But experience shows as many married couples who try too hard in a boat and have distressing personal arguments. There is more zest in competing when we do not battle the community as a family attack team. Of course, the whole family should be out in the race; but mixed about with friends in other boats. Wives should certainly compete against their husbands. When on occasion they win, there is elation in the parlor. When they lose, they enjoy the salutary pleasures of respect.

Foundations of Good Skipper/Crew Relations

It is fine to sail out to the starting line as part of a cheerful, expert group, dedicated to the humiliation of the enemy. When defeated, each member accepts the blame, resolving it shall never happen again. Such unity is not accidental, but is based upon:

Skipper responsibility—Choosing, training, and holding a fine crew is a function of the skipper's personality. He provides the boat and colors crew morale.

Equipment—Crews must enjoy the very best in sails and gear.

Enjoyment—Crews must be assured a good time. The best time results from maintaining a tight, alert organization; one that wins occasionally.

Basic atmosphere—Racing should be done in a cheerful, highly competitive manner. Crews must be trained to do as much as they can at all times. This means fighting for a gain on every point of sailing and on every leg. When leading by half a mile, both skipper and crew should work to make it half a mile *plus one inch*. During any race the pressure is always on.

Best Use of Man/Woman Power in Racing

In many boats the skipper is the Big Boss, and the crew simply rope pullers. Does this system tend to win races? On the psychological side, certainly not. From the practical viewpoint of getting jobs done, probably not. There are four essential racing tasks, which may be handled according to personnel on hand:

Overall command—Someone must always have the immediate and final say in a racing boat. Quick control is vital in close quarters, such as starts and on windward legs. The most experienced man normally makes these maneuvering decisions. As a rule he is the owner; but he does not have to be.

Helmsman—On most boats, particularly family ones, the head of the family steers. This produces good results *if* father is the best racer. But the tiller is by no means a male sceptre. Example: An expert husband/wife team from the Atlantic Class invaded Small Point once. He had strong hands and a heavy duff; so he did all sail trimming and hull balancing. The lady was an ace tiller-woman. They set their natural advantages to fine use, and were hard to beat.

Sail trimming—On most small boats the skipper trims his own mainsheet, feeling it affect his helm, while his crew handles the jib. It takes strong arms and hands to trim a mainsheet fast or to play it offwind, particularly one-handed while steering. It is better when all sail trimming can be left to the crew. Steamships have Chief Engineers, wholly responsible for adjusting the powerplant: sails need similarly focussed attention.

Hull balancing—The crew always balance; most helmsmen help, using the hiking stick. Good hiking is an art. It takes persistence, agility, and some nerve. In many rough water races the most experienced man should hold the boat level, not steer.

Some General Remarks on Crewing

While best results may accrue when the Oldest Dog aboard wields final authority, it does not follow that all others should be faceless command-takers. On most racing boats the Oldest

Dog also steers, for he is felt to have the clearest head in a jam. But it is quite possible that your boat may sail faster with some organization that uses his ability to more advantage. For example, once the hull is precisely balanced and all sails in perfect trim, she may move right away from the fleet with a teenager at the helm; one who has been taught to steer with finger touch, letting the rudder trail out astern, while accepting many small directions from the Old Man, who is watching the sails, to head slightly higher or lower. Again, if your boat's wisest racing man is also her heaviest, she may gain more stability-wise with his gluteous maximus (that's Latin, son) out over the rail, than from any deftness at the tiller.

No matter who handles the major jobs, every effort should be made to increase the tasks performed by each of the crew. Information is always needed on wind, on enemy maneuvers, and on one's own position relative to marks and crossing boats.

Number to Take, and Specific Jobs to Be Mastered

If not limited by class rules, an extra pair of hands (not attached to a fat, slow-moving body) can be helpful. A hundred and twenty more pounds will slow one just a bit downwind in light airs, but more than pay it back to windward in normal shifting breezes if the owner is an ambitious hiker. In addition to the pleasure of a new face, the practice of half training several replacements pays off when one's regular crew calls up an hour before starting time to say: "Johnny just fell out of a tree and I'm hurrying him to a doctor . . ."

The boat with a regular crew has a hundred yard lead over her opposition. She is always ready before the race, and it is a great pleasure for skipper and crew to come aboard and see each other fall to work, each knowing what to do and confident that the other will check on and back them up. No preparation on a racing boat is for one person to do-and-forget.

Routine, pre-start activities include:

1) Someone must go out to the boat each race morning to bail, take the sails, and to check for missing or inoperative gear.

2) Skipper and crew should meet on the dock well before race time. Big or late lunches are taboo. Rowing out to the boat, hoisting sails, deciding which sails to use, and all-hands early adjustments should be wholly without pressure.

3) Twenty minutes should be allotted to relaxed sailing about in the general starting area. This allows study of the course, decisions on best sail draft, and discussion of preferred position along the line.

The following activities will be handled by someone in each race:

a) Timing the start, and warning of other boats' pre-start positions.

b) Balancing the hull to assigned marks without order.

c) Adjustment of sheets to marks for present wind force, without order.

d) Checking out wind shifts on the compass, and routines for tacking on headers.

e) Watch for boats to leeward, and the movements of particular enemies.

f) Use of sighting lines in crossing situations and near marks.

g) Agreed tacking techniques as to weight shifting and handling of jib sheets.

h) Vang adjustments; sail flattening and bagging by downhaul; setting the jib sheet leads for point of sailing.

i) Preparing, breaking out, trimming and dowsing the spinnaker.

j) Jibing the spinnaker, or jib on its whiskerpole.

k) Bailing underway.

l) Taking the tiller as required.

A majority of these items should be left by the helmsman to his crew, who are less restricted in their movements. A fine crew will perform them all.

Crew Morale

Good crew morale is the key to racing success. The basic purpose is to *have fun*. And those who do, work harder and are more efficient than laggards. The degree of enjoyment in a racing boat depends upon the skipper. No one will sail long with a curmudgeon, or Big Boss. The following are weighty morale obligations upon skippers.

Good racing crews should be cheerful. If yours likes to drive past each opponent's house the morning of the race, shouting: "We're going to trounce you today!" he, or she, should be encouraged in this exuberance. Constant swearing by the skipper is a beginner's trait. Racers should appear to be enjoying themselves, not to be bewailing a just fate. The crew's comfort should be assured by foul weather gear, coffee, or such minor refreshments as are possible. Small rewards and rituals are pleasant in racing. If someone brings out fruit to be eaten after any outstanding job, such as rounding the windward mark first, it lowers tension. If, after a win, there is a tradition that all receive cokes at the store, or a hot buttered rum, these are pleasant stimulations.

Crews must be made to feel equally as important as the skipper, which they surely are. If there are two races and the first has been won, it works well to let the crew take the tiller for part of the second. They will often do quite as well; and the skipper may benefit by watching his boat from an unaccustomed angle. When one of the crew is assigned a job that involves the helmsman's acting upon his judgment, as when a turning mark comes abeam or there is question whether an opponent's bow can be crossed, it is well to follow his word. The boat then functions as a unit. Of course, the skipper holds final say; but if he goes against crew advice he should give his reasons. It is wiser to lose occasionally than to have co-workers feel their efforts are ignored.

Practice Suggestions for Skippers and Crews

In early season it helps to go out on non-race days to familiarize all hands with the boat and her gear. Maneuvering problems may then be resolved in a relaxed atmosphere. If the crew is competent, he or she should be encouraged to take the boat out alone when convenient. The day may come when the skipper is called away, and he may wish them to race it. In addition to pre-race checks of lines and rigging there should be bi-weekly end-for-end shifts of halyards, oiling of all cam-cleats, and a thorough bottom scrubbing. If the crew enjoy these tasks, by all means let them do them. It is their boat too.

Pre-race maneuvers with regular crew aboard are simple warm-ups in which all consider sail fullness and strategy for that race. After spinnaker sheet, guy and turtle have been set up, a few practice jibes may be undertaken, or any maneuvers that promise difficulty under present wind or sea. During this time the crew should do most of the sail handling and even steering, while the Old Man looks around. But when the warning signal goes, it is all business.

Sail and hull trimming routines should be practiced to bring performance to specified marks or standards during the race *without order*. A constant result is sought with jib sheet tensions and hiking out, so that if losing on a particular day, changes may be made from known positions. If a new crew is aboard, or the regular crew has inexperienced help, take a bit longer before the start to insure that the new hand understands routines and what is expected of him. A new crew wants to be told, regardless of experience, just as the skipper would if sailing for someone else. The regular crew should do most of the telling. Go through simple maneuvers, tack and jibe, set and jibe the spinnaker, while explaining why you make specific moves. If the job is difficult, as when jibing the spinnaker in a fresh breeze, the skipper may leave the helm to perform it first. The new crew will be interested and will often come up with a better way, particularly for him. Speed should not be expected at first; let him work for sureness.

A good crew is both alert to get the boat out ahead, and eager to keep her there. But the biggest gain is in *his, her, their,* and *your* added pleasure.

GAINS FROM A WELL TRAINED, SATISFIED CREW

A smooth working skipper/crew unit is worth 100 YARDS, whatever the race.

20 STARTS

The start of a sailing race is one of life's keenest excitements. A good competitor on closing his eyes and picturing himself in the last seconds of a run to the starting line, can hear the low "who-oosh" of enemy sails alongside and the thump of his own pulse as adrenalin quickens his blood. Non-racers do pretend that sweeter music rustles in a petticoat or in cash dropping into the family till; but these are delusions incident to natural survival.

One would think that the rush and positioning of starting boats would appeal to everyone, for starts indicate a sailor's style and flatter his ego when he gets away smartly under all eyes. Yet if planning and forethought are proof of regard, the start is not thought critically important. We often see boats arrive late in the area, observe few starts practiced, and find that sailors prefer to extemporize their dashes over the line, rather than to make them upon a system. Some fine performers do not get particularly good starts and will avoid fighting for top early positions. They seem to feel that since no one can predict what other wild men will do in the confusion, it is best to try for a relaxed getaway and to concentrate upon what to them is the key to winning: upwind ability.

How Starts Are Commonly Made and to What Effect

Let us study the positions taken and results obtained in an average Small Point Start to windward, then in one reaching,

220

and off the wind. The reader will contrast this to his home practice.

A normal Small Point windward start involves fifteen boats on a line a hundred yards wide, which, while not exactly square to the wind, is intended to be so. At least one boat dawdles in late, while several will barely make the area. Perhaps three skippers have come out early to study the line, sway up sails, and to pass pre-race insults designed to unnerve the opposition. While all eventually get the course from the starter's boat, only a few will look out along the first leg for soft spots or dark areas indicating fresher breeze, and not more than two or three study the scope and frequency of the wind shifts.

Few crews start on any system. Instead, they vary from race to race as if this were part of the fun; except that bargers tend to repeat a crime that has lately been successful. Most are inclined to hover a little behind the area where they plan to cross. All but a handful of the fifteen boats make their starts on the starboard tack. If the line clearly favors one end, a majority cross there. But some are sure to choose the poor end to avoid the press.

Commencing at what is the windward end of the line for a starboard tack boat, here are the results commonly obtained.

Bargers Above the Starboard Tack Buoy

Circling in an area fifty to a hundred feet above the starboard tack end of the line will be three or four boats, preparing for a barging descent. Some are chronic bargers; some are trying this heady maneuver just for the day. They will essay it upon a broad reach, hoping to flatten sheets above the buoy, while squeezing in or around anyone to leeward. One or at most two of this group get good starts; late bargers get no advantage; those who meet unyielding opponents fare badly and cause general confusion.

Bargers follow their exciting, dive-in system, knowing it to be a bit tainted, but trusting to luck, a bold front, and the certainty that they will never be very far from the line at gunfire.

If successful, they cross near the buoy with good speed. And it is this feeling of fast getaway that appears to attract them, rather than advantages of the windward berth.

Close Hauled on the Starboard Tack Just Below the Buoy

Approaching the line with sheets already snugged in, and on a course that lets them pass close below the buoy, are one or two helmsmen who are probably just a hair late. These are Men of Virtue. They know the rules state that they need give no room to windward boats, so over-consciousness of rectitude makes them stiff in maneuvering. But they have need for philosophy, for the Bargers are always above them.

Their starting practice is surely best on average, and in a tight, law-abiding class the only safe one. But since summer racing tends toward the flamboyant, they need loud voices with which to warn the Bargers that they mean to sink them. A variety of sarcasms also helps, such as: "Take your money out of the bank *he* works in!" or, "So it was *your* grandfather who shot Lincoln?" etc. . . .

A Formula Start Near the Windward Buoy

With about a minute to go, one or two boats will slide down across the line from its upwind side, then some thirty seconds before gunfire, jibe or tack back for it, using the Vanderbilt or similar formula for timing.

Such boats average to start well, and find clear holes if they exist. Their pre-start maneuvers are in less cluttered water on the wrong side of the line. But when they head down across it, they need the nerves of a Chinese Pirate; for they are on the port tack, plowing straight into a wall of enemies. Even when their turn-around is accomplished, they are sometimes overwhelmed before they recapture way.

Reachers Down the Line

Some three boats will reach down the line on the starboard tack at gunfire. These may be early bargers. Or they may be hacking along without plan. They are in danger of being

forced over early by leeward boats. But if their immediate vicinity is clear, they can start well. Because it is hard to tell the
exact location of the line from its center, they must sacrifice a
few yards to safety. But when the port tack end is better, anyone reaching toward it on the starboard finds his position improved the further he goes.

Starboard Tack at Extreme Port End of the Line

Several boats will be hard on the starboard tack near the
port end buoy. If this is the better end, such a choice may
work out perfectly. But the more favored that end is, the
harder it becomes to lay it on the starboard tack without becoming boxed in the far corner and unable to fetch out by.

Port Tackers

There are always a few boats starting on the port tack. Some
may be good sailors who like to live dangerously. And if they
find holes, a wind shift, or a favoring line, and can thread
through and around starboard tack boats without being protested, they get fine starts. This is markedly so when the port
tack leads into favorable wind or current. Their practice is
risky. For it requires quick hands on the mainsheet and accurate judgment of each enemy's intentions while sliding by his
stern; and if they become involved they are thrown out at once
like boobs before the multitude.

A few hopeful souls also try the port tack on the guess that
no one else will use it. In this they learn the facts of life early,
for they are sure to meet starboard tackers near their end of
the line. They will also hear green helmsmen scream, "Foul!"
while still fifty yards away.

Beginners Starting Late

Lastly, one or two novices, either through muddling or
timidity, cross twenty to thirty seconds late near the center of
the line.

Maximum Gap Seen in Windward Starts

Advantages up to 150 FEET are normal in windward starts, if we freeze positions at gunfire. This takes no account of subsequent vulnerabilities that develop as a result of being covered, pinned down, or generally limited.

The best *average* starts result from conservative, well timed approaches—if possible with wind clear in a hole of one's own, while the opposition is jammed up and fighting.

Reaching Starts

So far as even crossings of the line are concerned, Small Point reaching starts produce smaller gaps than those to windward—90 FEET being about the widest first-to-last separation at gunfire.

Two-thirds of reaching starters choose the line's windward end. Some barge, but not offensively, for there is less need to gain early speed in this way. Timing is simple. Boats ease toward the line with about a minute to go, killing speed by loosening sheets, then hardening in as the gap narrows and it is clear they are not early. One or two cross in reverse, then tack back under the Vanderbilt Formula.

During the last thirty seconds a few boats are sure to close-reach up the line, hoping to cause a jam near its windward end. As leeward boats with right of way, they do not have to bear off for the first mark until gunfire, so they delight in trying to pinch fast moving windward boats above the buoy. Their disadvantage is that the galloping windward brothers are often unable to dodge; so it is easy for the squeezer to take several into his cockpit, a questionable pleasure, even when performed legitimately.

Some always try the leeward end of a reaching line. And if this end has been properly advanced to give a slightly shorter course to the first mark, and *if* the ensuing reach is not so close as to demand pinching, their solitude can give early advantage. An absolutely fatal reaching start at Small Point is from the

middle of a square line. Boats starting there are slightly
blanketed by all to windward, so unless they find definitely
fresher air for the first two minutes and can veer up into the
lead, they face sure loss of two hundred yards through cut
wind.

A special curse applies to reaching starts on the port tack—
the skipper who makes a ritual of sailing the full line after gunfire on the starboard tack. Two-thirds of the fleet may be foaming away toward the first mark, yet he will persist in enforcing
his rights and will drive stragglers about while there is one left
to roar at. He won't win himself; but is he furious when hit!

Starts Before the Wind

Offwind starts at Small Point are occasionally made on narrow lines, and are dangerous in high winds when the course is
near a jibe. Boats may surge out of control at high speeds, or
make goosewing jibes due to lack of vangs. Helmsmen therefore tend to maneuver conservatively in rough going. Timing
methods are rudimentary: boats crawl toward the line with
eased sheets and simply "go for it" when they see they can.

Now and then pre-start trouble occurs between port and starboard tack boats running dead before the wind. But since all
are aware of the dangers of jibing, it is rare to see much jockey-
ing. Normal practice is to break out a spinnaker after the line
is crossed, and of course anyone who sets his earlier will be
converged upon. Leaders now swing out to windward or leeward to avoid being cut from astern, and since a few always
take a minute to get spinnakers drawing, this often happens to
them. The maximum gap between first and last at gunfire
seldom exceeds 75 FEET.

Basic Problems of Starting

Ask twenty average racers what makes a fine start, and
eighteen will reply: "Crossing right with the gun!" But Ted
Wells, patron saint of the Snipe Class, judges starts by, "Where
they leave me after four hundred yards."

View each start with Ted as an early step toward building up a lead, and these advantages become important in one:

Clear wind	Worth 75 yards in the first half mile over boats that are slightly cut.
Freedom to tack	If better conditions lie out to the right, starboard tack with no one just astern gives ability to swing over to port for a possible 50 yard gain.
Crossing at the favored end	The alert crew that spots a vulnerable line can pick up ten yards.
Crossing within 5 seconds of gunfire	Timing of this order puts two-thirds of the fleet temporarily astern.
Starboard tack	Worth a boat length over port in most crossing situations.
Having good way	Allows dodging interference, particularly in light air.

Were he skilful as Lucifer, no skipper could hope to make the *best* start every time. Because the slippery intermeshing of boats occasionally slips the worst duffer into a choice windward berth, it eases tension if crews understand that while it is their racing duty to start very well, it is the Lord who doles out those super-starts in which a boat plunges over the line, her stem barely nudging it at gunfire.

Small fleets reward aggressive tactics. Against five, or at most ten adversaries of lower skill, a smartly handled boat can take chances and skim through holes. But when all sail well, boldness at the starting line does not pay. In fleets of twenty-five, room for sinuous maneuvers will not exist and no galloping cowboy can force his way through without loss of hide. In large dinghy groups, such as the Larchmont Frostbites, a slow-starting procedure is in force. Instead of milling about, these well sailed boats line up early and crawl for the line with only enough way on to counter luffs or block those sneaking up fast from astern. A good start is possible to the expert; but only seldom is it the very best.

A Method for Fluid Situations

The start of a sailboat race poses a beautifully liquid challenge: for the helmsman, after choosing a spot for his crossing, must thread through enemy traps and changing winds, to arrive precisely on gunfire. It was Napoleon's mastery of such evolving situations that won him control of Europe.

Good starters reserve the flexibility to slip into late openings, but it clarifies the problem to present a system that has helped beginners to cross with the top third. Getting started is compressible into two tasks: the first involves the mighty brain, and so is *intellectual,* the second is *operational.*

The brain part may be accomplished promptly, once the line has been inspected for advancement of its ends and likely crowding, by selecting—

1) The best spot at which to cross
2) The manner of crossing. (By barging, reaching down the line, etc.)

In the operational phase the skipper maneuvers throughout his first four minutes so as to arrive with approximately *one minute to go* at a spot from which he could easily cross within forty-five seconds, if he were to drive over at full speed. During the last minute he then moves in, at first working off time by slow-sailing; but once adjusted to interfering boats and clearly not early, by buttoning down in a press for the line.

Practical Windward Starts

After entering the area a crew's first job is to check the ends of the line for undue advancement, since advantages up to a hundred feet can be involved. This is easily done by sailing to the center and luffing there head to the wind. With sails shaking in the wind's eye, a sighting is taken across either beam toward whatever marks delimit the line. When this is fair, both ends will extend straight out, forming a right angle with the boat's heading. But if one end lies forward of abeam, it is that much advanced, with the other a like distance astern. In theory, windward starting lines are laid out square to the wind, not to the course. To spread the fleet and stop crowding at the starboard tack end, the port tack end is often advanced several boat lengths. But lines are set by men, not angels, and winds shift, so their squareness must be verified.

Simple advancement of one end may not be a line's most important feature. Better sailing conditions can lie out beyond either end. If fresher wind blows out to the left, it can be reached by a starboard tack start from anywhere on the line. But if it is to the right, a start at the extreme right end may be needed to allow swing-over to the port tack without ducking under the sterns of the entire fleet. Again, if a jam-up threatens at the windward end, another crossing may give clearer wind, particularly if the line is fair throughout. Lastly, crews must be alert to spot the effects of a wind shift upon their selected crossing spot, since any veering of 10° upon a line a hundred yards long will advance the end toward which the new wind moves *forty-five feet.*

Once "where" a start will be made is known, the "how" remains for consideration, and as the diagram shows, the spot chosen upon the line largely prescribes its type of crossing. If this is to be the windward end for a starboard tack boat, for example, the line may be crossed by barging, or by a straight-in "Path of Virtue" start.

Starts by Area

Beginning with the Barger at the top of the diagram, let us examine the rewards and penalties of each type of crossing. Note that the barging boat comes down to her final starting course from above the buoy. Bargers may use a wide circle, but will try to force their way in ahead of, or between leeward boats close to the line. No experienced racer makes a practice of barging every start. But when early maneuvers spread the fleet, a barge may sometimes be used fairly as a tactic of opportunity.

When few boats start and it is clear that none can be within twenty yards of the windward end at gunfire, it may be possible to get away fast by revolving about the buoy just close enough in to insure a two or three second gap at crossing.

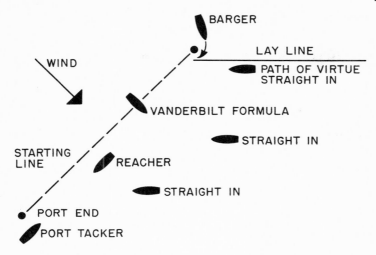

Because the barging boat has no rights whatever over anyone to leeward, she needs at least one and a half lengths of clear water to guarantee she will not be protested. She simply cannot force her way down and in. If the slightest proximity exists to any other boat, a barge will not pay. Even if the skipper gets away with it after suffering sharp comments as to his ancestry, it is bad manners to snatch from a novice room to which he is not entitled, while if the opponent he tries to squeeze is experienced, he will not get in.

The best approach on average in large fleets is along a line to the buoy just below the highest starboard course one can hold and still pass below it.

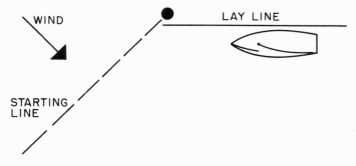

Here is a windward start, yet one that cannot legally be interfered with from above. It may be necessary to check-sail this "Lay Line" and to establish it by something on the water like a lobster-pot, for its lead is easily misjudged among milling starters. Any boat coming in slightly below it is well placed, since being already on her tightest course to the buoy she can hardly be luffed above it. If she allows just enough room to counter boats under her lee bow, she should be safe. Anything above is a slight barge, which still may be satisfactory if no one will be met at the line, or the helmsman can "S" to get down below it. But luffers to leeward spell trouble.

This approach may be likened to a biblical "Path of Virtue." It leads to good starts, if it is not undertaken too far out, when the virtuous path-follower may encounter enemies clogging the way to make him late. There are two limitations: bargers will surely be met near the line, who must be warned away like the sons of the Evil One they are; and the wind can easily haul 10°, which if it occurs to a strapped in boat a hundred yards out, may lift or drop her heading fifteen yards.

When the decision has been made to cross near the center of a fair line, a good start can be had in any patch of clear air along its length by a straight-in approach. The additional advantage of pre-start maneuvers in the largely open water on the line's windward side may be enjoyed by crossing in reverse under the Vanderbilt Formula. These swing-around starts average to give elbow room when crowds form near the windward buoy, but can seldom be made closer than twenty yards from it, since room will not be available there for back-tacking. If the line favors that end, the very best berth is therefore denied. A well trained crew is necessary to spin the boat around and get her moving in what may be narrow quarters before the gun.

Another start that gives good momentum, if the line is fair and the wind light, is to reach down toward the port tack end and slide over at gunfire. Dangers include any boats converging to leeward, which may force the reacher over early unless he is ready to drop under their sterns.

When the line greatly favors the port tack end, a straight in

starboard tack here can work well, provided the crossing angle
is not so narrow that boats driving far into the left hand corner
cannot squeeze out by the buoy. Practical limitations here are:
the likelihood of being blocked by port tackers and threaders,
who lose time for the virtuous starboard tacker, even when they
are excommunicated forthwith; and the fact that once over this
end one must be sure of good wind, since when it comes time
to tack back to port (assuming this will presently be necessary)
the entire fleet lies just above, all with right of way.

It is hard to justify a port tack crossing unless: there are few
boats on a wide line; the left end is far the better; the helmsman is an Artful Dodger; or he must move out to the right im-
mediately after the gun. In the last case a late port tack start
at the starboard tack end may be even better. A good mainsheet
man is a "must" on port tack starts. The skipper should be
quick to advise converging starboard tackers to "Hold your
course," and to make it clear that he will pass under their
sterns. They may not balk him as he keeps clear, so for this
interval he restricts their maneuvers. Much opportunism and
crew quickness are required in port tack starts. Tacking lines
help one to *know* he can cross an enemy without protest. He
must gauge such interval exactly, for all cards are with the starboard tackers.

Maneuvering During the First Four Minutes

Once a crew complete their "brain work" and know where
and how they mean to start, they can devote themselves single
heartedly to this end. Those whose planning ended shortly
after the warning gun have almost the first four minutes in
which to locate and proceed to a key spot, or area, from which
during the last sixty seconds they will make their timed run-in
to the line; while if they took two minutes to decide, only two
more remain in which to place themselves. The spot chosen
will depend upon the type of approach, and in each case it
must be close enough in so that the helmsman, if he so wishes,
could cross early. In a barge he will be somewhat above the

buoy; for any straight in or port tack approach, some sixty yards out; for a Vanderbilt formula start, approximately on the line, but headed across it in reverse; for a reach down the line, not too far from the upwind end.

Here the racer may ask why it would not be simpler to move to a spot from which he could smash in at full speed with everything drawing hard? The answer is that in competition several boats are sure to interfere. Also the wind may drop. So he holds back a fraction of time to work off by slow-sailing on his run in.

Early maneuvering toward a chosen spot should be precise, but plus or minus five seconds against a minute to go, is acceptable. Some skippers will circle during these first minutes within fifty yards of their spot; others will craftily slide back only at the end. The manner in which a boat eases toward her "one minute to go" spot as the seconds tick by is similar to the approach procedure of a light airplane coming in to land at a strange field. Flight patterns start from a set altitude, with the pilot flying a rectangular box that he widens out if he seems high, or closes in if he is losing altitude too fast. His expendable commodity is Altitude, while in sailboat racing it is Time-remaining. The careful helmsman holds back a few seconds, which he can drop away by widening out, or slowing down. His crew share in the problem of hitting a pre-selected spot behind the line accurately, and can help by calling out time-remaining from the watch, while freeing or hardening sheets according to whether they seem early, about right, or clearly late. They should also warn of congestions ahead that may force a change of plan.

The Final Run-in

When a skipper swings over for the line with only sixty seconds to go, he is delivering an offspring in regard to which all previous movements have been only affectionate preliminaries. One of his crew will call out time-remaining from the stopwatch; against which he mutters seconds-to-hit-the-line. If their run starts from anywhere near the proper spot for that start, he will be capable of an early crossing. The first half of his run-in may therefore be expected to include some slow-sailing to work off this time. Speed can be checked by luffing, by easing the mainsheet, by hauling the jib to windward, or by "S-ing." It is not legal to tow a bucket or a leg.

The Barging Run-in

With a minute or less to go the barger will be in the middle of a circular jibe above the buoy, or, if he is well behind the line, may already be broad-reaching on the starboard tack to squeeze in. In the first case the buoy will be close aboard as a marker against which he can widen out or close in if no leeward boat is nearby. In the second, if he can worm down to the lay line while still some distance away, the completion of his start may be as law abiding as the last days of a bad boy turned archbishop. His problem is not what he does himself; it is the reactions of others, all with right of way over him.

Path of Virtue Run-ins

Two-thirds of all starts are made with straight in final runs from key areas behind the line; a majority toward the starboard tack buoy, but if the line is fair, to any other spot as well. Some early slow-sailing is needed; otherwise the run will have been started too far out. Boats must always stay below the lay line and watch for enemies under their lee bows that may luff them above it. Those roaring up from astern are less of a problem, for time has a way of running out on cowboys. When time-remaining drops down to the same, or less than time-needed-to-hit-the-line, sheets may be snugged in and the boat speeded up to her best pace; the aim being to cross within two seconds of gunfire.

Last Minute Under the Vanderbilt Formula

Normal timing by this system starts at about a minute to go with the boat crossing the line in reverse. As the final countdown begins, a hole is sought into which she will tack or jibe back to the line. The formula tells when to begin this tack or jibe. Suppose that fifty seconds remain as the line is crossed in reverse, and also that a normal tack or jibe takes ten seconds. Time remaining (50 seconds) is divided in half, giving "25 seconds." To this is added one half of the time needed to tack or jibe (5 seconds). The answer, "30 seconds," is the *time-left at which to start* the swing back to the line.

The Vanderbilt system works fairly well on windward starts, but is less accurate than on reaches, for which it was designed, because: a) When sailing down before the wind the boat crosses the line at something approaching a right angle; but when returning to start she is hard on the wind, angled at 45° to the line, and so does not recross at the exact spot where her timing began. b) In descending to the line she sails faster than when coming back close hauled. Windward starts under this formula are consequently apt to be a few seconds late.

Last Seconds in a Reach Down the Line

If the line has been run at least once to establish how long this takes under the prevailing wind, it is simple to curve down past the windward buoy with something less in hand. A majority of the fleet will lie behind. The boat can be eased along the line, her crew counting out seconds, while all watch for others converging to leeward that might force her over. The helmsman will go under these sterns, calling out his intentions while still distant and warning away port tackers. Just before gunfire everything is trimmed in hard and good speed built up in a slot of private air.

Port Tack Run-ins

First class time-versus-distance judgment is needed here. All starboard tackers must be comfortably crossed, with crew agreement as to whether to tack beneath their lee bows or round under their sterns. No rigid timing patterns can be held on the port tack; some skippers like this. Except against novices, or on

an unfair line, port tack crossings return poor percentage results.

Control by Slow-Sailing in the Last Minute

Any type of run-in can be made more accurately and from
closer to the line if the boat is nudged along under good control by slow-sailing. Skipper and crew should experiment until
able to maintain tight, but slowed down courses. Easing out
the mainsail or jib may be tried, brailing up the jib, pinching
extra high, or even virtually heaving to with the windward
jib sheet taut. There is less danger than might appear from
boats overtaking fast from astern. If the slow-sailer's boom is
well out, the overtaker must establish his overlap far enough
out to allow hauling it in and still keeping clear. The overtaker
must also ease his mast up square with the windward helmsman
to gain mast abeam and the right to luff. Of course, the slow
boat must be able to counter converging luffs; but, in
accordance with Rule #40, these can only be made slowly.

If the stopwatch balance of *time-remaining* versus *time-to-hit-
the line* is called out regularly, it is simple enough when they
are even to speed up the boat. For their actual crossing, top
dinghy racers are said to make themselves a twenty foot hole of
clear air as follows: Approach to the line is, whenever possible,
to windward of a duffer, and with luffing rights (mast abeam)
over the boat upwind. Ten seconds before gunfire the windward boat is forced high by a slow luff, leaving four or five
yards of clear water down to the duffer, who it is hoped will be
too preoccupied to curve up too. Just before gunfire the helmsman drives off into this hole, builds up speed, then snugs in
sheets and hikes onto the rail for a fast crossing in relatively
clear air. At Small Point this practice is not always successful,
for too often it involves collision with a screeching windward
helmsman who either refuses to respond to the luff, or is unable to because boats above him have not "gotten the word."

Slow starts may be practiced alone from a hundred feet out,
then from well inside that. They are most useful in fleets of

more than twenty boats; their difficulty being that they require excellent crews.

Practical Reaching Starts

The reaching start is simpler than one to windward. But unless a reaching line is properly laid out with its lee end well advanced, boats must fight for berths near the windward end. This is not fatal, for all face the same demand. Shortly after crossing, many will luff out to windward in an effort to hold clear wind. If the lee end of the line *is* advanced and the ensuing reach is not too close, a berth there should be considered, particularly if it promises an inside lane at the mark. Should it seem probable that after crossing at the lee end a boat can tighten up and wi[...]dred yards be in the lead, that end may be risked; [...]se, it should be avoided. The worst possible reaching start is from the middle of a square line, or one that favors the windward end. Boats here sail with hopelessly cut wind.

One may barge down for the selected crossing spot in a reaching start, sail straight in for it, which will also be a barge as regards boats to leeward, or converge along a closer heading than can be maintained after gunfire. One can also cross the line in reverse and then tack or jibe back for it under the Vanderbilt formula. Barging a reaching start is not difficult against few boats on a wide line. But it can still lead to dangerous, fast moving pile-ups at the windward buoy; for again, the barger has no rights over boats below him. When they converge under his lee bow he must have room to swing behind them, remembering that it is only after gunfire that they are required to bear away for the first mark.

The boat choosing a conservative straight in approach to the line must also give room to convergers under his lee bow before gunfire. Any skipper on a close reach with no one below him has in theory the safe reaching start. His difficulty is that as he nears the windward buoy timing becomes critical. Hitting it five feet too soon is fatal; while arriving late by even thirty

that to the first mark, but after gunfire they must head away for it, at least until the line is crossed. Once clear of the line, a busy period follows in which spinnaker guys, poles and sheets are more important than luffing. The test of a downwind start is how much one gains over boats alongside in the first hundred yards through better spinnaker and mainsail trim.

Practicing Starts and the Impact or Rules Upon Them

Starting practice is both effective, and a great former of crews. And starts are fun to simulate, whether with imitation boats on a card table, by single boat on a short line, or by several making ten to a dozen crossings, with windward legs only two hundred yards long so that the best start inevitably gives victory in an abbreviated contest.

1973 NAYRU rules affect starts as follows:

1) Barging is not illegal: the barger simply has no rights and can never force a leeward boat to give him room.

2) Any boat may luff and be luffed *slowly* before a start. The fact of overtaking to leeward does not limit a luffer once she gains "mast abeam" upon a luffee.

3) There are still novices who believe marks on the starting line to be similar to turning marks out on the course, at which an overlap entitles them to room. This is a delusion. Windward boats may be pinched into the starting boat at any time before the gun.

4) After gunfire the leeward boat behind the line on a windward start may still head as high as full-and-by, but no higher, to pinch out windward ones. Starting on a reach or before the wind, she may head anywhere she pleases before the gun, but after it must bear away for the first mark until across the line.

5) Fewer collisions result if crews habitually call out their intentions to others converging upon them.

MAXIMUM POTENTIAL LOSS IN STARTING—

150 FEET

21 WINDWARD LEGS

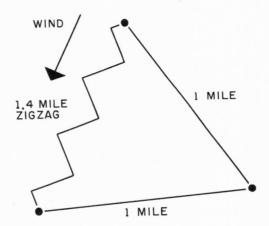

WIND

1.4 MILE
ZIGZAG

1 MILE

1 MILE

Sailors judge a helmsman by his skill to windward, much as aviators rate a pilot by his landings, for most can go wrong then. The upwind expert enjoys twice the time "his wonders to perform," as the reaching or offwind specialist. With course legs a mile long, the sailing length of one directly to windward is 1.4 miles due to the 90° zigzags of tacking. Progress to windward is slower than on other legs. Boats reaching or running at five knots cover a mile in twelve minutes; while the boat tacking upwind at about three knots, needs twenty-eight minutes for her 1.4 mile zigzag.

In view of the possibilities for planning and teamwork to windward, it should sober the optimist to consider how these legs are actually sailed.

At Small Point the owner or most experienced man steers the boat. He also tends his own mainsheet, which may be half cleated, or simply held, and makes all decisions without responsibility to his crew, who tend to become jib trimmers and weight movers. Silence, prompt obedience, and respect are the cardinal virtues of Small Point crews.

Gray matter is put to no damaging strain before windward legs. Small Point skippers await the start to see how they succeed, and if poorly, a decision is then made on splitting with the leaders. Few crews have plans for detecting changes in wind direction or velocity, or for tacking upon headers. It is assumed that wind will hold steady until it shifts. In tacking the precise instant when jib sheets are loosened or hardened in varies on each boat. Sail tensions accord with how the skipper feels about wind force. Half a dozen will sway up halyards just before the start.

Tiller techniques differ widely, as well among the expert as the poor. Inexperienced helmsmen do much pushing down upon the tiller. As each gust strikes they force the helm away to swing their boat into the wind, instead of allowing her to ease up to it through her own sail balance. Most Small Point helmsmen sit to windward, where their weight improves stability in a breeze. Perhaps a third, who have seen photographs of Briggs Cunningham steering *Columbia* from the lee side by her genoa jib, affect this big boat position.

Small Point skippers will cover an adversary directly to leeward, but not persistently. Close study is not made of the angle, or extent of disturbed wind off sails, their own or another's. So boats follow in one another's dirty wind, sorting themselves into groups, and each seeking the windward berth for its freedom of movement, rather than as a source of clear wind for themselves and foul air for the enemy. In crossings helmsmen rarely try for the lee bow position, but will swing down and astern of any starboard tacker whose bow they can not clear.

On rounding downwind marks with a windward leg to follow, a few will continue for half their lead, then tack in order to lie directly to windward of following boats. But they will not fight to hold this position.

Problems of Windward Performance

The job	Commonly best done by
Make spot decisions	Helmsman, in immediate control
Steer	Best helmsman
Trim mainsheet	Helmsman for small adjustments. By a full time trimmer for active maneuvers.
Trim jib sheets	Crew
Balance hull	All hands
Tack boat	All hands
Observe oncoming wind	Crew member most interested
Check compass for headers	Crew member most interested
Watch dangerous enemies	Crew
Watch under lee side	Crew
Decide instant to tack	Helmsman with crew advice
Adjust sails	Crew under helmsman's orders

This job-table assumes that the skipper is also the helmsman. In every racing boat someone must have immediate command and be able to initiate maneuvers under his own instant decision. Custom and practicality confer this upon the helmsman. But in small yachts it does not necessarily follow that the man at the tiller should do all thinking. Jobs will vary according to the number and competence of the crew. When only the skipper-helmsman is experienced, he tends his own mainsheet. But should a crewman have strong hands, it is a great aid to have him do it. With two reasonably good sailors, one light and the other heavy, as with a husband and wife, it often works best if the lady steers, while her husband does the hard work of sheet tugging and hiking out. The difficulty is that in most cases it is the husband who is the more aggressive racer, so the boat wins more with him at the helm.

There seems little reason to vary from the standard method of jib sheet trimming on tacks. Here the sheet is only released as the bow passes through the eye of the wind, and the lee sheet is then taken in smartly to just where experience says it should go. This can only be done time after time when sheets are clearly marked, and lead at the proper angle from their camcleats to the crew's balancing station on the windward rail. In a breeze when sheets are single part and the sheet tender's hands are small, there can be zero delay in the procedure.

Tacking is an all-hands operation. In the shift of crew weight it is important that everyone, including the helmsman, be exactly over the boat's centerline as she passes through the wind. As she pays off they will settle down smoothly, without jump or jerk. It is rewarding to practice tacking against other boats and to observe the slow-down that accompanies clumsiness. The amount of shoot to windward will vary with the hull momentum that can be maintained in present wind and sea. With a green crew ten minutes should always be spent to get tacking smooth as silk, and particularly on rough days when all must drop down from the windward rail, climb the other, get sheets in and cleated, watch opponents close aboard, yet insure that the boat recaptures way smoothly.

Thinking and Pre-Planning

A man should have his head examined for lumps who races a small boat to windward without studying the course. There are always spots where wind and current promise to be favorable. Against automatic passage through them, must be balanced the tactical advantage of making one's first long tack in the direction closest the mark. The man who stands away on his first tack, particularly if that needs to be only a short one, risks finding when he swings over for his long hitch that even a five degree wind shift has made his early tack entire loss. He also makes timing of his final swing over to the mark more difficult than if he had passed it close aboard and knew when to come around. Local conditions will occasionally make it unwise to adopt this standard method of laying marks. At Small Point the Middle Ledge buoy, which is turned to windward in southwest breezes, lies in lighter air and stronger tide than

the shore bounding the racing area. To tack for this buoy when
unsure of fetching it against foul tide is poor gambling, since if
it is not hit on the nose, any boat that has overstood slightly
will reach down fast through the lighter air and turn well
ahead.

Before each windward leg the crew member charged with
spotting wind shifts should venture a prediction as to the
quarter from which new wind may be expected to strike. Before the warning signal an estimate is needed of the frequency
and scope of the day's minor fluctuations. If this is forgotten,
tacks may be taken on presumed headers that will prove abortive. Everyone aboard must know the state of the tide and
where currents run most strongly. These will usually be where
water is deepest in the center of channels.

Hull Trimming and Adjustment of Sails

The hull is best trimmed to pre-tested marks, with each of
the crew knowing the order in which he shall move out upon
the rail and into the hiking straps. The helmsman will normally hike last. Someone should be delegated to heel the boat
5° to leeward in light airs to fill the sails. Fore and aft trim
and centering of weight will be designed to keep minimum
rudder forces. Close-hauled sheet settings for both jib and
mainsail are identifiable by bits of colored yarn woven into
the sheets so that they may be cleated exactly, or slackened by
known amounts to suit wind strength.

Tiller Work

If the tiller is pictured as a magic wand, capable of producing sailboat speed, its strongest spells will be worked to windward. On windward legs sail trim is fixed, and positioning of
the rig to hauling winds is by the helm; on other points of
sailing a boat normally heads straight from buoy to buoy, with
maximum sail power obtained by constant retrimming of her
sheets. In three respects the tiller habits of good helmsmen
differ from those of beginners:

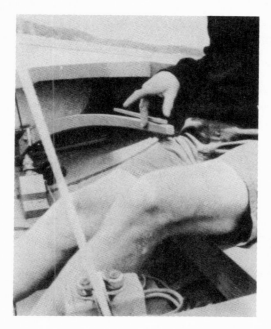

Finger tip steering for well balanced boat. Hiking stick not in use

1) The good sailor grips his tiller lightly. Two fingers are quite enough to steer a balanced boat. Pressure is largely one way: a holding back against the boat's natural tendency to luff. To pay her off, some pull is supplied in gentle finger tugs that are as quickly released. When a tighter heading is desired, finger pressure is simply removed and the boat allowed to seek the wind of herself. Contrast the tiller grip of an average beginner, which is a fist operation. He steers in both directions. To head off, he jerks the tiller to him. When a gust strikes, he forces it down hard, oaring the boat up into the wind to spill pressure from her sails. When such a push-down sets more than 10° of rudder blade across the boat, the higher drag slows her noticeably.

2) The expert, using minimum rudder force in one direction only—to head the boat off—guides her along the edge of the

wind. He encourages any tendency to eat out to windward, only dropping her head with a slight finger pull when he senses her as climbing too high and about to run out of wind. His job is to produce only enough rudder force to nudge the hull off and keep her moving. This presumes a sail balance in which weather helm is only 3°–4°. Once the boat is moving well, her tiller pressures become minimum. Where three-quarters of the time the expert's rudder blade trails, and predominantly so in light airs, the beginner, who is never sure where his wind sits, sculls constantly to find it. When his sails starve, he jerks the tiller to fill them. When they harden and the boat heels, he pushes down, making such large eddies that ripples of water-stall show far back in the wake.

3) Lastly, in tacking, the experienced racer starts his turn with an easy push-down, preferably in a spot of wind that will allow him to complete it with good drive. As the bow starts to swing, his rudder is centered, and in passing through the wind it virtually trails. In approaching the new course the tiller in a fine tack will lie about where it would be if the boat were well underway—holding a few degrees of weather helm. An active shoot to windward is desirable. The boat should move well in curving up into the wind, and should keep some of her forward way as she drops off, particularly in lumpy seas and high winds. Tacks started from overheeled positions are difficult to complete smoothly. The beginner's tack begins with a jammed down tiller that is held hard-a-lee. The boat squirms and stops. If the start was from a 20° heel, or from a reach among high waves, she may go into irons. Should she pass the wind's eye with her rudder still uncentered, she will pay far off without recapturing speed. A big heel normally follows as the new wind strikes, then a wide "S" curve that loses twenty feet.

Pointing or Footing?

Under Sail Tests we concluded that within narrow limits equal results can be obtained by heading high or footing fast, and that the beginner's best compromise was to *keep his boat*

lively. A useful routine for encouraging liveliness to windward is:

The helmsman lines up his masthead fly with the headboard,
glancing up every few seconds to hold it there.

He tugs the tiller gently with two fingers, releasing all pressure, then repeating the tug until the boat's head drops and she
is *felt to move.*

As she comes alive faint vibrations will steal to his fingers
from water passing the rudder. At this instant he relaxes all
pressure, allowing her to coast up into the apparent wind.

At the first suspicion of the hull's going dead, and even if
the masthead fly still indicates a proper course, enough finger
pressure is restored to pay off and revive the sensation of movement.

Tiller Sequences in Changing Winds

Once the beginner develops a light touch, learns to keep his
boat footing, while checking the headboard-to-masthead-
fly angle so that she eats up well, he will still find old timers
beating him, but by lesser amounts. The reason is that the ancient mariners are quicker in adjusting to wind changes. In
Chapter 18 we considered the standard wind variations met
along a course. Since these will recur until eternity, we need
only to summarize their more important demands upon a
helmsman.

Action required by shifts in wind direction—Whoever is watching to windward for the dark traces of new wind will call them
out, particularly when they change the headings of other boats.
As each shift approaches, the careful helmsman will ease toward his next course at least five seconds early; for to await the
new breeze is too late and donates five clear feet to anyone
who anticipates its angle.

As velocity freshens or drops—The commonest steering error
lies in failure to appreciate that whenever wind freshens or
fades with *no change* in direction whatever, an altered course is
still demanded.

As a shelf of stronger air moves in, the good helmsman prepares to:

Luff slightly until his boat picks up speed.

Bear away gently when she stabilizes.

Bear away a bit more as she moves back into normal wind.

Climb up to first heading as a last correction.

Roughly the opposite applies upon gliding into a lull. And because the lull's first effect is subdued, giving a lower, rather than a better heading toward the mark, many sailors simply *hate* lulls and do nothing to gain in them. Now the helmsman must:

Bear off slightly until hull speed drops.

Return to about his first course in the body of the lull.

Ease considerably higher upon emerging into normal wind.

Drop back to first course upon recapturing speed.

In both cases there was a flowing "S," with the knowledgeable helmsman gaining slightly in each bend over those who steered straight on. The first bend was *up* when the wind freshened; it was *off* when it faded temporarily.

Practice in circular puffs—Passage through the rotary puffs and flaws that are characteristic of offshore winds requires warning from someone as to which face of the rough new gust is about to strike. Tiller anticipation partakes both of a luff for the stronger wind, plus a sharp correction for whatever its angle of approach is to be. Here, as in all windward course corrections to changing winds, the reader will observe that the skill difference between expert and untutored helmsmen lies in the expert's readiness to act just *before* each shift arrives. The beginner is not only slow to eat high into freshening winds, but when at last he does scull up parallel to the rest of the fleet, he expects the new heading to last. When it does not, and his sails flap, he is late again in bearing away.

Tactics

The keenest member of a crew is its best tactical observer to windward. His, or her, job is to advise in a steady flow of reports

what each enemy is up to, and how successfully. Watch is necessary to leeward, particularly when on the port tack. If this is
difficult in a breeze because of a low boom, a wide plastic
window may be set into the foot of the jib or near the mainsail luff. The extent and angle of wind shadows of all boats
close by are prime crew concerns, as are wakes and the best
spots at which to cross them. If in the lead, advantage should
be taken of any defensive aid, such as swinging one's dirty wind
into the virgin sails of pursuers. When it is not quite possible
to cross a hostile bow, preparations should be made early to
take the safe, lee bow position. At least one and a half lengths
of open water are needed to tack squarely in an opponent's
course; for he needs not to even start keeping clear until you,
as overtaken or leeward yacht, fill your sails. It will commonly
pay a starboard tack boat with a port tacker passing close astern
to make a covering tack as soon as the latter is clear. This holds
the port tacker below until the first boat is ready to swing back
to starboard; for should the port tacker be allowed to proceed at his pleasure, when next they meet, assuming no wide
gain by either, he will be on the starboard with right of way.
There is a theoretical defense for the port tack boat against being so covered, in that as soon as she clears the starboard tacker's stern and sees him start into the wind, she should tack too.
Under Rule #41.4, when two yachts close together tack
simultaneously, the one to starboard, or in this case, the ex-
port tacker, has the rights.

Hailing for room near shore is so common on windward
legs that all must know how to claim it. But it may not always pay to shout proudly: "I demand room under Rule 43!"
A visitor at Small Point who did this so infuriated the locals
that they roared back he was a "Bonehead sea-lawyer!" and
refused to comply.

One should plan to hit windward marks on the starboard
tack; but when forced to do so on the port, with starboard tackers to be met in the vicinity, overstanding by $1\frac{1}{2}$ boat lengths,
an insurance policy costing five seconds, allows one to duck
below the first few and still clear the buoy. Let any starboard
tacker see that you can barely fetch a mark on the port tack,

and he will stand on just enough to put you about, or if you pass beneath him, to make you miss it.

Practice Maneuvers for Windward Legs

These items have all-hands value on windward legs, and may be practiced on non-race days:

To Be Demonstrated by the Skipper:

Hull trim that will be required. Crew seating to maintain it, and progression to the rail and into the hiking straps.

The complete tacking operation. Particularly as to smooth weight transfer and snugging in of the jib sheets.

Sheet tension desired in various winds by placement of colored threads in the camcleats.

Sail curvature desired and how to change it.

Width of jib and mainsheet leads on the deck, according to wind strength.

Selection of sails for the conditions.

Warnings of other boat movements, and on the approach of gusts.

The light tiller touch for a new helmsman, and the "no-push-down" technique as the boat heels.

Regular Crew to Be Proficient in:

Reports on areas of better wind, and enemy movements.

Information on headers from the compass.

Data from tacking lines.

Tacking as a unit against another boat. Both to go upwind, one in frequent tacks, the other in few, with the multi-tacker largely holding her ground.

Crossing beneath another boat's stern to be practiced until the crew can get the mainsheet in hard to use the up-slant there. Similarly, the exact lead needed to tack under another's lee bow to be verified and the maneuver repeated until its success is automatic.

Efforts made to hold a faster boat in one's wind shadow. The best local skipper to be asked to sail alongside through a specific number of tacks. If he escapes, ask him why.

MAGNITUDE OF LOSS SEEN ON WINDWARD LEGS

Once out ahead, well sailed boats increase their leads. Common losses for every mile sailed up wind are:

900 FEET

But beginners who pinch badly can drop back:

1500 FEET

REACHES

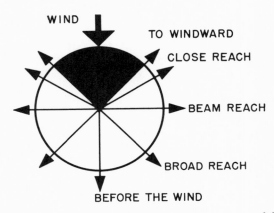

WIND

TO WINDWARD

CLOSE REACH

BEAM REACH

BROAD REACH

BEFORE THE WIND

The reach as a point of sailing covers two-thirds of the wind's spectrum. Reaches are classed as: Close, when a mark can just be laid without tacking. Beam, with the wind squarely from the side. Broad, with a quartering wind, but the jib still drawing. It is on reaches that sails develop their greatest push and give a hull top speed. In a ten knot breeze the working sails of a Small Point One Design show roughly this ratio of forward thrust to speed:

To windward	10 lbs and 3 knots
Close reach	15 lbs and 3½ knots
Beam reach	40 lbs and 5 knots
Broad reach	35 lbs and 4½ knots
Before the wind	30 lbs and 4 knots

An evil companion of high forward thrust is even higher side force, which if unchecked, will produce over-heeling and a slow boat.

252

It was formerly thought there could be no passing by class boats on reaching legs. Reaches were sailed straight from buoy to buoy, and with all moving fast there was no time for a break-through. Anyone trying to drive by to windward would be luffed, while if he curved down to leeward, he met the leader's nubbly wake and windshadow. For modern planing dinghies and catamarans the reach is considered a vital leg. The first International 14 to climb up onto her plane scoots away from the fleet. A fresh side breeze is needed to make these light hulls get up and go, but they are willing to zigzag 45° off course at a 40% fee in extra distance, which the doubled speed of planing quickly repays. Displacement boats, however, still constitute a majority of racers, and until lately their reaching legs have been considered processions. Today genoa jibs give livelier speed on close reaches; on beam and broad reaches flat spinnakers reward expert sail handlers, while on gusty days the reaching technique of "Off in the Puffs, Up through the Lulls" encourages threaders to dart about, stimulating profanity and delight.

Popular regard for reaching, nevertheless, still sees it as paying thinner dividends than windward work or running free under light sails. But since all boats go fast, reaching legs are enjoyable.

How Reaches Are Actually Sailed

The tasks performed by skipper and crew on reaches are much the same as to windward. The owner, or most experienced hand, assumes the tiller. In small boats he also tends his own mainsheet. The crew always trim the jib, while if a spinnaker is set, they raise and dowse it. Reaching crews generally hike out. Certainly they absorb most of the cold water that slops aboard. Crews are not expected to be brainy or super-alert, and because all boats hold similar courses there is less need for them to warn: "Here comes trouble on the port tack!" or "That hammer-head is trying to pass us again."

One might expect reaching legs to be sailed as straight lines, after allowance for set of tide. But because following boats inch out to windward in the hope of passing there, and leaders must protect their wind, a reaching fleet tends to curve into a bow, offering ten or twenty yards gain to the helmsman with the fortitude to steer a direct leeward course. In the matter of reaching spinnakers, skippers wait to see whether the leader sets his and how it draws; and since it is trickier to break one out in the open on a broad reach than when sheltered behind the mainsail off the wind, several boats are likely to make a mess of this.

At Small Point only the better crews widen out jib sheet leads and mainsheet travellers on reaches; while still not all use vangs, because: "They get in the way all the time." Mainsheets are rarely played in and out to anticipate the ever-changing angle of apparent wind. Crews do not warn their helmsman of approaching gusts to reduce heeling. Steering is his job, not theirs, they say. Lacking routines on who hikes out first, whenever a sharp gust strikes twenty boats, ten of them will roll sideways and down. Class "C" sailors and below enjoy this and associate it with speed through the water.

Green reaching helmsmen simply aim at the next mark, then fight weather helm with rudder across the boat, not by slackening sheets or shifting crew weight aft. On high wind reaches when a spring scale has been attached to the ends of Small Point tillers, readings up to "20 lbs" are common, or about the drag of a snowshovel nailed across the keel.

The average Small Point reacher attempts all passing to windward. If in danger of being passed there himself, he may luff half heartedly, but never into the wind's eye, as the British delight in doing to "tag someone out." A few chase puffs, driving off with them, then easing up through the following lulls. They have read that this is a crafty stratagem, rather than confirmed its worth by experience. Such squirmings and wormings are commonest in fresh winds, when with all footing fast through breaking seas they produce delusions of grandeur.

Problems of Reaching Performance

Two factors limit reaching speed:

1) The control of a reaching sailboat is in a sense opposite to that to windward. Where the windward working boat fixes her sails and steers a changing course, adjusting to shifts of apparent wind by tiller, the reaching rudder, ideally, trails and the boat is held on a *straight course* by repeated hardenings and freeings of her sails. Because apparent wind angle on reaches moves far more as a result of gusts and lulls than from slants in the basic wind, on puffy days reaching sheet work is constant and demanding.

2) The sails on a reach lie well out to leeward, where they produce strong turning and heeling couples. Unless skill counteracts both effects, reaches, with their high speed, offer great potential *loss of speed* through hull drag and inefficient rig angle.

Although most racing cockpits are too small for interchange of helmsmen on short legs, there are theoretical advantages to the Harvey Flint system of putting the best sailor on the mainsheet, while a junior takes the tiller and simply holds the boat's nose on the buoy. Here the sails steer. The best man sets them to maximum power angle, then tries to maintain this through shifts of apparent wind. A strong mainsheet trimmer can produce fine reaching gains. Playing the sheet actively, he comes in and out, on word from the steersman when the helm hardens, but predominantly under his own judgment of the sails, which he studies from his hiking post on the rail. During the average mile of reaching he will take in and let out slack sixty times. Should an opponent luff suddenly to leeward, his sheet hardens ten feet in that first second.

Reaching legs demand active weight shifts by the crew, both to limit weather helm and to hold the rig up and driving through gusts. All must be prepared to hike without order to retain an agreed maximum heeling angle of, say 10°.

The bearing of each upcoming reaching leg is worth checking before the start to determine whether it will pay to chase puffs, and if so, how widely. If one bears away 10° for half a leg, then back to the mark, it costs 2½ extra yards in a hundred. Bearing off 20°, then back, costs 7½ a hundred over the straight course. But in either case if the turn back to the buoy is long delayed, penalties can reach 15% and 35%, as dotted lines in the diagram show.

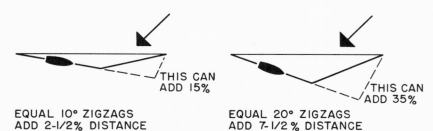

THIS CAN
ADD 15%

THIS CAN
ADD 35%

EQUAL 10° ZIGZAGS
ADD 2-1/2% DISTANCE

EQUAL 20° ZIGZAGS
ADD 7-1/2% DISTANCE

Racers generally agree in not setting their reaching spinnakers unless the wind is a hair aft. With a 20 knot apparent wind dead abeam, Small Point spinnakers contribute dangerous heeling and only a little extra speed; while in light air whenever the wind draws slightly forward they backwind the mainsail enough to slow the boat. Experienced crews who plan to use one, lay out halyard, sheet, pole and guy before the reaching leg so that no one ever has to clamber up onto the bow to pass spinnaker gear around the jibstay. Their spinnaker gear sits ready in its turtle or box, clipped down to prevent sliding overboard from a canted deck, and they have perfected an all hands routine for passing the pole up and down in order to lessen its potency as a harpoon and perhaps save the skipper's front tooth or favorite eye.

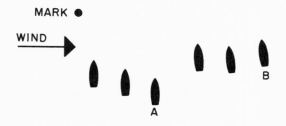

MARK ●

WIND →

A

B

When after two-thirds of a leg, boats are still fighting side by side, the helmsman in boat "A" should start working for an inside berth at the mark. If he is to swing up past other sterns, a short period of braking or of stubbing progress may be needed, by pulling the jib hard to windward; for it is better to be 5 yards late at the turn with a chance to tack squarely around into clear air, than to be carried 50 yards below, as is "B."

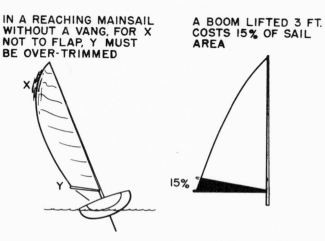

IN A REACHING MAINSAIL WITHOUT A VANG, FOR X NOT TO FLAP, Y MUST BE OVER-TRIMMED

A BOOM LIFTED 3 FT. COSTS 15% OF SAIL AREA

How to lessen heeling is a major reaching problem. Rollover is automatic in boats without vangs because of their need to over-trim the lower half of their mainsails, as in the first sketch. The second shows how the vang retains all effective sail area. Let a boom lift only three feet, and 15% of a mainsail's plan form disappears. In a blow when the boat must be sailed upright and driven fast, widening jib and mainsheet leads out to the rail also reduces heeling; first, by freeing the jib/mainsail slot, and secondly, by converting mainsheet tension into downpull upon the sail's after leach, which flattens that entire section and cuts its drag.

When trimming the mainsail on a broad reach, even if a vang holds the boom and headboard in one plane, the masthead fly-to-headboard angle is less useful as a guide than when going to windward. Upwind, the headboard and fly lie close together, and it is only necessary to keep them so. On wide reaches the fly swings well to leeward of the headboard, and with each shift of apparent wind this gap opens and shuts. The standard method of checking mainsail trim is for the sheetman to pay out until some spot on the sail, such as a sensitive part of the luff, begins to tremble. He then trims in slightly. Because a sail *looks* right, does not mean it is not too firm. It will warn by shaking whenever apparent wind draws ahead, but when it slides aft, the sail can overharden without the trimmer's knowledge.

On reaches an *Out-in* sequence of the mainsheet as the wind freshens, or *In-out* as it fades, replaces the small "S-ing" tiller shifts to windward. As explained in the chapter on *Wind,* upon entering a gust the educated sail trimmer expects to:

> Pay out the mainsheet
> Pull it in
> Pull in a bit more
> Pay back out to first setting

While on moving into a lull, he or she will:

> Pull in the mainsheet
> Pay out a little
> Pay out still more
> Pull back in to first setting

Angle of the spinnaker pole keeps step. With its pole close against the jibstay on reaches, a modern spinnaker sometimes draws better if the outer end is allowed to rise and encourage spread of the leaches. Leading the spinnaker sheet wide through a snatchblock at the end of the mainboom can defer the point at which it backwinds the mainsail, and becomes detrimental.

Because baggy sails give speed in soft air reaching, both clews and luffs should be adjustable while under way for extra fullness by easily slackened outhauls and downhauls. Across the wind there is little loss from parasitic drag, so in the interests of reaching with the boat upright, crew heads and tails may protrude freely. The closer the reach, the more dangerously a spinnaker can heel the boat. Several Small Point skippers have capsized when lowering them as a result of halyard or sheet snarls and their attempts to ease pressure by normal luffing, which the tugging spinnakers made impossible. In this predicament, before rolling over, a skipper must head *off with the wind,* not up.

In heavy going an alert helmsman can reduce heeling by bearing off smartly just before each gust strikes.

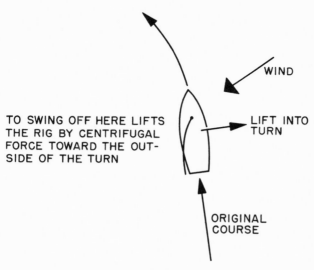

TO SWING OFF HERE LIFTS
THE RIG BY CENTRIFUGAL
FORCE TOWARD THE OUT-
SIDE OF THE TURN

WIND

LIFT INTO TURN

ORIGINAL COURSE

As the diagram shows, a quick pull on the tiller that drops the boat's head, generates enough centrifugal force (always acting toward the outside of a curving path) to lift the rig against the oncoming wind. Such stiffening is short lived, but valuable; the boat sits up well and can be luffed back to her course as the strong wind passes.

A Puff Chasing technique may also be tried whenever wind patterns of varying force dot the reaching leg. The principle is that by bearing off in each patch of fresher wind, one remains in them slightly longer than if the straight course were held. Next, upon emerging into a lull, by heading a like amount above normal, one passes more quickly through it and so into the next strong patch a bit sooner. Efforts to stay longer in strong air seem to produce more gains for displacement hulls under light conditions than under fresh, for when it is blowing hard, every course is a fast one and all may be near hull speed to begin with. Here is the pattern in its simplest form:

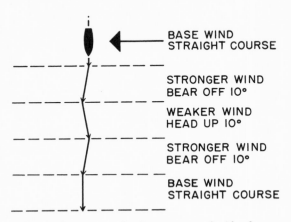

Here we have beam-reached across a shelf of stronger wind, then one of weak, then another of strong, but always of the same direction. The mathematics of Puff Chasing work out roughly thus: By bearing off 10° we stay 5% longer in the two strips of stronger air; and by heading 10° *above* normal, we cross the span of weaker wind 5% more quickly. The losses lie in extra distance sailed, which for these 10° zigzags cost only 2½%.

At first sight it should seem profitable to sail 2½% farther in order to stay 5% longer in strong air, and 5% less in weak; for our improved speed should be greater than 2½%. And some puff chasing experts *do* make it look that way, particularly on light days. Of course the matter is more complicated in a race, for wind seldom marches along in precise cuts of strong, weak, then strong. Again, the direct course to the mark may be the fastest reach, so all blind zigzagging is at lower speed and for the sake of cutting capers.

When attempting a break-through to windward skippers

must be skilled in the "mast abeam" maneuver, and ready to screech out loud and clear when this position is gained. It is worth a few inches to be steering from well forward: for Rule 38.1 stops a luffer when you, at your "normal station and sailing no higher" than he, reach his mast. A good mainsheet trimmer will keep the sail coming in and the boat driving throughout the entire procedure, while if being passed to windward, the same strong mainsheet arm can hold all but the fastest opponents astern.

If attempting the same breakthrough to leeward, extra speed is needed, first to push through the enemy's wake, then to escape his windshadow, which now drops well below what slides off his sails to windward. But NAYRU rules are here an aid, since under Rule 39, no one may bear down below his proper course to the next mark to interfere, after boats are within *three overall lengths* of each other. This would appear to limit Puff Chasing by windward boats, for those to leeward may well term such zigzags a "bearing down" upon them. Again, under Rule 38.2, once across the starting line, a boat overtaking to leeward and barred from luffing during that overlap, can, once she is forward of Mast Abeam, create a new overlap by widening out a hair beyond *two lengths* to leeward. Now if she angles back up, she is free to luff.

Reaching Practice Routines

1) It will reward both skipper and crew to go out alone and learn to reach their boat with minimum rudder. After selecting a mark, the bow is kept on it by trimming the mainsheet and shifting crew weight forward to increase weather helm, aft, to reduce it. At all times the hull is held level; while as each gust strikes, the helmsman bears away slightly to produce a counteracting centrifugal force.

2) An imitation reaching leg may now be sailed with compensation for current and a narrowing of this angle as the mark is closed. The following will be performed automatically: Outer jib and mainsheet leads in use; the mainsail flattened by

vang; a good man on the mainsheet, and active hull balancing by all hands through gusts and lulls.

3) With two boats reaching side by side, one will chase puffs, while the other holds the straight course. All hands on the puff-chaser now study force and dispersion of the wind patterns. Trimming sheets and hiking without order, they await word from the helmsman on when he will zig, and when zag. Puff chasing may not always gain, but trying it indicates to a crew the reaching activity needed on a winning boat.

4) Getting the spinnaker up and drawing on closer and closer reaches, until the tightest on which it improves speed is known. Dowsing the spinnaker on a reach must be fast, with care that no lines snag. To reduce the danger of a capsize, when they do, *head off*, not up.

Widest Gains Seen on Reaches

300 FEET A MILE on gusty days over boats without vangs.

23
BEFORE THE WIND, AND LIGHT SAILS

Twenty years ago racers considered running before the wind a "slide downhill in the sun." The only speculation was whether it would pay to reach out to the side at higher speed. Today the parachute spinnaker enlivens downwind legs. Boats run fast under these dramatic, multi-colored mushrooms; skill is needed to break out and keep them tugging; and because it is the crew, not the skipper alone, that tends them, the heady wine of competition fires the gullets of a wider group. Light sails are highly publicized, with Arthur Knapp stating that they win most of his races. George O'Day, the 5.5 Metre Class Olympic gold medalist, is hailed in the press as "Downwind O'Day." A master spinnaker tender can pick his berth in the Bermuda Race.

Among class boat sailors, however, skill close hauled still outranks ability downwind. The top manipulator of light sails does rank above the fast reacher.

How They Sail

Small Point skippers with green crews are likely to hop forward to hoist their own spinnakers, although few stay there to trim them down a full leg. Such assumption of all duties is open admission that the boat is not ready for tight competition.

When the last leg is a run to the finish, widely different courses are taken after the mark. Those in a cluster fight each other; leaders, by veering out to keep clear wind, close followers by chasing them to deny it. One or two hold low, or jibe away to what they trust is a faster heading. Because the blanket is even more popular in downwind racing than at a bundling party, and cutting an enemy's wind gives fierce joy, boats within striking distance of another's stern always aim for it, praying to collapse the front runner's sails and to drive by his windward side. When a pursuer overestimates the strength of his wind shadow, this attack may fail; but even its threat causes an off-course bend to windward by leading boats, which in turn encourages the second flight to head straight home to leeward.

Though greatly improved by 1973, downwind techniques in the Small Point fleet used to suffer from equipment deficiencies. Boats without vangs needed to hang a crew member out on the mainboom. Whisker poles were often too short, with spike ends that slipped out of jib clews—oars propped against the deck served others. Even today spinnaker gear is still diverse, and a good number of boats dispense with spinnaker topping lifts and forward guys. In light air these poles and sheets are heavy. enough to collapse a Mae West bosom into a dangling bed-sheet. Spinnaker sheets and guys average to be too short to reach from the billowing clew back to the stern, then forward to a trimmer's hand, for which two overall lengths of the boat are needed. Since 75% of the Small Pointers set their spin-nakers flying from sailbags, those who scorn a swivel at the top, often get theirs up twisted and have to claw it all down for a new start.

The helmsmanship of tail-enders before the wind is charac-terized by over-steering, with little effort to anticipate the rhythmic swing of a running boat's head. The wind may veer, sigh like a bride, or whistle "Yankee Doodle"; swells may lift first the stern, then the bow. Still they head straight on, until what asked only minor correction, demands a strong tiller pull. Heavy weather jibes under such harsh ruddering can produce dangerous broaching-to as the boom slaps over; while it is in the excitement of massed overlaps near the finish that weekend sailors achieve their most heroic and spinnaker-thrashing "snafus" due to inexperience with that paraphernalia.

Problems of Downwind Sailing

When parachute spinnakers are used, legs before the wind tend to be visualized solely as exercises in breakout, trimming, and dowsing that sail. Speed through the water under working sails on the several points of sailing is approximately at factors of: 3 to windward, 4 running free, and 5 on a beam reach. Because the close hauled boat zigzags, her time over a leg is further slowed to a factor of 2. The running boat, in contrast, speeds up under her parachute spinnaker, but not so much as popularly imagined, since a well handled competitor under only mainsail, jib and whiskerpole drops back less than a hundred yards a mile.

There is a feeling of warmth and reduced wind when running free. Where the close hauled boat, slanting at five knots into a fifteen knot breeze, whips nearly twenty knots of apparent wind into the faces of her crew, before it, her five knot hull speed is subtracted, so they feel only ten. Although spinnakers are termed "light sails," a fleet that can stand up to half a gale to windward without reefing, can carry spinnakers before it in the lessened apparent wind. Downwind skippers have few tiller/sheet corrections to make because of freshening or fading apparent winds. They do have to retrim both mainboom and spinnaker pole whenever true wind veers, but since it and boat-course virtually coincide, whether wind-force climbs or drops, its angular relationship with wind-over-the-bow alters very little. Where close hauled and reaching boats repeatedly suffer unbalanced apparent winds, and must correct by tiller or sheet, the running boat simply speeds up or slows down.

Small boat crews enjoy their freest movements before the wind, but their busiest moments. The hull sits level, with exposure of heads and ears to parasitic drag now favorable. The first job is to trim it for least resistance through the water. About 5° of heel to *windward* seems to be the best side to side angle to keep rudder forces low. Light sails become the prime concern. A crew is expected to have spinnaker pole, guy, and sheet laid out ready for use, to brail up the jib, to break out the spinnaker from its turtle, sail bag, or paper bag, and once it is drawing, to maintain level of the pole by its setting at the mast. If another leg follows, they put the jib back into operation near the downwind buoy, dowse and muzzle the spinnaker, and repack it for future use. Sitting well aft, the helmsman sees the fly angle well enough to trim the pole and guy himself. But his crew must jibe the spinnaker and help him horse in his mainsheet during emergency luffs. Certainly they should warn him of approaching enemies, state how he is positioned relative to wind shadows, and keep an alert eye for patches of fresher wind.

Some closing in by following boats may be expected on runs. Finish lines are usually off the clubhouse near shore in areas of deteriorating breeze. Once squared away around the last mark, the massed sails of a fleet spread their widest, and such a fence of mainsails and spinnakers can starve the wind of boats well out ahead and suffocate a single leader only four lengths clear. Choosing a course will involve knowledge of tide and of spots likely to furnish brisker air. Some prefer to reach downwind rather than to stay on the straight slide. Going out and back 20° costs $7\frac{1}{2}\%$ in extra distance, while widening to 40° makes the price 25%; so the helmsman must *know* a specific deviation will produce speed in excess of its extra yardage.

Once a crew has its spinnaker drawing, there is a tendency to concentrate upon those sensitive curves and to neglect mainsail trim. Yet each shift of the masthead fly that asks movement of the spinnaker pole must see the mainboom keep step. An aid to downwind trimming of both mainsail and spinnaker is a masthead fly with a colored ball as its counterpoise. The standard fly is invisible down in the cockpit when it trails out before the mast, but such a colored knob clearly warns by its angle whenever the wind swings in over the end of the mainboom, which will cut mainsail power 15%. It is important that the vang hold the mainsail flat and fully extended, but in light air too tight a vang can prevent the mainboom's going out all the way. As a further refinement, if the mainsail has been bagged by slackening its outhaul and downhaul, the gooseneck should be lifted and locked several inches high, otherwise vang tension will draw it back down and take fullness from the luff.

The basic spinnaker rig for small boats is shown herewith. The pole has quick-release end fittings that open remotely. Light Brummel hooks make good halyard, sheet and guy attachments that do not snag on stays. Each corner of the spinnaker should have its swivel. The pole is normally hooked

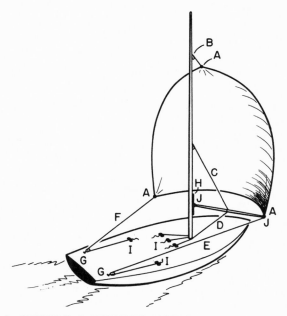

A- SWIVELS & BRUMMEL HOOKS
B- HALYARD 6" ABOVE JIBSTAY
C- TOPPING LIFT TO SUPPORT POLE
D- FORWARD GUY TO HOLD POLE DOWN
E- GUY
F- SHEET
G- FAIRLEADS WELL AFT WHERE HULL IS WIDE
H- TRACK OR EYES ON MAST
I - CAMCLEATS FOR HALYARD, LIFT, FORE GUY,
     SHEET & GUY
J- QUICK-RELEASE POLE END FITTINGS

over the guy itself, then pushed directly out against the sail's tack, although some spinnakers have two inch rings at either end into which the pole snaps directly.

Any system of hoisting and breaking out the spinnaker is satisfactory, provided it guarantees that everything goes up uncrossed and the sail is drawing the instant the windward mark is passed. Three methods commonly used on small boats are:

Flying—A majority of small racing boats set their spinnakers directly from sailbags, which are often tied to the foredeck. This does away with the nuisance of packing, and if the sail is hoisted in the lee of the mainsail it offers simplicity. It also offers uncertainty, for twists can develop. However, if the head of the spinnaker has a swivel, these can usually be worked out with the right blend of tugging and profanity.

Turtle—The Turtle, or folding box, allows convenient place-ment of a spinnaker forward, and puts it well in the clear at break-out, largely eliminating twists. Turtles were designed for boats with deck space forward of the jibstay, such as the In-ternational 210s. Some skippers pack their turtle and leave it

Spinnaker in box with all corners correctly rigged for quick release

on the bow throughout the race; some who are wind resistance conscious, only clip it there before the downwind leg. A plywood box with slotted sides has been developed for use on the Small Point One Designs. Such a box, when hooked to the deck near the lee shroud, allows hoisting the spinnaker outside the jib. In packing, the sail's three corners drop into appropriate cuts, and it is unnecessary to flake it down to any degree. First the red, or port lower corner, fits into the red slot; next the packer feels up along that leach, straightening as he goes until he comes to the head swivel, which he drops into the blue slot. Lastly, he proceeds down the right hand leach, to its green or starboard corner, which fills the green slot. Having three corners and two sides of a triangle without twist, the foot must also be straight.

In stops—It is rare to see a small spinnaker stopped up in thread, although this is standard on large boats and allows hoisting well before the mark. A substitute is the kraft paper bag with its bottom corners cut open for the two feet of the sail. After halyard, sheet, and guy are hooked on, and the sail wedged in tightly enough so that it will not flop out before being pulled, the packed paper bag is hauled aloft, where it swings out of the way as the mark is neared. When the pole is up, all that is needed is a tug on sheet or guy, which rips the bag and allows it to fall overboard; the sail drops and is whisked out by the wind, drawing at once; while, if sheet and guy have not intertwined, there will be no twist.

Spinnaker Preparation

Before the start it is generally possible to predict the side upon which the spinnaker will first be used, and to hook its halyard, sheet and guy there together on the deck. The ends of each line attaching to a spinnaker should be marked with colored tape for quick identification: red for the port sheet or guy, green for the starboard, and the halyard any other shade, such as blue. This eliminates error in snapping them into the sail. During the race a wind shift may make the side chosen for the halyard the wrong one. But it is easy to pass all three Brummel hooks around the jibstay if they are joined together. With the halyard taut enough to prevent the lines dropping under the bow, if the sheet on the side that is being left is freed, and pull given on the side to which it must go, all three hooks pass smoothly around, without recourse to crew weight on the foredeck. There is more challenge when only one item, such as the halyard alone, is on the wrong side. But by tying on a light weight, such as a shoe, and slinging this out ahead, it can be made to swing back down the desired side of the jib.

Breaking Out the Spinnaker

When near the windward mark all hoisting and breaking out of the spinnaker is best performed by the crew under their own timing and routines. The tendency is to delay until the mark is alongside, which is far too slow.

Hooking on Halyard, Sheet and Guy—100 Yards Out

After the box has been clipped to the deck outboard of the lee jib sheet, the three Brummel hooks are snapped into appropriate corners of the sail. With plenty of time to check that spinnaker sheet and guy both lead clear of the jib, and that the halyard goes up free all the way to its block, whoever is responsible will now sing out: "All leads clear!"

Getting Up the Pole—50 Yards Out

The pole is placed on the deck, where if flat-sided, it will not roll. Some like to have its end fitting open upwards, others down. The spinnaker guy is now snapped into the end fitting, and the pole lifted by its toppinglift and fixed to the mast. Once the forward, or down guy, has been adjusted, the spinnaker sheet should be cleated at some approximation of its first setting, so that during the seconds when the sail is breaking out, attention may be diverted 100% to pulling the pole aft by its guy. The pole is now ready; and if *all its lines are snug*, it will not swing wide during a tack to touch another boat to leeward.

Hauling Up the Sail—Beside the Mark

Getting the spinnaker aloft takes only a few seconds when the halyard has a camcleat. A mark is needed on the halyard to warn when it is up to within a foot of the top, so that the hoister never has to look aloft. All hoisting should be complete before the mark is turned, and in light air this can be done by holding both leaches together and allowing the nylon center to flap gently without opening.

The Break Out—Immediately After Rounding

A pull of some six feet on the loose guy now snugs the spinnaker clew out against the pole fitting and draws the leach forward and clear of the forestay. A few more feet swings the pole aft to its right angle versus the masthead fly. At this point the helmsman of a two-man crew may wish to take over pole control, while his helper sits forward on the lee side to watch the sail and tickle it into lifting by the sheet.

Brailing the Jib

It only remains for the crew to reach forward when convenient and brail up the jib. A simple brailer is a foot of elastic shockcord with a snap-hook on one end and a clothespin on the other. The hook goes into the eye of the jib clew, the cord wraps around the jibstay, while the clothespin fastens back over the jibsheet, where any sharp pull will release it.

Spinnaker Trim

Standard spinnaker trim keeps the pole as a direct extension of the main boom, and both at right angles to the mast-

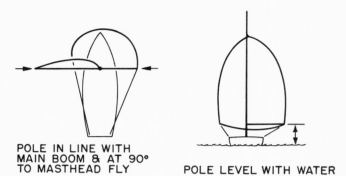

POLE IN LINE WITH
MAIN BOOM & AT 90°
TO MASTHEAD FLY   POLE LEVEL WITH WATER

head fly. The pole is also held parallel to the water by altering its height at the mast. Modern spinnakers draw best if they are encouraged to lift, spread their leaches, and assume the shape of a half apple. This means that the pole attachment to the mast may look unnecessarily high.

Some feel that a spinnaker will splay itself out more powerfully if, as the wind rises, its halyard is loosened so that the top of the sail moves forward into fresher air well clear of the mainsail, or as much as twenty-four inches. The relative importance of spinnaker sheet trim versus that of pole and guy is also questioned. A few crews neglect the sheet, even fasten it and attempt all trimming by pole angle. Both are important tools and needed to stop curl-in of the edges. Rarely can the helmsman forget masthead fly angle for five seconds without damage to spinnaker trim. Once a spinnaker collapses, it can cost ten seconds and loss of a boat length to get it hard again. Whenever edge pucker appears, a sharp tug upon sheet or guy, or upon both together, will harden it momentarily.

Since the guy leads inboard from a rigid pole, it is unimportant how far aft it goes. The spinnaker sheet, however, should not only run to the widest point on the deck, but having it lead far aft may promote lifting of the sail. On many boats the boom is so low that it forces a spinnaker sheet down and destroys all benefit of such aft lead. Here it can help to rig a snatch-block in the end of the mainboom, which will give spread to the spinnaker sheet. The spinnaker will pull best when its maximum area is on its own side of the boat, unshadowed by the mainsail. This asks a pole of full class length.

Jibing the Spinnaker

There is little loss in the standard small boat spinnaker jibe.

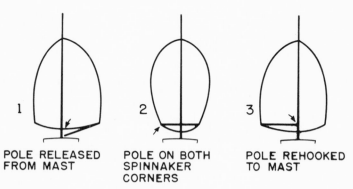

POLE RELEASED
FROM MAST

POLE ON BOTH
SPINNAKER
CORNERS

POLE REHOOKED
TO MAST

First, one of the crew reaches forward as the mainboom crosses over (ducking the vang) and unhooks the spinnaker pole from the mast. This leaves the pole fast only to the old guy-end of the sail. The pole is now clipped over what was the old sheet, and will be the new guy, and snugged out against the sail. At this intermediate point it is attached to both clews. Lastly, the other end is freed by its remote control cord, and hooked into the mast. When the new guy and sheet are both trimmed, the jibe is complete. The maneuver should be run through time after time, first to one side, then back to the other, until it is quite automatic and can be completed, with the sail handler's attention elsewhere, *within 8 seconds.*

Some skippers prefer the free-wheeling jibe in which the pole never leaves the mast. Instead, as the mainboom goes over, it is unclipped from the old guy-end of the spinnaker, then lifted or dropped inside the jibstay and rehooked to the opposite corner. With a wide foretriangle the pole can easily pass the jibstay; with a short one, it must point to the stars.

The trick in all spinnaker jibes is in rehooking the pole over the new guy and easing it out against the sail, without having to pull the spinnaker clew down into the cockpit and collapsing it. A long ape-arm or light bamboo stick will help to snag the flying spinnaker sheet as it lifts far out to leeward.

Spinnaker Dowsing

After his first battle with a spinnaker in heavy weather, the beginner is likely to view dowsing as a melodramatic experience. To tug a surging nylon monster in under a low boom, while the downwind mark looms alongside, the boat over-heels, and an iron vang compresses his chest, seems to demand superhuman balance and skill. Some who fight to smother a still-drawing spinnaker have their skulls creased by flying swivels, or tow it all overboard. Nevertheless, dowsing a spinnaker *can* proceed smoothly, given only practice and the care to see that all lines run freely.

In under the boom—Taking a spinnaker in beneath the boom to leeward is standard lowering, and the only type practical when the wind is not squarely aft. Distance out from the mark can be reduced with experience, after a start at some fifty yards, in this fashion:

Unbrail the jib and set its sheet for the next leg. Release the guy, so that the pole seeks the forestay and the spinnaker flags off to leeward. If the end fitting on the pole is opened, a few extra feet of guy are gained which may be just enough to take all bag from the sail; but if it still tugs hard and away from the sheltering mainsail, it may pay to let the entire guy snake out through its camcleat and fairlead, providing of course, that it will not whip away to foul a leeward boat. The pole may now be disregarded and taken down later.

With arm or boathook, snatch the spinnaker sheet, which will be pointing straight away from the lee rail. With the other hand, pull the spinnaker halyard free from its camcleat and commence lowering. Draw the corner of the flagging spinnaker into the cockpit, while paying out halyard a foot at a time.

As the halyard runs out, the sail will slip down. Once started, it slumps fast. For the first few pulls it may seem that everything must be blown back and overboard, particularly if the boat is heeling. It must not be ripped against boom fittings. But if draft has been destroyed and it is kept close to the mainsail, the spinnaker will now race straight in with little or nothing touching the water.

Take down and stow the spinnaker pole. Unsnap sheet, guy and halyard, hook them back together, and reposition for future use. If necessary, repack the sail.

Down over the windward bow—When the wind is directly aft, Arthur Knapp suggests this dowsing, which brings the spinnaker down with so little tug that it may be carried almost up to the mark:

Unbrail the jib and set its sheets for the next leg.

Lean out to leeward, grasp the spinnaker sheet, and pull it in enough to unsnap its Brummel hook from the corner of the sail. The spinnaker will now fly out dead ahead of the boat, without draft, and held only by its halyard and pole.

Drop the pole into the cockpit, and snatching the guy as it leaves the pole, start lowering the halyard. As the halyard pays out, pull the spinnaker down aboard, first by the guy, then by the foot of the sail when it can be reached. It will pass in through the open gap to windward of the jib in an area of fine visibility, and with no more fuss than a large flag—*provided* the wind is dead astern.

Replacing Halyard, Sheet and Guy, and Repacking the Spinnaker

In many races the spinnaker is used several times. So after a first dowsing the crew must repack it and reposition its lines, all of which involves an understanding of where those lines presently lead.

Note that after a conventional under-the-boom dowsing, the spinnaker halyard, sheet and guy all run into the cockpit *aft* of the lee shroud. In replacing them upon the foredeck it is very easy to wrap the halyard inside, and *around* the shroud, which will royally foul up any subsequent hoisting. Also, if the guy has been allowed to snake out completely, it must now be rewoven and its Brummel hook slipped back out around the jibstay.

After a down-over-the-bow, or Knapp dowsing, halyard and guy lie on what was the windward side. But the old spinnaker sheet, having been detached to leeward at the start, must now be passed outside the lee shroud, then forward and around the jibstay to rejoin them, or they around to it, according to where the spinnaker will next be used.

Repacking the spinnaker in its turtle, box, or paper bag, is no problem if the receptacle can be firmly seated and the boat is not in heavy going. Any free half minute will serve.

Tiller Work and Tactics Before the Wind

If a relief helmsman is available, *if* there is room in the cockpit to exchange helmsmen, and *if* the hated enemy are not too close and too crafty, it sometimes pays to relieve the most experienced sailor for duty on light sails at the start of a spinnaker run. But whoever steers, all hands try to ease the boat's rudder by actively trimming both mainsail and spinnaker against the masthead fly.

During a jibe, with the crew busy at the spinnaker, the skipper hands in his own mainsheet. And if he will half rise, wedging the tiller between his knees, he has both hands free to pull it. The trick is to get the mainsail in fast, steering just high of the jibing course; then in dropping down to it as the mainboom slams over, to curve back a few degrees, while paying out the mainsheet *even faster* on the new side, as a counter against the boat's strong surge into the wind. A vang is needed to hold the boom low. If it flips high enough to let the mainsail leach wrap about the lee shroud, a goosewing jibe, followed by a capsize, may result. If it lifts only a few feet in crossing the centerline, it can crash the permanent backstay and shiver the mast. When the breeze is not heavy, the mainsheet may be handed in and released all in one piece without bothering to take it in through its blocks. In very light air the mainsail may be *jerked in hard,* which nudges the boat a foot or two ahead. But it should be paid out ever so gently in order not to press the sail against a cushion of air and lose the gain.

In the matter of tactics, the best skippers try for clear wind and minimum involvements running free. All boats are handicapped by their light sails, and the decision to luff a single opponent who is gnawing at one's tail, can hold back only him, while losing several lengths to fifteen others. The time to luff and start aggressive spinnaker jibes is just short of the finish line. Only if one's own crew is clearly superior to the fleet can offensive operations be undertaken down an entire leg. All hands should practice using their windshadow as a dagger. But when overtaking dead before the wind they must remember the danger berth from which none can escape.

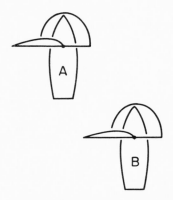

Boat A is about to be blanketed, yet she can luff head to the wind with the certainty of striking boat B, or of wrapping her up in her own spinnaker. Such a luff should be started before A is greatly slowed by B, and during it, A's spinnaker pole must slide smoothly forward to keep her footing.

Any helmsman wishing to pass to leeward should know Rule 39, which stops a windward yacht from bearing off to block him when the boats are within *three overall* lengths. Also, as already explained, once a leeward overtaking yacht draws forward of Mast Abeam, to gain luffing rights she has only to jibe away, then back, or to widen out beyond *two lengths,* both of which give her a new overlap and the right to luff.

It is well to plan downwind legs that will insure a starboard tack at the finish. If one's own crew is agile, a quick lurch there toward any port tackers can make them jibe into a delightful turmoil of flapping sails and twisted sheets. Converging sharply from the lee will bring similar confusion to windward boats. While all are calling out, but none knowing exactly who has luffing rights over whom, the happy spinnaker tender who keeps his boat driving can cause more ruin than Casanova in a girls' convent.

Downwind Practice Routines

These downwind maneuvers should be run through until execution is perfect within the times assigned:
The Whiskerpole—Setting and removing a whiskerpole—3 seconds. Jibing it—5 seconds.
Preparing spinnaker halyard, sheet and guy—These three lines to be clipped together in one spot on the side where they will next be used. Shifting them to the opposite side to be practiced; also tying a weight to the spinnaker halyard and swinging it out ahead of the jibstay, and so to the other side.
Breaking out the spinnaker—The spinnaker to be hoisted in varying wind strengths: flying from its sailbag, from turtle or notched box, and from a paper bag. All lines to be snapped on 100 yards out. The pole to be in place 50 yards out. Once the spinnaker is up, it should break out without twist time after time, and draw well within—5 seconds.
Jibing the spinnaker—This routine to be practiced until release, rehooking of the pole, and subsequent trimming of the new guy and sheet are automatic. The helmsman will hand in his own mainsheet, insure that the boom does not lift in crossing, and check the boat's tendency to broach as she swings onto

her new jibe. Because this maneuver sharpens downwind attack and defense, it should be letter perfect within—8 seconds.

Dowsing the spinnaker—Both under-the-boom and down-over-the-windward-bow. The sail to flag away flat, and its halyard to slip freely, so that everything is down in the cockpit and nothing drags overboard—10 seconds.

Repacking the spinnaker—To replace the spinnaker in its turtle or box, free of twist for later use, by matching the sail's colored tablings into the proper slots, and exploring two leaches, or one leach and the foot—30 seconds.

The effect of wind shadows—With a friendly boat alongside, wind shadows to be passed through and directed against one another, until their possibilities for harm are established.

Luffing and combatting luffs—Two boats running side by side under spinnakers to determine the closest approach that can safely be made to the leeward boat's windward quarter, should she luff head to the wind. Luffs to be carried from simple feints to 180°, with each boat trimming sails in an endeavor to hold speed.

Gain vs loss from off course reaching—With two boats running side by side, one to hold the direct course, while the other reaches away, then back at progressively wider angles. The deviation at which best gains are made to be noted.

WIDEST LOSSES OBSERVED BEFORE THE WIND

300 FEET A MILE for uncontested sailing.
But 450 FEET A MILE when trailing boats fight luffers, collapse their own spinnakers, or tow them overboard.

24 ROUNDING MARKS

The garden sailor pays small attention to rounding marks. A mark is something to be shaved closely, but not hit.

Racers like to approach windward marks on the starboard tack for its right of way. Since experience tends to err toward safety, we see more windward marks over-stood, than under-stood. Exact timing of the final swing-over to fetch is by sea-man's eye, with less than one in fifty using tacking lines or any sighting device.

Downwind marks are brought close aboard and when the helmsman sees his bow is well by, he puts down the rudder. The result is a "U" path, with the mark alongside at the start and well to windward at the end. There are frequent fouls at downwind marks, since it is easy to dog a leader's stern so closely that when he shifts his helm and slows in the act of rounding, a follower surges up and can only try to wedge in between him and the mark. Sloppy sheet-to-tiller coordination distinguishes second flight boats at marks. With a windward leg coming up, the skipper whose attention is diverted by enemies may end ten yards low, while boats just astern cut well inside.

Some Problems of Mark Rounding

Upwind marks—To limit the chance of over-standing, experienced sailors like to sail their first long hitch in the direction closest to the mark. When forced by local geography to stand away early, their safeguard is to *know* from experience, not from guess, exactly how far to go. Eighty per cent of a fleet make their final slant to a mark under protection of the starboard tack. If there are strong reasons for coming out from the left it may still be possible to thread into a line of starboard tackers fifty yards below the buoy. The closer in this is attempted, the more it becomes a red rag to starboard tack bulls, who will struggle to prevent it, although they may not balk. A perfectly timed tack that barely fetches a mark 400 yards away usually conceals one or two lengths of over-standing that the helmsman regains by heading low and footing fast. From one hundred yards out a practiced seaman's eye can be accurate to within ten feet. Most skippers bring windward marks abeam, or slightly aft, before tacking. Choice of the instant at which to come about involves several allowances: tide may be fair or foul, which from a hundred yards can make a course fifteen feet too high or low. In heavy swells government buoys have a nasty habit of jumping out toward passing boats, so a six foot clearance is little enough. If the wind has been shifty, the normality of present heading may be suspect, and a helmsman well below his proper course may be unable to fetch a mark brought directly abeam. Occasionally a boat is fortunate enough to have no one above, but several below her who can not tack until she does. In this case she should defer coming about until there is no risk whatever of failing to fetch. When she does tack, the others will probably stand on for a length to clear their wind, all of which will be loss if she can round with started sheets.

Downwind marks—The manner in which sailboats turn causes major difficulties in rounding downwind marks. The green helmsman thinks as he follows in another's wake, that should the leader turn sharply, he may do the same, while holding his interval as if the boats were toy railroad cars moving along a track. This is not so. The turning maneuver of any boat, from skiff to ocean liner is a complicated process due to the fluid medium that supports her. When a sailboat's helm is put down she squashes sideways and slows down. A phenomenon that the Navy calls "Advance and Transfer" occurs, in which the boat heels and pivots about her rotation center, a point not always clear to the helmsman. Now as the bow swings up, her stern goes broad, blocking any close following boat until she regathers way and curves about the buoy.

This marked slow-down in sailboat turns puts close pursuers in jeopardy. If they sit off the leader's counter without an agreed overlap, they must suddenly kill way, which is impossible running free. One thing is certain: as the leader's helm goes over at the mark his stern will swing wide, and the follower, catching up six feet in a hurry, faces emergency selection from: a) Squeezing above the leader, either between him and the mark, or above the mark. b) Ramming into his quarter. c) Veering out to leeward, assuming others there are ready to give him room. Any contact constitutes an open foul under Rule 42 1(b)(i) which warns a boat clear astern to anticipate the maneuver of rounding.

The Fastest Track Around Downwind Marks

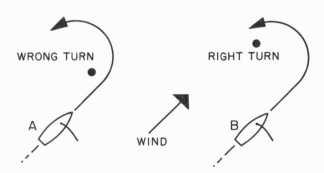

Marks are normally rounded in a "U," with the mark passed close alongside at the beginning. By shaving close by, the helmsman feels he will prevent others from cutting inside him. The disadvantage is that when this turn is completed, he lies well to leeward, as in A. But the end of B, the proper turn, leaves a boat squarely beside the mark with nothing lost downwind. To achieve this advantage a helmsman must know the size of his turning circle. At good speed it will average about one boat length, so he must start his swing that far to the side if he is to end by, not below the mark. In close quarters, with an adversary directly on his tail, a skipper may fear to swing so far out, lest the other cut in and establish an overlap that entitles him to room. This makes it vital to hold a pursuer clear astern until the mark is reached. 1973 NAYRU Rule 42 2(a) continues to prohibit edging in after the leader is within *two overall lengths* of the mark, unless, as in 42 2(b) the following boat has just completed a tack within two lengths of the mark and established its overlap, or in any case, after he is too close to obstruction to give room safely. About forty feet out therefore becomes a critical spot at which the leader of two small boats must either shake off, or concede, a continuing overlap. If clear here, his problem is reduced to executing his turn so that the follower can only swing in astern or below him, and so be subject to backwind. Now as both boats descend the last few yards to the mark, if the follower holds out to windward, or in his wake, the leader is not forced to widen out for the proper 'U' turn, since the follower can do no better. But the moment the follower swings wide, the leader must do so too, since if he stays close and lets the other make the proper turn, he will end to leeward, pinned down and unable to tack.

From the follower's standpoint, once it is clear he has not gained his inside overlap at two lengths out, he must prepare to leave half a length for the catch-up that will result when the leader puts down his helm. In veering wide, he hopes that the leader scrapes close by the mark and makes the improper turn that leaves him to leeward. If this happens, the follower swings high inside and into control. But should the leader know his business and turn correctly, the follower will find himself squarely astern, fluttering in backwind, and must tack free at once before he slows down and finds others sliding up to make it impossible.

It is important to maintain good speed in hardening up around downwind marks to close hauled courses. This asks a smooth rudder force, so main and jib sheets must come in just a mite ahead to lift the boat to her tightest angle. One of the crew will tail in the mainsheet to established marks. No helmsman can swing his boat up smartly single handed on tiller and sheet, while with one eye he watches the opposition, with another the masthead fly, and with a third gauges the final heading. Boats astern enjoy the advantage of witnessing a leader's progress. If this is bad, they will surely pinch high inside to escape his backwind and to hold him in their lee.

Rules Problems at Marks

Windward marks produce few complicated hassles, although on occasion boats that pinch and try to squeeze in between opponents, lose way and strike the mark. The 1973 Rules no longer allow an underwater part to be grazed, even the ground tackle.

Rights of a port tack boat approaching a downwind mark on the inside are similar to those of an overlapped windward boat rounding an upwind mark. They are both entitled to *room in the rounding* and to nothing more. Either may be carried the wrong side of the mark if the carrier does not turn it herself.

Monumental jams at downwind marks accompany late demands for room by followers who have made no allowance for the slow-down of leaders in the rounding maneuver. The followers charge up and can only avoid contact by pulling along a leader's windward side. They now try to force between him and the mark, screaming all the while for "Room" as if they had established a proper overlap at two lengths out. Competitors nearing marks should always obtain voice agreement as to their relative positions. The helmsman with his hands full may wish to delegate such shouting to his crew. The leading boat will certainly pass word back that an overlap has *not* been established at the critical two-lengths. It is even more important for a follower to secure agreement that one *is* established and that he expects room. If no agreement is obtained and a collision ensues, the Protest Committee can only decide under Rule 42 2(d)(ii), that it *was not* established in time.

The first boat around a downwind mark may not safely tack with less than a one length lead. If she goes over from port to starboard, she must fill away on her new course and still leave a boat astern opportunity to keep clear. If from starboard to port, she must clear the other entirely. In no case does a following port tacker even have to *start* keeping clear until the leader's sails fill on her new starboard tack; nor does she have to be a slippery eel then. If the follower only *thinks* he had to dodge before that time, the leader must be disqualified for tacking too close. Any leader who suspects he is short of footage for a safe tack should apply enough backwind to drop a follower into his wake before coming about. When the course to the next mark lies back to windward through a press of boats under light sails, a leader will be well advised to hail loudly from fifty yards out. They will be deep in their own distractions, and even if they do not hit him, will be delighted to blanket him and make him think they may.

Practice Routines for Turning Marks

Skipper and crew should devise and check-sail a method of sighting windward marks a hundred yards distant that will establish the instant at which to tack for them. A safety factor of half a boat length on the starboard tack, and one and a half on the port to be allowed. Error must not exceed fifteen feet.

On reaching and running legs, efforts to gain the inside berth must be started within 200 yards of the mark. To slow down and ease across sterns may require abnormal sheet trimming.

Offwind practice by two boats to establish the normal catch-up in that class when a leader's helm is put hard down to round. The boat following six feet astern will attempt to stay in track without collision. If this is impossible, how to cut wide is learned.

Two boats to approach a downwind mark, one fighting to gain and the other to prevent an inside overlap. Both crews to exchange information and to give or refuse room according to rights established up to two boat lengths out from the mark.

A pattern for rounding downwind marks to be practiced, involving the proper "U" turn, in which a boat ends beside the mark as her swing is completed, not as it starts.

Two crews and their helmsmen to practice smooth round-

ings of a downwind mark until they can keep their boats footing fast as they climb to tightest effective headings. The crews
to firm in sheets, the helmsmen to check masthead flies, until
the loss in yards between a good and a bad rounding is clear.

Two boats after rounding a mark in column to establish the
minimum separation that will let one swing over, either to starboard or port, and still clear a follower just astern. As a variation, the safe interval to be halved and the leader to apply
backwind in an effort to widen out to safe tacking distance.

LOSSES OBSERVED AT MARKS

At windward marks—60 FEET when port tackers are blocked,
or when boats fail to fetch.

At leeward marks —45 FEET when boats round poorly and
let others sneak in above them.

25 LIGHT AIR

Racing in light air is not thought a separate technique. Sailors reared in the fresh breezes of Buzzards Bay and Cape Cod scorn Long Island Sound for its drifting matches and think these make the sport a guessing game. Long Island Sounders, however, feel that their search for zephyrs stimulates the intellect and introduces an element of mind over matter.

Few racers change their basic methods in light air. They simply curse the lack of wind. Those who expect gentle going set their lightest sails, bagging them to some degree, and often when a breeze blows up during the afternoon they regret the choice. When the weather looks unsettled, one or two "scientists" will telephone the Weather Bureau or local airport for a forecast, hoping to crystal-ball the direction of any new wind. After the start these watch the horizon for signs, particularly for steamer smoke, and will ease toward parts of the course where fresher air has been met in the past. The average competitor struggles through a light wind race, trusting to luck, expecting his own to be bad, and watching other boats to see which are unjustly favored. When those at a distance find livelier air, skippers with pliant dispositions edge toward them. But the majority, who take pride in their own devices and prefer winning once to placing second five times, plod straight along, hoping the Lord will eventually favor them as they deserve. Which He commonly does.

Problems in Light Air

How to progress in light air repays study, if only because of its frequency. One summer race in six begins in faint going, few are cancelled, so to win a season's championship, better than average finishes must be obtained on glassy water.

Calms are exasperating. But it is the best fighters who win in them. They stick out the annoyance, keep alert, and don't hack about in their boats. The problem becomes one of getting all of what wind there is. A boat that can snare one lift that eludes the fleet will ghost out thirty yards. Let her slide into several, and she will lie an uncatchable hundred yards toward the next freshening slant, which is most likely to appear from the general direction of the old wind.

In light going it stimulates a crew to prospect for wind. On sunny days air often whispers in at right angles across a beach as the heated land sucks it off cooler water. When wind blows off a rocky shore it takes little magic to predict a dead spot below each steeper pitch. Whenever a soft breeze angles in against a high island, it tends to reinforce and to swing parallel to the sides. As they crawl along, crews should search out the dark traces of surface wind. Passage may be sought among them, but it is not necessary to sail through the middle of each ruffling. Close alongside may do, for the wind can be blowing there six feet over the water, as the masthead fly will indicate.

Racers are inclined to view wind marks on a glassy surface as capricious and likely to ease along with available breeze. If we visualize wind as moving in horizontal strata, this may be unrealistic. Down-knuckles from a stream of active air twenty yards overhead often persist in one spot for minutes. Sailors who picture wind as one compact mass, think that traces to windward must come on to them. But those ripples may show an elbow that curves down there alone, much as a burble on the surface of a brook reflects some snag behind and below it. In practical racing we get more wind by easing toward its signposts, than by trusting these will come to us.

The masthead fly is a valuable sail trimming check, particularly one on a boat fifty yards distant. Cigarette smoke whirls away accurately, too, if kept clear of the downdraft beneath the boom. A cigar, or piece of 4th of July lighting punk fastened to the shrouds, is even better, and can counsel sheet adjustments when the sails seem incapable of any thrust at all.

Equipment

A light boat and a flyweight crew are thought best in zephyr sailing. Yet some heavy boats ghost well when the sea is flat and they are sailed to hold good momentum. Under drifting conditions bottom slickness pays its best dividends, and barnacles or algae are criminal cargo. Since any small boat can be heeled against the club float, and only a scrubbing brush is needed to remove them, the twenty minutes by which a weed laden boat otherwise loses can be better spent here.

The largest, filmiest working sails with the widest roaches that will stand are aids in a near calm. Yet sometimes then a midget spinnaker can be made to swell and draw when all fat Mae Wests collapse. Light weather cut by sailmakers is on the full side, so to windward, if outhauls are fully slack, it is possible to over-bag a sail until pointing ability is lost. A special light air jib with flowing curves can ease its boat along while others "stand and wait." Fishcord sheets help jibs and spinnakers to lift and pull. Some small boats that omit the spinnaker pole toppinglift, find under flat conditions that the weight of even a light pole droops these sails. Flexible battens, thin at their inner ends, form the mainsail leach into smoother curves. The masthead fly must be sensitive and fairly large.

Light Weather Sailing Techniques

Boat speed in "light calms" results from full sails, sheeted well out, and the boat kept moving. It is fatal to pinch with sheets trimmed extra flat, as for strong winds and smooth water. The very expert Mrs. Pat Duane sets the stops of her Flying Dutchman mainsheet traveller to windward, then trims gently to the center of the boat to keep a rounded sail. Extremely high headers do not slide well when it is glassy. By contrast, the fast footer who appears to be eeling along well below course can move toward any new wind that appears. One Small Point One Design, not otherwise outstanding, may be seen ghosting away when everyone else lies dead. Her mainboom sits far out as if for reaching. As she gains momentum and points higher for twenty yards her sail comes in gently, only to be eased out again as she drops off, slowing but still moving.

Leeward heel 5° lets sails hang to their designed fullness. Some experts sail upright in a calm; but their records generally show them to be more successful in high winds. Movement within the cockpit must not be permitted to slat the sails; in an oily swell the vang is a useful preventer. Because a jib is more sensitive in light air than a mainsail, some helmsmen choose a lifting spot on the jib luff and steer by it from the lee side. The masthead fly is then difficult to see; but once a boat is whispering along, her loosened jib makes an acceptable heading gauge.

On first sliding into each glassy expanse, some forward shift of apparent wind must be anticipated, which will force a lower heading. Compounded to crawling speed, such a drop-off in course is exasperating, but it will plague all boats, and part of the loss may be regained by carefully easing up into the face of every catspaw. When the next mark lies in a mirror of calm it can pay to overstand by as much as fifty yards down any arm of fresher wind that will permit subsequent approach under slightly started sheets.

Raceways of foul tide, which in light air stop a boat dead, must be avoided. Conversely, it is doubly pleasing to float along in fair tide. When a mark sits in foul current it should be passed several boat lengths before tacking to round; such precautions may seem ridiculous until one drifts helplessly down upon one. The watchful skipper who notes an expanding glassiness beyond the starting line will thereafter sail no more than twenty yards from his crossing spot; in extreme cases twenty feet may be too much.

Tiller action in lulls is the gentlest possible; one finger being enough to guide a trailing rudder. When tacking, the helm should go down smoothly, leaving no ripples. Retention of hull momentum is important, and when the crew shift their weight, it should be done cautiously. When possible, tacks may be started within a puff to insure recapturing way. Jibing in calms can be done without loss by tugging the mainsail in hard, then easing it out very slowly. This will urge the boat a foot or two ahead. The opposition will grow sarcastic if it is done repeatedly near the finish line; but any single jibe must be performed to advance, not hinder the boat.

A minor relaxation in Racing Rules is conventional in dead calms to the extent of poling boats apart and clear of marks, but this does not apply when there is steerage way. In very light air a port tacker about to swing over to lee-bow a starboard tacker, must allow for the extra slowness of the maneuver and the fact that the other does not have to even *start* to keep clear until he fills away; perhaps a matter of twenty seconds.

Practice Routines in Light Air

Since luck is a critical factor in exploiting new wind, experienced competitors do not expect to shine like the Star of Bethlehem in every light weather race. On occasion the most arrant plumber will bumble home first, while top sailors sit becalmed. This pleases the tailenders and keeps them racing.

Pre-Race Matters—The boat's bottom must be absolutely clean —if possible, sponged off the morning of the race.

All non-essential items will be removed. To hold weight low, the purist skipper may order his crew to eat a light lunch and leave their shoes in the dinghy.

Sails should be adjusted to smooth, easy curves, using flexible battens and light jib and spinnaker sheets.

During the race—The value of any light weather practice is most clear when two boats sail side by side, one following it, the other doing exactly the opposite. Such matters include an outboard trim of sheets to keep the boat moving easily; footing, not pinching, to conserve hull momentum, and all tacks made to retain headway. In the search for wind, areas known to contain more of it to be passed through, and dark surface traces sought out. Cigarette smoke and the masthead flies on nearby boats seen as the prime wind indicators. The progress of boats on either side of the fleet to be kept under study, and own path adjusted without warning opponents nearby.

Maximum Light Weather Losses

Two boats will occasionally drift around a mark side by side, one find wind, the other a vacuum, and the first glide away to win by a full leg.

But average loss under drifting conditions through pinching and relaxed concentration is in the nature of:

100 FEET A MILE

26

HEAVY WEATHER

Those who enjoy smashing through high winds and breaking seas are classed with Tarzan and the Missing Link. Best equipment is thought to be a heavy boat, a heavier duff, and undersized sails.

It is the old timers who glorify racing in heavy weather, particularly those who have been to sea. They think it the most exciting, character-building part of the sport. Ladies do not like storms. They get wet and their hands hurt holding sheets. Children either delight in, or fear them. Parents worry about their offspring being mashed in collisions and crushed beneath falling masts.

How They Sail in a Gale

If it is stormy outside the harbor, those obstinate enough to race, put on their best face, sway halyards up hard, bring no special equipment except an odd slicker, and plan to keep sails as flat as possible. Caution will be observed at starts and marks when seas are cresting badly and gusts go over forty. Some undertake a bit of feathering, but not on a practiced basis, for the old fisherman's idea, that the best man carries the most sail, endures. There is much scrambling, hiking and yelling, and what bailing is possible. All get wet, and a fifth of them enjoy it.

One boat in four will experience gear failure. The commonest thing to break is the jib halyard, which wears as it goes over the halyard sheave on the mast. Occasionally at downwind marks we hear an ominous "Cra-ack" as of monster eggshells,

293

when overlapped hulls kiss in rounding. Once a season some beginner capsizes in a goosewing jibe, or fills up after failure to ease his mainsheet in a gust. Officials who start a race under gale conditions always are criticised when the fleet struggles back in, doused and bedraggled; especially if it rained hard earlier in the day or the sky was black at gunfire. They should have known better!

Problems of Heavy Weather Sailing

If we had to choose between skill in heavy and light weather, we should certainly take the light, since drifting matches out-number days when the sea roars for giants. Probably not more than two races will start in big blows each summer, while waves high enough to swamp a poorly sailed boat may build up dur-ing three more. Often when it storms or a thundersquall threat-ens, small boat contests are put over. Even a twenty-five knot breeze—in which a flag rattles straight out—can cancel them.

But when the taunt of "Come on, chicken-heart!" prevails, and the sky looks dark, it is best to check all gear. The most dangerous failures occur in stays and mast tangs, which should be examined at the dock. Jumper struts and jumper stays are easily checked and tightened there. Main shroud turnbuckles will occasionally be found to lack cotterpins or to have loos-ened on one side of the boat. If sheets show wear where they chafe in their camcleats, they can be changed end for end. Of course the boat will be sponged dry, and buckets and bailing cans supplied for emergency use underway. If a big sea is run-ning outside in which the mast might conceivably be lost, a good towline and anchor are necessities. Slickers are important for the crew who sit forward and absorb green water. At Larch-mont the boys who fear a dunking warn: "Don't bring your good watch, bring your mother-in-law." Lastly, when the wind is really howling in the rigging make sure that a committee boat will follow the race, and discourage beginners from com-peting. Have them crew for others.

Hulls—A heavy hull is thought at its best in rough weather on

the grounds that it will hold more momentum through breaking waves. But it may be that weight is only *less* handicapped
then and that a logy boat appears faster in a seaway because she
reflects her owner's aptitudes; most heavy weather experts being
indifferent to extreme lightness. A broad bottomed crew on the
rail certainly helps a boat to carry sail to windward; and in a
gale this can mean first place, since hulls reach and run the
other legs quite evenly. Weeds on the bottom are least penalized on high wind reaches when all approach hull speed like
motorboats; but to windward roughness still drops a boat badly.
Sails—The flattest, smallest working sails are best when a boat
should be carrying two reefs. Even a narrow roach makes for
heeling. Use stiff battens and enough halyard and outhaul tension to form wrinkles. Bowing the mast by tightening the permanent backstay will also remove belly and let the boat point
higher. Working sails that win at ten knots are simply too fat
to lug at thirty. Their full curves generate so much drag and
heeling that the boat squirms and falls off. Even if the helmsman is good enough to keep her moving, it will soon exhaust
him, while boats with flat sails drive easily by at a third the
effort to their crews. If unfortunate enough to be caught with
full sails in a half gale it is important to cut mainsail drag by
widening the traveller so that sheet pull flattens the leach. A
taut vang upwind gives similar drag reduction. Whenever possible the vang should lead down to the butt of the mast, where
its pull on the boom is downward, rather than a side thrust
against the gooseneck that will soon shear off the mast track
and its screws.

In rough going the jib is the basic driving sail, and should be
cut flat, or at least trimmed so. When jib sheets are single part
it makes their handling easier to use an over-fat set, provided
these will pass through the blocks. Books on sailing do not agree
on the best high wind inboard-outboard location for jibsheet
leads. But Small Point experience leaves no doubt that when
the aim is to foot through breaking waves, rather than to point
extra high, they should be pushed out several inches.

Race Committees about to send a class away in winds approaching their sea-keeping limit sometimes restrict use of the parachute spinnaker. The new Rip-Stop nylon seldom tears, however, and skippers may be trusted to make the safe light sail decision. If able to stay upright on the beat to windward, they should be able to carry a spinnaker home in the lessened apparent wind; while if it is really snoring and all boats plough away before it at hull speed, any light sail seems a Don Quixote gesture.

Tiller Techniques in High Winds

Steering a small boat in thirty knot winds is thought to involve control practices similar to those in average weather, but requiring more nerve. This is not so. Heavy weather racing is a different skill. The men who win when storm signals are flying often do not place well in light air. Ted Wells remarks that long after he was an international champion he had to learn to "luff in the puffs" and to accept defeats from friends who knew how to ease upwind when it blew. It is not just a matter of using weight well. The best heavy weather skippers often do little hiking at all. They steer actively, some holding their tillers upright: their boats sit level, foot fast, make few tacks, and breeze right along.

Uffa Fox and other British dinghy sailors improved small boat high wind techniques when they discovered that a reefed boat could never win over a full course. For windward legs on which their open 14 footers were overpowered under full sail, they developed a wind-spilling system for the mainsail that they call "Flagging," and we call "Feathering." The more proficient dinghy skippers ease their mainsheets twelve to fifteen inches, still keeping mainsails flat by vang. They and their crews may sit on the rail or inside the cockpit. They sail along upright, planing when possible, but making little spray or fuss and almost no leeway. Others who fight to use full sail power may roll far over, plunge and drift downwind. Still the featherer heels amazingly little, while gaining up to ten yards in every hundred.

Control in standard weather—Until a boat overheels, she will not slow down. So up to the point where her hiked-out crew can no longer hold her to a ten or fifteen degree list, it pays to extract all possible drive from the rig and to sail her hard.

As wind increases—A second set of flat sails lets the boat sit up, and asks less skill from her helmsman. Serious racers always have these ready. If caught with full sails, draft may be reduced by widening out the mainsheet traveller, by tightening downhaul, outhaul, and permanent backstay, and by the vang.

In overpowering winds—In extremely high winds, when no effort by skipper and crew can hold the boat level to windward under full canvas, even if this is flat, the problem becomes how to limit sail power to what the hull can accept on something approaching her best sailing lines. The accomplished featherer achieves this by 1) Flattening the mainsail by its vang, while easing out sheet until the luff lifts and power comes only from the general area of the battens. 2) A flat driving jib. 3) Active, but narrow rudder blade movements.

Why Feathering Works

When a crew learns to spill a desired fraction of mainsail thrust, heeling can be checked and the need to hike reduced. A flat jib and the batten area of the mainsail furnish enough power to move the boat fast upwind. In "feathering," a mainsail is eased enough to let its luff swell while the battens stay hard. With a vang or widened mainsheet traveller holding the leach straight and cutting drag, boom and headboard are wide of light weather settings, yet the hull points normally high. The helmsman next rudders in small active arcs to keep his boat barely upon the edge of her sail power requirements. When this knack is acquired, she will hold speed and heel hardly at all.

The end result of feathering is escape by the rig from the tremendous heeling couple of her full mainsail that otherwise rolls her over, slows her down, and strains her gear. The hull slides on easy lines; her keel or centerboard hang straight down to limit leeway. The barndoor rudder, which an over-heeled boat must brace against her path to prevent surging into the wind, is eliminated. It is worth noting that the lively tiller movements that make feathering effective in a gale are not so well adapted to light going. Feathering is like a pushshot in golf, which is fine for keeping a ball low under rough winds, but which is not extremely accurate, when accuracy can be more surely gained by standard means.

Crew Responsibilities in Heavy Going

The heavy weather crew must shift weight smartly, yet avoid mutual interference. Foot cleats and hiking straps give confidence in clambering onto wet, tilted rails. Seats built with a gap into which feet may be hooked are superior to either in a seaway.

Someone must always spy out the competition to leeward. A Mylar window in the mainsail helps when the boom is low and all hands are on the windward rail. The level attitude of a feathered boat, which simplifies around-the-compass observation, is another argument for this technique.

Desperation bailing from the rail will occasionally hold a boat in the race. When a foot of water slos-shes in her bilges, each bucketful weighs twenty-five pounds and all of it rides to leeward. A bailing can on a stick, plus a wide hole in the floorboards are necessary. Spray boards are comforting in a seaway, but being clumsy, are seldom used.

In high winds it helps to have a hamfisted crew member trim the mainsheet. His coming in-out-in through gusts and lulls may supply enough drive to let a boat fight clear of her enemies at times when the helmsman finds the tiller a full time job. If the mainsheet is to lead forward to someone on the rail, its camcleat must swivel.

Foul weather clothing is a necessary part of a racing boat's gear for the lift it gives her crew's morale. Similarly, a thermos bottle of hot coffee can keep them fighting the good fight when all are drenched and shivering.

Maneuvers in a Gale

To lose all headway when tacking in a gale of wind can produce a dangerous knockdown, not to mention five yards of below course "S-ing" to regain speed. Whenever possible, tacks should start in a smooth spot, never into the face of an onrushing wave. Tacking speed can be increased if the rudder shifts as the boat starts down the back of a swell; an additional safety feature in such downhill tacking is that when the boat lies head to the wind she now rides low between the crests and is less exposed. As an aid to sureness in regathering way, the mainsheet may be slackened, then returned to established marks as she comes up to speed. Fewer than normal tacks will be taken when a boat is plunging and may go into irons, and any guess on fetching marks must be reduced to a sure thing by judicious overstanding. This applies doubly to crossing the bow of a right-of-way boat, which in a blow is always capable of several lengths of extremely high heading.

Because there is danger on reaches of surging out to windward in an unexpectedly fierce gust, the mainsheet must be quickly releasable. When dead before a gale the bow will sometimes dive under and the boom roll high, threatening a capsize to windward. Rapid weight shift aft is then required of the crew, followed by return to original station. Excess rudder, applied late, will be useless. The helmsman must always be ahead of his boat, using small firm pressures.

High wind jibes are not difficult with a tight vang. Without one, the boom can flip upwards until the mainsail leach wraps around the lee shroud in a goosewing jibe, or the boom strikes the backstay as it crosses, which may take off the mast top.

Both going up and coming down, spinnakers flap less in the lee of the mainsail. Setting one in stops now has advantages. A roll of mending tape should be aboard for emergency tears.

Extreme closeness to overlapped boats at marks is unhealthy; at least fifteen feet of separation being advisable when both must jibe. Marks themselves have an evil habit of waltzing out of swells when passed close aboard.

A small sailboat can be made to surfboard down tall breaking seas, as *Gretel* did when she passed *Weatherly* in the second
race of the 1962 *America's* Cup series. The trick used by Wai-
kiki beachboys of slanting across the face of a swell to pick up
speed will merge the boat with the wave. At the last second, if
her counter can be swung directly before the crest, as the wave
breaks the boat will lift with everything boiling beneath her,
and be carried as much as two hundred yards down course. The
danger is in broaching; so tiller action must be quick, constant,
and never wide enough to produce drag.

Practice Routines for Heavy Weather Racing

With an expert—Small sailboats may be safely raced in bad
weather if crews are willing to learn by doing. On stormy days
the best local high wind sailor should be asked to skipper, while
all hands study his use of helm, trim of sails, and preferred
sheet location.

Side by side—Once the reasons for the better sailor's high wind
practices are digested, two class boats may go out together in
a blow to sail side by side without interference, one to feather,
the other to strap everything in and drive hard. How far the
feathering boat's mainsheet must be eased for her to slide along
upright under jib and battens will soon be clear. This spot
should be marked for later use. After some minutes the boats
exchange techniques, the featherer to heel down, the driver to
feather. Specific advantages are then confirmed.

Why high wind racing is a separate skill—While in standard
weather the racing purpose is to trim the rig, then interfere
with it as little as possible by rudder as the boat eats out to
windward, in a gale the helmsman plans to interfere continually. He aims to con his boat to that exact angle versus the wind
at which all power is produced that the hull can absorb; but
not an ounce more. Quick, but restricted tiller shifts keep the
mainsail luff barely swelling. Active steering through wave tops
and away from steep faces that seem about to break is also
needed.

In a storm the major task to windward is on the helmsman. When he feathers expertly his crew may sit inside the cockpit. Their jib is sheeted flat, their mainboom out to known marks, but held down by its vang so that the headboard-to-masthead fly angle is wider than normal. The helmsman knows that he cannot ask his hull to accept the full brunt of the wind, but that by steering with small, quick movements he can hold a satisfactory power angle. Once the trick of level sailing is learned, it is as if all hands might drink tea. The boat foots along, while opponents roll far over, showing their keels, plunging and sliding off to leeward.

On reaches, the jib is still the balance sail that lightens helm. If the mainsail is held down in one plane by its vang and the sheet eased to the worst gusts, it is possible to steer a direct heading without a rooster tail spurting in the wake.

Racing after this fashion in high winds can be fun, and acquiring the skill makes a man feel stronger than nature. It also makes sailing in storms safer by reducing punishment on boats and gear.

HEAVY WEATHER LOSSES

Accidents can drop a boat out completely. But normal high wind loss through inexperience is:

150 FEET A MILE

27 LOCAL KNOWLEDGE

While it is conceded that an ability to predict currents and local wind patterns would benefit sailboat racers, few carry the sport to that degree or think the human skull a fit depository for such insight.

Not one helmsman in twenty buys his local current tables for study. In Maine, or wherever there is high rise of tide, most will know the water level at race time, but rather as something to aid or hinder in returning to their mooring than as an ally around the course. The amateur consensus is that strongest current runs off points of land, with back eddies in their shelter. When gentle winds from a specific direction have proved flukey in the past, or a new breeze blows in several times from one quarter, it is assumed that nature will repeat herself. Fresh winds and favorable set found under a shore are expected there again. The few contestants who cross the starting line with plans to sail a certain path under, let us say, an easterly breeze and slack tide, will hurry elsewhere if they fall behind.

It will be observed that racers do not separate the favors of an area into wind and current components; nor do they map the exact set of any current. They simply decide that an area is a good place to sail in. Having gained there in the past, they return with hopes for the present.

The Racing Problem in Changing Local Winds

Each racing area enjoys sailing winds whose habits may be learned from its better sailors for the asking. Generally speak-

302

ing, along the New England coast southeasterly winds are light, and when they die out, the new breeze appears from the southwest. Northwest winds jump 15° from minute to minute, but hold fresh and gusty from that quarter for hours. The passage of air-mass frontal systems with their major wind shifts can be roughly timed from newspaper weather maps, but a telephone call to the local airport gives better accuracy.

It is questionable whether knowledge of Aerology is as useful in racing as ability to adjust to what the Lord momentarily provides. Improved finishes reward the keen eye that studies the course at the start, and that detects signposts of wind change thereafter. Any surface darkening in the intermediate distance or boats heeled actively are telltales it may pay to steer toward. The tilt of a government nun buoy can betray current beneath her religous form as foul as the devil's tail.

Streaks of altered wind—When prevailing winds strike a high shore they often straighten out and run parallel to it for some distance. While the steep western sides of islands in Maine bend southwest wind to more northerly courses, whenever shores are flat, the heat of the day is likely to suck air in at right angles as an advection breeze. A dependable but seldom used wind shift is the slant that comes out of a thunderstorm when it is still some distance away.

In the matter of changed velocity, whenever prevailing winds squash in against a high land mass, for several hundred yards offshore they tend to reinforce and to blow slightly harder. But the centers of bays that exhibit this side strength are often short of wind. Sailboats will now play such sides to the fullest and only tack out for a center mark when sure they can fetch it, particularly when tide will be foul at the mark. When gentle winds blow off the shore, boats must swing well to seaward of any tall bank that is lined with trees, for a direct course under the land may have no wind at all.

Occasionally competitors will be seen sailing into coves or bays, where if Justice were to triumph, they would run completely out of wind; yet presently they emerge with a fine breeze and favoring slant. When such an accursed development takes place, no matter how illogically, the area should be examined after the race. The flow of natural wind is subject to no man's dominion, and works its wonders in "mysterious ways." It may seem unjust for any wind to blow there at all, but it should be used the next time out.

Protection against wind shifts—The most obvious defense is to see new wind coming and to sail toward it in order to be first at the trough. Some years ago Messrs. Calahan and Trevor published an interesting study on how to benefit from wind shifts in sailboat racing. Their instructions were complicated and involved areas and lines that they named after themselves. Standard defense on windward legs is to stay upwind of the closest enemy, both to foul up his supply and to receive any shift that he does.

If the reader will take two matches and a ruler and lay out various courses with wind shifts on the dining room table, he will find that his safest protection against any change up to 90° is to stay *between the most dangerous adversary and the mark.* When out to one side of the course, and either to windward or squarely ahead, there are shifts that will cause the leader of two boats to lose nothing, part of her lead, or even put her astern. In no case can the leader gain. She either loses nothing, a little, or a lot. But if her advantage is always maintained to place her *between* the follower and the mark, any shift that reaches both boats at approximately the same time, leaves her lead largely intact.

From the pursuer's viewpoint, opposite tactics are required. If a shift is expected, it will pay to sail to leeward or astern; never with a leader blocking approach to the mark. The position chosen, assuming the leader allows it, will favor the side from which new wind is expected.

Tides and Currents

Tide is the rise and fall of water. Current the flow. It is the speed and direction of current that concern sailors.

Current direction—The government Current Tables may be

purchased for the local sailing area and checked against experience. If the little arrows prove "amusing but confusing," ask a fisherman to sketch in his corrections. Lobstermen, who must set their traps with warps of different length, know both depth and flow intimately.

Textbook pronouncements on current say it runs fastest in the centers of bays. Maximum depth on the chart *should* therefore confirm the lines of fastest flow in the current tables. Tiderips may be expected off points, with fast reverse eddies beneath them. Currents do not necessarily change at high or low water. Some persist for hours, or never change at all. Within fifty feet of Hermit Island in the Small Point racing area a narrow ribbon of current moves continually southward.

The boat that could ride local currents perfectly might float around the course with her sails down. The rub is that both flow boundaries and speeds are inexact. In some areas such as Larchmont, where there is high volume of commercial shipping, current tables have been verified. But the Maine Coast is dotted with islands and "Y" forked tidal streams. One might predict that the current would race up the deep centers of bays, then slow as it cut into the branches; but the current does not seem to have read the tables. "Lee-bowing" on the basis of a map can look scientific. Yet shift a set only 5° toward "Dead Pig Reef," and you end up with the chickens. The racing skipper who gives his whole attention to charts may be neglecting more pressing matters.

Current is important on windward legs where boats move slowly, and where there is choice of paths to use or avoid it. Reaches and runs, being straight, subject a whole fleet to the same water and make wide diversions profitable only in light air.

Racers need only understand that there *is* a current effect. "Who gained by going where," then becomes an all hands' concern. If filing such information in the brain seems difficult, those old enough to be beyond the spell of the petticoat, may divert a little black book to this use.

Current speed—The speed of current can be roughly estimated from the dip of lobsterpot buoys and from the tilt of government nun and can buoys. In very light air, ripples ducking away from a slanted mark will warn a skipper to overstand when the flow is foul.

The fastest water masses do seem to run in deep channels, and the slowest over shallows. Skippers occasionally defeat a tide-bound fleet by skimming over a mile of barely hidden rocks. Your correspondent has tried this hair raising maneuver and never gained thereby; although enemies always seemed to come up hand over hand when *they* sailed over ledges to avoid a tide. Gain should be balanced against possible loss. A stranding will surely lose thirty seconds, even if the boat can be pushed off without damage; and thirty seconds means dropping back four or five places in a close race. Speed through the water is always low in extreme shallows, for hull drag rises and large eddies tug at the boat.

Swells and Waves

Big swells form as a result of storms, sometimes hundreds of miles at sea. Half a dozen waves may furrow the upsloping back of one monster swell. As a rule swells need not be avoided; although a boat dipping between their crests suffers some loss of wind against another sailing in the lee of a point in smoother water.

Waves several feet high slow sailboats materially, and since the hulls of different classes pass through them with varying ease, it can pay the small, boxy types to go wide to avoid a pounding. Waves form quickly when a fresh breeze drives down against the tide. Chop is steeper in shallow water than in deep; witness Buzzards Bay, where small sailboats fighting to windward gain when they find a lee and easier going. On reaches and runs there is less of a slowdown, since waves and boats move together and impact is cut.

Skill in steering among wave tops partakes of the quick rudderings of the heavy weather expert. Footing fast, not pinching is required. A boat must always be driven off steep rocks or the faces of islands where confused rip-raps climb and duck, and can shake all wind from sails in light weather. Tacking in high waves is an art. The crew get soaked and a sloppily handled boat may go into irons.

Waves are a lively part of racing, and one of the "x" factors whereby one man beats another. The best way to handle them is to copy the helmsmanship of those who win in them; drive straight through with a good full; avoid them when possible.

Obstructions

Sailors who like to live dangerously can build up a reputation as cutters of rocks and shearers of points. There are always spots along a course where by holding within a foot of breaking shoals, one can gain. Manmade obstructions that must be passed close aboard include fishpounds, which are dangerous in high seas, since their long corner lines extend unseen to snag keels.

The best short cutting is done by those who *know*, not by those who guess. Skippers who wish to gain through daring may well spend a non-race afternoon in an outboard boat, exploring all turning spots and outlying rocks whose unseen threat forces boats to round them respectfully. If the tide's range is high, such scouting is best done at low water. Race gains of two hundred yards can reward the helmsman who slides by a spouting ledge while all others pass it wide.

When the black shadows of rocks begin drifting close by underneath, the crew will be glad to keep a sharp lookout. It may somewhat ease their nerves to heel the boat and reduce her draft; and after a grounding she will slide off more quickly if one of her crew is ready to dangle over the lee side from half way up the mast to cant her on her beam ends.

There are always sharp criticisms and objections when someone wins a race by shaving an obstruction dangerously close; and with justification. The enterprise that digs out secrets of local pilotage is commendable. But races are sailed to be won by superior skill, not by risky gambles. In the last analysis, it is

the Race Committee who are at fault when a course is laid out
to reward cutting through unsafe water.

Practice Maneuvers in Local Winds and Tides

Wind and Tide are interesting theoretical fields of limited
practical application to racing. Winners average to be those
who are alert and who *use* such matters on occasion; not the
long-haired scientists with shiny domes who invent them. A
useful knowledge of wind and current can be gained by asking
winners where they sail and why; talking to fishermen; examining government charts and current tables.

Before the race, all hands should decide where it has proved
best to sail in the past in like weather. *At the start,* watch is required of who goes where, and how successfully. But your own
boat should follow the best racers. *During the race,* there will
always be room for individual choice, and particularly to windward in a blow when less punishing seas may be found by
those who will look for them.

Conclusions on Weather Phenomena

Current and wind variations are phases of Natural Science,
controlled by the Lord for His own purposes. The racer's purpose is to get around the course first. If able to make the two
coincide, he may well say, "Amen." But if not, he needs only
remember that we are placed in sailboats to suffer and to learn,
and that "Art Is Long."

LOSSES DUE TO OMISSIONS IN LOCAL KNOWLEDGE

100 FEET A MILE

28

TROUBLES WITH RACING RULES

Few sailors deliberately flout the Rules, which they know are devised for their safety. It is a satisfaction of sailboat racing that pirates never flourish in it long.

While hassles over rules are rare in experienced classes, violations in summer racing spring from a desire to inject zip and spice into the contests (particularly when fouls draw minor penalties), and inexperience, compounded by a poor lookout system.

Commonest Rule Snags

Most racers know the current NAYRU Rules in principle. But any quiz shows not more than one in ten to be secure on all points. A surprising number of old timers flunk each test with grades around 30%; yet out on the course their experience lets them foresee jam-ups and sail clear. Rule violations are common at—

Starts, when massed boats maneuver with all thoughts on getting away fast; and when those who have made barging descents feel that after the gun they are somehow entitled to room at the windward end, as if at a turning mark with an inside overlap.
Windward legs, when port tackers forget to watch under their sails for those on the starboard, or respond too late when hailed. In crossing situations, when port tackers overestimate their chances of skimming by. When port tackers swing over to starboard and call: "Right of way!" to those following on their quarter the instant their sails fill. When local conditions reward

close tacking along a shore and there is confusion over the right to hail others about as boats stand into danger.

Reaches, when helmsmen bear off to sit on the wind of those passing to leeward.

Off the wind, when luffs must be curtailed as an overtaker moves too close alongside, or invokes the Mast-abeam limitation too early. In collisions at downwind marks when those clear astern surge up on a leader who has altered course in the act of rounding; or when they try to force inside after he has reached the mark and turned it widely.

How Strictly Should Racing Rules Be Enforced?

In good racing the NAYRU Rules are enforced without question; although 60% of sailors do not protest a small violation that they feel was unintentional.

In areas where racing is carried out independently, leniency is often practiced on the idea that the gentle approach gives most enjoyment. Some fleets assess minor penalties, such as loss of three points for flagrant fouls; but no one is expected to drop out. Ten years of this "friendly" system at Small Point, Maine, has convinced all hands that it is *not* the way to run races. Violators do not learn, or even try to improve. Fouling becomes chronic. It is discouraging to youngsters to be pushed and rammed by elders, who in other matters expect deference from them. It is dangerous when sailors using such license compete elsewhere. And in the end it is less fun.

There is no surer way to spoil a class than to call no fouls whatever. When this occurs there are early starters who refuse to return; jams at marks; boats damaged in high winds.

Disqualifications Cure the Wicked

There is little difficulty in learning the Rules, and none in abiding by their spirit. Once a sailor knows he will be thrown out upon losing a gamble to squeeze by any right-of-way opponent, he simply allows the necessary six additional feet. If three points in the standing are all he can lose, he will gamble for the fun of it and glory in bluffing through. Half the time he will not even be protested; while at worst he draws a growl from someone who will bluff him back at their next crossing.

Consistent rule enforcement makes races more interesting, as against the grab-bag they become when bold skippers snatch advantages their skill has not entitled them to. The cure by disqualification is sure fire. One prompt heave-ho for a rule beater under the jeers of the fleet is more health-giving medicine than a quart of Lydia E. Pinkham's "Vegetable Compound" ever was for a moonstruck maiden.

When a racing group decides to call all fouls and to ask violators to drop out, it does face the problem of requiring its sailors to read the rules, and of assigning someone to adjudicate fouls. In consequence, one or two officials undertake what may prove an embarrassing responsibility.

Semantics in Racing Rules

Writers of regulations for quick moving vehicles—Air Traffic and Racing Rules—must translate abstract principles into action. Out of words they must compose dictates that will be easily understood, direct the mind in danger to safe procedures and start proper physical response without delay.

Some can, if they study hard, master rules from a book. Theirs is an intellectual skill; and only after much racing will they bypass thought to swing their boats instinctively out of trouble. Racing Rules thirty years ago did not suggest the desired action, but descended a full staircase of steps from the printed order conferring a right, down to the security in a race it hoped to give. There were "Privileged" and "Burdened" vessels, plus some burdens on the privileged. The rule identified a point of sailing and gave it precedence. But it did not command an action. To tell a beginner on the port tack, "I have right of way," did not warn him before the boats crashed, "Tack now," or, "Go under my stern."

Harold Vanderbilt's simplified rules cleared the racer's uncertainty as to who was doing what. The wording of Robert

Bavier's books helped to initiate desired responses, when for "Starboard tack yacht has right of way," he substituted "Port tack yacht *keep clear"* The 1973 NAYRU Rules, now all but identical with those of the IYRU, seem involved, but the gist of their maneuvering sections is fairly easily grasped. However, their attainment is still a mental skill, a comprehension-to-action sequence that asks sailors to:

Read and digest the printed text.

As trouble develops select the rule governing that emergency.

Hope the adversary does the same, but hail if he does not.

The 7th (1973) edition of YACHT RACING RULES AND TACTICS by Gordon C. Aymar explains and illustrates the rules, their application and difficulties with diagrams and photographs.

A Naval Solution by Simplification

Ever since Moses stumbled down Mt. Sinai with his tablets, rule givers have puzzled over how to enforce safety by printed words. The ultimate demand upon a set of instructions faced U.S. Navy radar picket destroyers off Okinawa when Japanese suicide bombers flew over. Fire Control procedure then required that the Gunnery Officer call his anti-aircraft battery on the intercom to identify incoming targets as follows:

"Air target—
Relative bearing 125,
Target angle 45.
Open fire!"

But when Baka Bombs came gliding for the bridge it was found that no order in excess of two words could be understood, and that the only command that insured proper action was:

"Open fire!"

"For Christ's sake!" was sometimes added hopefully.

Visual Aids, Doggerel, and the Loud Voice

Racing Rules cannot be chopped down to single words, for they govern too wide a sailing spectrum. Yet there would be fewer collisions if visual association technique speeded the brain's decisions to keep clear. For each basic complication a picture flashed for two seconds on a screen might show the critical state, as seen by a helmsman's eyes. The danger would be shown as he and his crew observe it from their cockpit, never as a map, or diagram, suitable only for seagulls. When the flash died, the novice would be expected to start action— *now*. Unable to delay, he would form visual concepts of danger areas, under the boom, or out ahead when on the starboard tack. And he would learn correct evasive action as a physical response.

It would be equally easy to print a pack of cards, each illustrating a different threat as seen *from* a racing boat. The backs could state suitable action and quote the governing rule.

Short doggerel verses helped mariners of the 19th century to sail out of trouble.

> "If two lights you see ahead,
> Port your helm, and show your red"

was typical. This field is as fertile today, and soon the poets of Larchmont may chant to their children:

> "Under the boom—
> Give the dog room."

Or:

> "If he's out clear ahead,
> And we hit him—we're dead."

Steamers reinforce their whistle blasts with white puffs of steam to confirm their course changes visually. NAYRU Rule #35 now *requires* that racers hail before making any course change, except a luff, that may not be foreseen by others. Those who misdoubt their rights in an emergency need only to shout to a nearby skipper what they propose to do and expect from him. If in error, they will receive prompt correction. It will also reduce fouls if skippers add the name of the boat from which they wish action. As, *"Thunderbucket!* I am holding my course. So *you* keep clear."

A Single Principle That Avoids Trouble

The average racer can study a diagram of two competing sailboats, or set up problems with mock boats on a table, and after

ten seconds judge who has what rights. Those familiar with the
Rules can place the blame for a collision in such stopped positions at once. But racing is not a series of stopped positions.
Rather, it is a fluid, continuing action, in which boats move
along like heavy trucks without brakes. As situations tighten,
the problem is to know before proceeding, who will be at fault
if contact comes.

Collisions seldom result from flat violations of established
rights, particularly when relative positions have endured for
some time. A port tack boat does not sail straight into a starboard tacker, nor does anyone drive up from fifty yards clear
astern to ram a leader's quarter. Fouls occur after position
shifts, when it is doubtful as to the instant a new right applies.
As a right of way yacht assumes her new course, a gap of seconds often follows before her subsequent rights are established.
Examples are: when tacking close under an opponent's lee
bow; when swinging over to starboard directly ahead of a close
following port tacker; or when forcing an overlap near a downwind mark.

If competing sailboats, about to ease into new positions,
might tell from a single principle who would be responsible for
a foul, maneuvering would be simplified. A skipper, aware that
the decision must go against him, would give room or abort.

The Anti-Cowboy Principle

When racers converge, two characters are always present:

The Pious Man, who is going about his business, and who as
the crisis develops, continues to do so.

The Cowboy, who closes in, crosses, or tacks near the Pious
Man, hoping to clear him or to take up a new position.

It is easy to say which is which. The Pious Man simply goes
along piously. It is the Cowboy who puts danger into the mix,
who precipitates the trouble.

The "Anti-cowboy Principle" now states:

"In any dispute over a foul—whether on closeness, or timing, or contact—the *Pious Man is always right*. The Cowboy is *always wrong.*"

Race Committees have no choice whatever. If the Pious Man *thinks* that the Cowboy crossed so close on the port tack that he had to bear off, the Cowboy goes home. The Pious Man does not have to *even start* keeping clear until the Cowboy fills away under his lee bow, or comes over to starboard ahead of him. And then he does not have to be an acrobat. If the Pious Man is slightly spastic and thinking about the stockmarket, the Cowboy still must be at fault in the eyes of a Committee. The Cowboy can never win a close decision, unless the Pious Man freely concedes he was wrong.

Consideration of the safety bias in 1973 NAYRU Rules will wisen many a Cowboy. Rules 32; 37 3; 41 2 and 3; and 42 all make this clear.

We conclude with this sage distillation of today's Racing Rules:

"The Cowboy who comes close
And makes trouble for the Pious Man,
Will lose every protest,
And should stay clear while he can."

Practices That Lessen Risk Under NAYRU Rules

Before the start—A majority of starting line collisions follow failure to see other boats to leeward.

When on the port tack, watch out *everywhere!*

Establish a course along which the windward end of the starting line can barely be fetched on the starboard tack (the Barging Line). Then approach below it, unless there are few competitors.

After the gun, the mark at the windward end is not a turning mark where an overlap gives room. Since no boat to windward may force down in, a leeward boat that can fetch such a mark full-and-by may squeeze all others into a tree, so long as she does not luff above close-hauled.

Windward leg—Apply the Anti-cowboy Principle in crossings and when tacking close.

Advise others of your intentions. If about to round under a jittery starboard tacker, call to him: "Hold your course."

When someone passes beneath you, it is illegal to balk him, but a covering tack is allowed the instant he is clear.

Reaches—Never bear off to prevent a boat within three lengths from passing to leeward.

Before the wind—Beware the Bermuda Luff, in which an overtaken boat pinwheels around head to the wind, and do not sit in the vulnerable area just off anyone's quarter. British born sailors consider this an insult, and will "Tag you out" here repeatedly.

When overtaking to leeward, luffing is not permitted during that overlap. But once forward of Mast-abeam, a new overlap may be created, either by jibing, or by widening out two lengths, which does give luffing rights.

Overlaps must be established early at downwind marks, plus agreement that they exist. A mark is "reached" when the leader is two lengths out, or can no longer safely give room. Followers will catch up at least six feet when the leaders helm goes down, and must anticipate by readiness to swing wide.

LOSSES SUFFERED THROUGH INEPTNESS UNDER RACING RULES

More small losses are suffered under the Rules by the timid than by the bold. Sometimes the bold are disqualified to the joy of all present. But green sailors who always let a gambler force in ahead, drop—

50 FEET A MILE

29 _Summary of Losses in the Race Itself_

Point of sailing	Most staggering loss in feet per mile
Start	150′
Windward leg	1500′
Reaches	300′
Run under spinnaker	450′
Rounding marks	
Windward	60′
Leeward	45′
Light wind	100′
Heavy wind	150′
Local knowledge	100′
Trouble with Racing Rules	50′
Total loss possible in tactical sailing	2905′

SECTION V

RACE-RATING SAILBOATS AND CREWS

30

A, B, C, D AND E RATING CLASSES

It was an announced purpose of this book to set up Race-Rating for sailors and their boats. Early tests on the speed effect of Hulls, Sails and Fittings showed that these items of equipment could produce a *widest* gap of 1500 feet a mile. 2905 feet of loss was also found possible in bad tactical sailing.

There would be inaccuracy in simply totaling these amounts as a sub-basement for Race-Ratings. Under the 2905 foot tactical loss figure, sailors would be charged in one race for failures in both light and heavy going; while widely different penalties for windward, reaching, and running legs are lumped together without prorating them over the distances they actually govern. But it is easy to derive a well proportioned view of tactical skill, leading toward A, B, C, D and E ratings, if we picture a triangular race with one mile legs, into which all losses fit as they occur. Here the clumsiest sailor drops back 150 feet in his rotten start; 1500 feet after a sour windward leg; 60 feet when in irons at the windward mark; 300 feet by his careless reaching; 45 feet when wide at the downwind mark; 450 feet in a sloppy spinnaker run home; 125 feet through faulty adaption to light or heavy wind, by averaging their costs; 100 feet by ignoring local conditions; and 50 feet for poor use of racing rules. His total slow-down is "2780 feet" over three miles: of which we retain only a third, or 926⅔ feet, for the convenience of a one-mile rating. Say, *925 feet,* for a round number.

It now remains only to add the accepted "1500 feet a mile" equipment loss for Hulls, etc., to come up with a "2425 foot" All Bad, or rock bottom figure, from which handicapping efforts may begin.

How About That Size?

2425 feet of drop-back a mile is a slabsided loss—almost one foot in every two sailed. Before cementing it down as the cornerstone of a Class A, B, C, D and E Race-Rating system, it seems wise to confirm the existence of such gaps in practical racing.

At Small Point every other week, boats trail by the better part of a full leg over a three-sided course. Perhaps they have only sailed poorly; perhaps they have achieved some king-size foul up. And at least twice a summer the winner of a flukey windward-leeward race can glance back as he finishes to spot a baffled beginner still struggling near the halfway mark. This laggard may have pinched so high in the faint air and foul tide that he lost all heart and headway, or he may have grounded temporarily. But whatever his failures, he was trying.

So it seems that the "2425 feet a mile" ultimate loss when *everything is 100% sour,* does stand up.

Do the Proportions Check Out?

Sailboat texts often rate Skipper and Crew, Hull, and Sails for importance at: 40%, 30%, and 30%.

On breaking down the "2425 foot all-bad performance gap," it is interesting to find that its proportions are: Sailing Skill of Skipper and Crew, 38.1%; Hulls, 30%; Sails, 22.7%; and Fittings, 9.2%. Add Sails to Fittings, for a Rig Total of 31.9%, and we are in good agreement with the wise men of nautical literature. Of course, such closeness is luck, when so many figures are approximated.

Five Rating Classes

A, B, C, D and E Race-Ratings cannot reflect the full 2425 foot gap over a mile of racing, for working handicaps must distinguish normal competitive levels, not freak inefficiencies.

Golfers rate from par, up to about a score of 120; not to 200, just because some arch-duffer is capable of shooting that high on an unlucky day.

For an easily remembered interval that covers just over half the widest possible racing loss, we set the gap between classes of sailors at "100 feet a mile," and between classes of boats at "150 feet a mile." This conforms to the textbooks' weighting of Handling at 40%, against the remaining 60% for Hull and Sails. It also allows quick computation of the distance whereby a Class A skipper in a Class A boat should defeat, let us say, a Class B skipper in a Class C boat over each racing mile—one "100 foot" interval being chargeable between the skippers, and two of "150 feet" between the boats.

31 RATING THE BOATS

Most losers will concede that their boats are slow. And in this they are generally right!

We now offer a painless questionnaire that Race-Rates sailboats into Classes A, B, C, D and E. The reader who finds these questions arbitrary may resent low classification of his boat upon verbal distinctions that to him seem irrelevant. But the questions have been made arbitrary to reflect the rigid payoff that all receive at the finish line, where, as Saint Peter says when his door clanks to: "Son, you either have it here, or you don't!"

Boat Rating Directions

Twelve sets of questions follow, each allowing a sailboat to be rated Class A, B, C, D, or E in one respect, and carrying a penalty in "feet per mile" *below perfection*. For a final rating, total these penalties, and find the boat's position in Column 1 of the next table, with her Class and General Characteristics beyond.

Rating Table

Total loss in feet	Boat Class	General Characteristics
0–140	A	Has the best of everything; all tested, proved and adjusted
140–270	B	In good shape, but not always checked to be so by the owner
270–470	C	In fair shape, but keeping it so is given little thought
470–600	D	Some shortages or deficiencies exist
600–740	E	There are evident shortages due to ignorance

	Loss in
On Hull Weight	*feet-per-mile*

Class A   0
The skipper knows his exact minimum class weight, and has checked to determine that his hull is almost precisely that.
Class B   20
Minimum hull weight is known, but the hull is somewhat over it.
Class C   40
The skipper does not know his proper class weight, but the hull looks in good shape.
Class D   60
Hull appearance is fair.
Class E   80
Hull appearance is poor.

Hull Shape

Class A   0
The hull has been checked against class blueprints and found to conform in all respects.
Class B   5
The hull has been checked and found to conform fairly well.
Class C   10
Hull unchecked, but looks all right.
Class D   15
Hull unchecked, and showing minor evidences of differing from the class plans.
Class E   20
Hull has plain, if minor, curvature or deadwood differences.

Bottom Condition

Class A   0
The bottom is beautifully smooth. The owner sees to this himself, and keeps it so throughout the season.
Class B   40
The bottom is good. The owner sees that the boatyard cares for it in the spring.
Class C   80
The bottom seems fair. The boatyard has simply been directed to keep it so.
Class D   120
The bottom is only fair. Once well painted, it is forgotten.
Class E   160
The bottom is poor. Any copper paint the yard prefers is used, and allowed to deteriorate through the season.

	Loss in feet-per-mile

Hull Trim

Class A   0
Keel and/or ballast is known to be exactly in accord with blueprint values. Best sailing trim is known and maintained on each point of sailing.

Class B   10
Best trim angles have been determined, but are inexactly maintained.

Class C   20
Trim is simply guessed at.

Class D   30
Little thought is given to trim.

Class E   40
The boat is clearly out of trim.

Leeway

Class A   0
Underwater profile, including the centerboard, has been carefully checked against class plans and found to conform.

Class B   10
Lateral profile looks all right, although the boat is not the closest winded in the fleet.

Class C   20
Lateral profile is disregarded.

Class D   30
There are minor differences in fairings or underwater profile from the class plans.

Class E   40
When examined in the boatyard there are evident differences in underwater profile from the fastest boats in the class.

Rudder

Class A   0
The rudder is exactly to class plans in plan form and in gap beneath the hull. Its trailing edges are beautifully thinned.

Class B   5
The rudder is good, but not as finely thinned as several others.

Class C   10
The rudder looks all right.

Class D   15
The rudder is somewhat off shape. Its edges are unthinned.

Class E   20
The rudder is clearly small, off shape, warped, and has gaps between its sections.

	Loss in feet-per-mile

The Sails

Class A — 0

The sails are from the winningest sailmaker of the class. They are not more than two years old, have been checked for exact dimensional agreement with the class plans, and are used only in winds within ten miles an hour of their designed curves, which means that two sets, or preferably three, are available.

Class B — 40

The sails are by the best sailmaker, but are unchecked against the plans. An extra flat set is used in high winds.

Class C — 80

Sails are by a good sailmaker, unchecked and used in any winds. They look all right.

Class D — 120

Sails are by a maker with an undistinguished record in the class. No exact trim settings are used. They seem adequate only.

Class E — 160

The sails have evident shortcomings. The same set is used in all weathers. Neither dimensions nor best trim angles are verified.

Rig Balance

Class A — 0

The rig is exactly balanced for weather helm to windward in light air. Sheet settings are verified for each angle of sailing. The mast is straight, stiff, and light.

Class B — 25

The rig has proved well balanced in competition. Best sheet settings are known. The mast looks good.

Class C — 50

The rig performs adequately, but careful tests have not been made to balance or improve it.

Class D — 75

There is evident weather helm. The mast bends and its jib-stay slackens to windward. Sheet settings are by guess.

Class E — 100

The rig is evidently unbalanced and requires strong tiller pressures in a breeze. Stays are unevenly adjusted. Sheet settings differ on opposite sides of the boat.

Parasitic Drag

Class A — 0

Rig windage is at a minimum. There are no extra halyards.

Loss in feet-per-mile

Class A (*Continued*)

Weight of fittings aloft is the least possible to give adequate strength.

Class B   5

An effort has been made to reduce windage and weight aloft.

Class C   10

Lines and fittings aloft are of average size or smaller.

Class D   15

Little attention has been paid to weight or windage aloft. The rigging is simply functional. Mast diameter may be large.

Class E   20

Weight and windage aloft are disregarded. Large and extra halyards are used. Neglect of windage may be shown by cockpit combings higher than called for in the class plans. The boat is burdened aloft.

Hull Fittings

Class A   0

Everything is aboard that will aid a crew in determining trim. The tiller has no slop. A good hiking stick and hiking straps are fitted.

Class B   5

The boat is well equipped, but there is nothing "fancy."

Class C   10

The boat is outfitted for plain sailing.

Class D   15

There are minor equipment shortages that handicap the boat in competition.

Class E   20

The boat must be raced bare. Nothing is aboard to assist in gauging trim or in balancing the hull.

Sail Fittings

Class A   0

The rig has all facilities for adjustment and control of sail shape. The vang is excellent.

Class B   20

Many equipment items are aboard, but not the very lightest, or best.

Class C   40

The boat is equipped for normal racing, but in close competition lacks precise adjustments. There are few camcleats.

Class D   60

The bare items for sail control are aboard, lacking adjustment facilities. No vang is fitted.

Loss in
feet-per-mile

Class E   80
No underway sail adjustments are possible. There are
major shortages.

Convenience Items

Class A   0
Everything is aboard, ready to use. The masthead fly is
sensitive. The crew enjoys the best of foul weather gear.

Class B   5
Equipment is good, but basic.

Class C   10
Only essentials are aboard.

Class D   15
The boat can be raced, but without comfort or convenience.

Class E   20
There are serious shortages. No effort has been made to
assist or relieve the crew.

What To Do Now

A return to the Rating Table on page 324 with the boat's
Total Loss figure, will yield her Race-Rating.

32

RATING THE SAILORS' SKILLS

Sailors tend to over-rate their abilities by about one skill class. Those of minor talents think winning to be largely luck, and do not credit anyone with firm superiority over them in particular aspects of racing. It is only the experts who expect to gain or lose by like amounts in like situations.

To sweeten the pill of competing under our limited personal skills, these questions cover policy and practice throughout a race. Class A sailors will not miss more than one of a group; Class B, up to three; Class C, six; Class D, eight; while Class E may miss them all.

Questions That Highlight Racing Performance

Before the race   *Yes-No*

1) Does someone go aboard the boat on race mornings to oil blocks, check all gear, and bail?   _____

2) Is the boat cruising about in the racing area twenty minutes before her start, so that the crew may study conditions and plan strategy?   _____

3) Are several sets of sails brought out, and the best for expected wind strength hoisted, after careful check of what is blowing?   _____

4) Are any green crew shown maneuvers they will be expected to perform; and are special operations that will be faced that day run through, as well as those that have given trouble in the past?   _____

330

5) Does the crew have a sound idea of weather expected for the day, and is this confidence based upon study of a weather map, or a telephone call to an airport *upwind?*   _____

6) Have the frequency and scope of wind shifts been measured, and before sailing down to the starting line is a careful look taken out along the course and an estimate made as to the spots where wind will be most favorable?   _____

7) Is spinnaker gear laid out ready on the side where it first should be used?   _____

8) Five minutes before the warning gun are working sails given last trim adjustments for existing wind?   _____

9) Is flow of tidal current near the starting line observed, plus any spots of dead or fresher wind?   _____

10) At the warning gun is everyone relaxed, do all lines run clear, and is the boat quite ready to go?   _____

The Start

1) Is an early head to the wind luff made near the center of the line to identify advancement of either end?   _____

2) Does the skipper explain to his crew the type of start he plans and where he will cross the line, taking into consideration the number of competing boats and the line's width?   _____

3) Does one of the crew—not the helmsman—call out "Time-remaining" from the stopwatch, and is this count brought down to actual seconds in the last minute?   _____

4) Is the approximate spot from which final run-in to the line will be made located on the water by something such as a lobsterpot buoy, or by bearings?   _____

5) During the early minutes does the boat ease to-

Yes-No

ward this area, staying out of trouble, but always ready to shift plans if a jam threatens up ahead?

6) In drifting conditions does the helmsman hug within fifty feet of the line?

7) When starting his final run-in, does the skipper control speed by slow-sailing?

8) Does one of the crew keep a close watch for right-of-way boats, particularly those converging to leeward?

9) Just before gunfire, can the crew speed up the boat without order, snugging in sheets and hiking on the rail?

10) Is the starting aim to cross in clear air, and once over the line, to move out toward areas of better wind?

Windward Leg

1) Is the crew trained to balance the hull to assigned levels, moving out to the rail in sequence without order?

2) Are jib and mainsheets trimmed to marks, and are both sails adjusted for fullness as wind force varies?

3) Does the helmsman use a gentle tiller touch while easing the boat up to her best angle against the masthead fly?

4) Is the helmsman familiar with the need to luff in the gusts and bear off through the lulls?

5) Does someone watch distant wind, wind about to strike the boat, and does he or she warn when the compass indicates it may pay to tack on a header?

6) Is the first long tack made in the general direction of the mark, unless there is sound reason for doing otherwise?

7) Is the crew's tacking so smooth that almost no distance is lost in the process?

8) Is defense against backwind maintained, attack on nearby boats by backwind made as possible, and any enemy to leeward watched constantly?   _____

9) Does the crew use sighting devices and know exactly when it is safe to cross an opponent's track and when to lee-bow him? Does the helmsman call, "Hold your course," when he means to pass astern?   _____

10) Is it normal practice to stay with the better sailors, not to split tacks with them?   _____

Reaching

1) Is level hull trim maintained without order by an understood sequence of crew weight onto the rail?   _____

2) Is the boat steered more by mainsail trim than by rudder, even through gusts and lulls?   _____

3) After flattening the jib and widening out its sheets, then bagging the mainsail, does someone devote full time and both hands to mainsheet trim?   _____

4) Is the mainsail kept in one plane by its vang and by widening out the mainsheet traveler?   _____

5) Is puff-chasing attempted, once it is clear that a certain off-course heading will pay?   _____

6) Does someone watch for and call out the approach of gusts and lulls?   _____

7) Are reports made on enemy movements and progress, both on boats alongside, and on those out to the flanks?   _____

8) Have defensive luffs been practiced, and in bearing off in an attempt to pass, does the helmsman know the best part of a wake to penetrate?   _____

9) Does the helmsman "bear off in the puffs" to keep his boat on her feet?   _____

10) Is the crew skilled at setting and dowsing the reaching spinnaker, and do they all know exactly when it pays to carry one?   _____

Running Under Light Sails   *Yes-No*

1) Is setting the parachute spinnaker, or adjusting jib
and whiskerpole, an automatic procedure that insures
these sails drawing as the *mark is passed?*   ———

2) Is bagging the mainsail, and its exact downwind
trim always attended to?   ———

3) Is the hull heeled slightly to windward to reduce
rudder forces?   ———

4) Are spinnaker pole and sheet constantly adjusted
against the masthead fly so that collapse of the sail
rarely occurs?   ———

5) Is the spinnaker encouraged to lift and spread its
leaches by raising the pole at the mast, and by easing
its head out forward of the mainsail by halyard?   ———

6) Are spinnaker and mainsail jibed smoothly in high
winds?   ———

7) Has dowsing the spinnaker been practiced both to
leeward and straight ahead, until the sail comes down
without draft in a matter of seconds?   ———

8) Does the crew know how closely it may approach
an overtaken boat's windward quarter, and can it
keep the spinnaker drawing throughout defensive
luffs?   ———

9) Is someone delegated to report on the progress of
all enemies, particularly those close astern?   ———

10) When starting downwind, is a course chosen that
will lead through the most favorable current and the
freshest wind?   ———

Rounding Marks

1) Are congested windward marks normally ap-
proached on the starboard tack?   ———

2) In the interests of laying windward marks closely, does the crew practice with sighting lines under varying conditions of wind and tide?   _____

3) When approaching a mark, is current estimated by its lean, and the flow of ripples from its base?   _____

4) When forced to approach on the port tack, is an insurance policy of 1½ lengths of over-standing paid to boats coming in on the starboard?   _____

5) When it is clear that a mark sits in light air and unfavorable tide, does the helmsman over-stand it slightly, in order to foot down fast on his actual approach?   _____

6) Has the crew practiced establishing and denying overlaps two boat-lengths out from downwind marks and does someone always confirm or deny them in a loud voice before the helm goes down?   _____

7) Does the helmsman make the proper "U" turn at a downwind mark that leaves him beside the mark at its completion, not below it?   _____

8) Is the pivot point of the class known, and exactly how much a boat ten feet clear astern will catch up when a leader squashes sideways in rounding? Has escape from this predicament been practiced?   _____

9) After rounding a downwind mark, do crew and helmsman combine by sheet and tiller to bring the boat to her highest course against the masthead fly without stubbing her progress?   _____

10) Does the helmsman know through practice exactly what his lead over a boat in his wake must be before he can tack in her path?   _____

Light Winds

1) When drifting conditions seem likely, are light weather sails always on hand?   _____

Yes-No

2) When crossing light patches with "average sails," is the crew experienced in fattening sail curves with out order?   _____

3) Do all hands understand the need to keep the boat moving in "light calms," and to avoid flat trimming of sails?   _____

4) Is a "Wind finder" aboard who searches the intermediate surface for new air, and always warns of its approach?   _____

5) Are cigarette smoke, tell-tales, and the masthead fly in use, plus observation of the masthead flies of other boats?   _____

6) Is the boat heeled slightly to leeward to fill her sails?   _____

7) Is the hull kept quiet to prevent sail slatting?   _____

8) Are fishline jib and spinnaker sheets on hand?   _____

9) Is the flow of any tidal current considered in selecting the best light wind course?   _____

10) Is distant smoke studied as a fore-warner of wind change, and does the crew know the quarter from which a new breeze is most likely to strike in?   _____

Heavy Winds

1) Are flat sails available when conditions warrant their use?   _____

2) Does the crew know how to flatten sails already set by outhaul, downhaul, mainsheet traveler, and by bowing the mast?   _____

3) Is it trim doctrine to sail the boat flat, using hiking straps and hiking stick?   _____

4) Does the helmsman "feather" in high wind, and is his mainsheet marked for this purpose?   _____

5) Has the helmsman studied the heavy weather tiller methods of the best sailors in his fleet, and can he

keep his own boat footing fast in a half-gale with their small, active tiller shifts?

6) Does the helmsman ease up and off through breaking crests to lessen pressure on his boat?

7) Can the crew execute safe high wind tacks between the swells?

8) Can the boat be bailed from the windward rail?

9) Is heavy weather gear and hot coffee aboard?

10) Are spare bits of line, tools, safety cushions, and a towline, all aboard?

Local Knowledge

1) Is height of tide at starting time always known?

2) Is the crew familiar with both speed and direction of current flow around the entire course?

3) Are all areas of wind diversion known, so that they may either be sailed through, or avoided?

4) Is the position of any submerged rock or ledge established, particularly those off turning points?

5) Before the start, is the crew in general agreement on the best local areas through which to sail?

6) In light air, are rip-raps off steep shores avoided, and in heavy going does the skipper hunt out smooth water in a lee?

7) When risking a short cut through shallows, is the boat heeled to lessen her draft, and does one of the crew keep a sharp lookout for rocks?

8) Has someone been delegated to report on the progress of boats far to either side of the fleet?

9) Has a careful low tide check of the racing area been made on a non-race day from an outboard motorboat?

10) Is a notebook kept of unusual racing results, obtained by boats that sail abnormal courses?

Racing Rules Yes-No

1) Does at least one person know the NAYRU Racing Rules *completely?* _____

2) Do the crew occasionally set up rule problems on a table? Do they understand the safety bias of all racing rules, by which the man who *initiates* a complication is always at fault in any dispute over "time when?" _____

3) Are danger bearings on all points of sailing understood as something to be visualized, not deduced —under the boom, when two boats are on the same tack? Is one of the crew delegated to keep watch on these bearings? _____

4) Does the skipper always hail approaching boats to clarify his intentions? _____

5) Are rules peculiar to the start all clear? An overtaking yacht's right to luff once she gains Mast-abeam? Luffing before and after the gun? _____

6) Going to windward, does the helmsman ask others crossing his bow on the starboard tack to "Hold your course," until he swings clear astern? _____

7) On reaches, does the helmsman avoid bearing off to sit on the wind of a boat passing within three lengths? _____

8) Running free, can the helmsman always stay clear if an overtaken boat luffs him head to the wind? _____

9) Does the helmsman overtaking to leeward, know how to establish a new overlap that gives him luffing rights, once he is forward of Mast-abeam? _____

10) Do all the crew know their rights and obligations when hailing for, or being hailed for room, as they approach a rocky shore? _____

Skill Rating for an Entire Race

A rating based on all "No" answers given above finds these negatives according to skill level:

> Class A — less than 10
> Class B — less than 30
> Class C — less than 60
> Class D — less than 80
> Class E — 80 or more

"I Want Another Chance!"

A few Class D and E racers, disgruntled at their low seat on the totem pole, may object to the many feet and feathers we have perched above them. Their easiest confirmation is to ask several opponents where *they* think they should rate. Competition breeds honest answers.

Again, the man who likes arithmetic might sharpen his pencil, isolate each part of the race for its full loss capacity, then puzzle out a new self-rating based on his last five well-remembered races, or his next five.

As a start he would halve the maximum gap for each part of the race to bring it down into normal handicapping range, then further separate it into 60% for Hulls, Sails and Fittings, and 40% for Handling. Five more even slices, and he would have A, B, C, D and E rating classes, reaching from perfection to a bad Class E. Now he would check his own loss on starts and mark roundings, where boat-speed plays little part, before determining how much he gained or fell back over one mile segments of windward legs, reaches, or runs, where it does. Light and heavy winds, and passage through non-standard local conditions would weight his totals when applicable.

Any Race-Rating so derived must be ponderous, even when accurate. But after a dozen races, the rater could not escape a good insight into his own abilities.

Fortunately, quite painless proof of sailing skill can be had in one afternoon by those willing to submit to the testing fires of the Short Race.

Verification by the Short Race

In addition to high-lighting the skill of skippers and crews, these abbreviated contests are the greatest fun imaginable. Their one negative effect is to shoot all alibis full of holes.

Pass the word for four, or at most five, boats and their crews to come out. One should be at least Class B, although Race-Ratings are surer when the "touchstone sailor" is Class A. The course will be windward-leeward, never more than 500–600 yards out to the turning mark. While an occasional box course is amusing, the heart of short racing is the single windward leg. Starts are by three minute whistle, on a line fifty yards wide. The first few races may be sailed by crews in their own boats; but once all know the course, it adds pleasure to switch crews and boats on a round-robin schedule, which is easy to draw up for four or five.

Short races give tight finishes, with about fifty feet between sailor classes, and seventy-five between boats. But ratings are best obtained by totalling the number of opponents beaten after a group of races, then comparing them to what the Single Class A skipper did.

Short races test sailors to their fullest. Any ten seconds of duffering or inattention, and that race is lost. The challenge then repeats, and next time the crew may know their lesson. Although the start appears to govern, the lone Class A helmsman invariably squeaks through, a winner on percentage.

Conclusion on Skill Ratings

The value of Race-Ratings is in the help they give young and serious racers to uncover deficiencies. Some old timers dislike having their techniques appraised, and see in this an invasion of privacy. But ratings do not harm the great run of sailors, who will ignore them anyway. Most sailors *know* they are great lovers; they *hope* to be successful in business in order to take care of their families; but when they lose a race they *assume* that because they are as talented as their friends, it had to be through bad luck. There is nothing wrong with this assumption as human nature. It simply stops all racing improvement.

33 VALUE OF THIS MATERIAL TO SAILORS

An effort has been made to show the factors making for speed in sailboat racing, as well as for slowness. Should a reader now wish to make speed checks on his own boat, it will be interesting to see whether he obtains figures similar to those found at Small Point. He will need some equipment: to weigh his hull, platform scales or a steelyard; to tow it alone, or against sisters, a suitable towboat with spring balances, and an accurate speedometer, such as a calibrated pram. It is quite possible that he will greatly improve upon the methods given.

The purpose of amateur tests is not micrometer accuracy, which is beyond those without costly equipment, but understanding of the broad amounts of force needed to sail at various speeds. What diminishes or raises this force is equally important.

Better Race Results

Sailors who wish to place higher will do so more surely by concentrating upon their tactical skills than by equipment tests. The better racers are always ready to help them, and it costs nothing to go out and practice. Learning to make a sailboat go fast is twice as easy against a trial horse, for sharp and pokey practices then stand out. For a skipper and crew to improve, takes what athletes call "desire." They must keep records of what-happened-when, and above all, study their bad results, for five seconds of racing error lose more than ten of cleverness ever regain.

341

What This Book Hopes to Show

This text has tried to picture racing, not as it ought to be, but as it is. We have used the Small Point class as a mirror because it is against WHAT IS that the reader must compete. Let us recall in parting that while to you and me the scientific approach may seem useful, to the great majority it is so much confusion. We must respect their prejudices.

In the broader survey, no matter how much one longs to win, it is best not to seek only that. There is fierce delight in slicing first across a finish line, but in time this can easily be felt by anyone who will stay at home and master his own boat. The most victory hungry helmsman will concede that in Stars, Finns and Olympic classes he can find dedicated racers whose lives mould around competition, and who will certainly beat him (most of the time) even if he lives for the starting gun, as they do.

So in the end, after reaching skill levels that are personally satisfying, we turn to developing the sport.

The Ultimate Values Sought in Racing

We conclude:

Sailboat racing can never be the even-up proposition that the majority like to think it is—if only they wanted to work at it too. Those who deserve to win, soon do. As to individual potentials—it is clear that a majority of sailors can never be really good. No one can improve who does not want to take trouble.

In the justice of this result, and in the healthy life of sailors lie the benefits of yacht racing. Its infallible leveler is that quirk in human nature that makes us all want to sail by our *own methods,* even when those are manifestly wrong. There is something in the combination of open water, wind, and sky that confirms individuality and swells each heart to its largest when it is following its own hopes.